THE RECORDINGS OF ANDY KIRK
AND HIS CLOUDS OF JOY

OXFORD STUDIES IN RECORDED JAZZ
Series Editor Jeremy Barham

THE RECORDINGS OF ANDY KIRK AND HIS CLOUDS OF JOY

GEORGE BURROWS

OXFORD
UNIVERSITY PRESS

Oxford University Press is a department of the University of Oxford. It furthers
the University's objective of excellence in research, scholarship, and education
by publishing worldwide. Oxford is a registered trade mark of Oxford University
Press in the UK and certain other countries.

Published in the United States of America by Oxford University Press
198 Madison Avenue, New York, NY 10016, United States of America.

Library of Congress Cataloging-in-Publication Data
Names: Burrows, George, 1975, author.
Title: The recordings of Andy Kirk and his Clouds of Joy / George Burrows.
Description: New York, NY : Oxford University Press, [2019] |
Includes bibliographical references and index.
Identifiers: LCCN 2018042796 | ISBN 9780199335589 (hardcover : alk. paper) |
ISBN 9780199335596 (pbk. : alk. paper)
Subjects: LCSH: Twelve Clouds of Joy (Musical group) | Kirk, Andy, 1898–1992. |
Jazz—History and criticism. | Twelve Clouds of Joy (Musical group)—Discography.
Classification: LCC ML421.T83 B87 2019 | DDC 784.4/165092—dc23
LC record available at https://lccn.loc.gov/2018042796

1 2 3 4 5 6 7 8 9

Paperback printed by Webcom, Inc., Canada
Hardback printed by Bridgeport National Bindery, Inc., United States of America

TO ALICE, MERRYN, LEONA, AND KATE

CONTENTS

SERIES PREFACE

THE OXFORD STUDIES in Recorded Jazz series offers detailed historical, cultural, and technical analysis of jazz recordings across a broad spectrum of styles, periods, performing media, and nationalities. Each volume, authored by a leading scholar in the field, addresses either a single jazz album or a set of related recordings by one artist/group, placing the recordings fully in their historical and musical context, and thereby enriching our understanding of their cultural and creative significance.

With access to the latest scholarship and with an innovative and balanced approach to its subject matter, the series offers fresh perspectives on both well-known and neglected jazz repertoire. It sets out to renew musical debate in jazz scholarship, and to develop the subtle critical languages and vocabularies necessary to do full justice to the complex expressive, structural, and cultural dimensions of recorded jazz performance.

Jeremy Barham
University of Surrey
Series Editor

ACKNOWLEDGMENTS

SO MANY KIND and generous people have supported the writing of this book that I fear I will forget to thank at least one of them. So, I offer the following vote of thanks with the caveat and apology that it extends to all those that helped me in this endeavour.

I am especially thankful for the financial support that I received to conduct research for this book from the Faculty of Creative and Cultural Industries of the University of Portsmouth through their Research Accelerator Fund and Conference Support Fund. Furthermore, the university funded a period of sabbatical to complete the writing of the book and during that period, Annie Sanger-Davies, Sandra Philip, Thomas Neil, and Darren Daly covered my lecturing duties. I offer particular thanks to them as without their work this volume would not be in print.

I am thankful to all my academic colleagues at the University of Portsmouth and elsewhere who provided moral support and understanding when the going got tough in researching and writing this book. I am especially grateful to Chris Danowski, Erika Hughes, Colin Jagger, Laura MacDonald, Ben Macpherson, Matt Smith, and Nik Wakefield for putting up with my ruminations and frustrations about my work on the book in our shared office. Such ruminating often spilled over into our technical office where Walid Benkhaled, Russ Percy, and Greg Smith were always on hand with good humour. Nicholas Gebhardt, Professor of Jazz and Popular Music Studies at Birmingham City University, and Catherine Tackley, Professor of Music at the University of Liverpool, were a great source of encouragement and inspiration to me when we talked about the project at various conferences and business meetings.

I am also grateful for the helpful feedback I received on presentations on this topic from colleagues attending the *Rhythm Changes* conferences and other symposia at which I presented my ideas.

I owe a particular debt of gratitude to William Everett, Curators' Distinguished Professor of Musicology of the University of Missouri—Kansas City (UMKC), who helped me with accommodation and good company during several research trips to Kansas City. I was greatly helped in my research there by Chuck Haddix, an authority on Kansas City Jazz and Curator of the Marr Sound Archives at UMKC. He generously lent me his index to the *Kansas City Call*, made available rare recordings and Interviews, and proved a mine of information about all things musical connected with the city and region. Similarly, Kelly McEniry and Stuart Hinds of the LaBudde Special Collections department of the Miller Nichols Library at UMKC were very helpful in supporting my research and in securing permissions for several of the images that appear in this volume. Through them, I made valuable contacts at the State Historical Society of Missouri Research Center and the Kansas City Museum.

Elsewhere, Emily Sanford of the Bentley Historical Library of the University of Michigan helped me access their Andy Kirk Papers, Maristella Feustle of the Music Library of the University of North Texas and Doug Reside of the New York Public Library provided copies of stock arrangements, and James Hershorn, archivist at Rutgers University's Institute of Jazz Studies, helped me access their Mary Lou Williams Collection. Hershorn also introduced me to Father Peter O'Brien, shortly before he died. O'Brien formed a direct link for me with the Clouds of Joy because he had acted as Mary Lou Williams's manager during the 1960s and co-taught courses on jazz history with her during the 1970s. Through Williams, he met Kirk and he told me that he had always felt that Kirk needed more attention for what he had achieved.

I still feel honoured to have talked with Father O'Brien about this project, and I found him to be warm, funny and deeply supportive. When I met him, he said that he thought Williams would certainly have appreciated my project and that meant a lot to me because I have always been acutely aware of my own situation as a comparatively privileged white-European scholar writing about this topic at such a remove from the time, place, and conditions that Kirk and his musicians experienced. I am sorry that this book did not appear before O'Brien passed away in May 2015, but I hope he would have approved. Meeting him certainly spurred me on to make the book appropriately meaningful in his memory and Williams's too.

I am especially thankful to those kind souls that gave their time to read drafts of material that appears in this book. In that regard, I am

ACKNOWLEDGMENTS

indebted to the wisdom of my retired colleagues from the University of Portsmouth, Denis Reeve Baker, Dave Allen, Sue Harper, and John Craven, who all offered an editor's eye, useful advice, and encouragement. So too did my dear friend Ian Tipping, my ex-colleague Dominic Symonds (Professor of Musical Theatre at the University of Lincoln) and my musical brother-in-arms at Portsmouth, Colin Jagger (Director of Music). However, special thanks for reviewing my writing and generally putting up with me during the project are reserved for my wife, Kate Burrows. She not only helped me clarify my argument, but she also managed our three wonderful little girls and our household affairs so that I could get on with writing and editing when it really mattered. I hope I have repaid all of them with this volume, in which any shortcomings are all of my own making.

THE RECORDINGS OF ANDY KIRK
AND HIS CLOUDS OF JOY

TROUBLESOME
RECORDINGS
JAZZ STYLES, MASKS, AND RACE

THIS IS THE first book-length study of the recordings of Andy Kirk and his Clouds of Joy. Although this all-black jazz band is not as well-known today as the contemporary bands that were led by the likes of Count Basie, Louis Armstrong, Jimmie Lunceford, Earl Hines, or Fletcher Henderson, the Clouds of Joy competed with those groups and enjoyed a similar high profile during the later 1930s and early 1940s. Through many of the fine records that they made between 1929 and 1949, Kirk's band came to exemplify big-band jazz of the so-called Southwester Territories of the United States, and especially that of their cultural hub, Kansas City.[1] They made numerous radio broadcasts and recordings in

---

1 In *Early Jazz: Its Roots and Musical Development*, Gunther Schuller maps the Southwestern region as extending from Denver, Colorado, in the west, to Chicago, Illinois, in the East, and

the prewar period, and in 1942 their record of 'Take It and Git' secured the very first 'No. 1' spot on the 'Harlem Hit Parade', the original incarnation of *Billboard* magazine's pioneering R & B chart (Whitburn 2004: 18). In 1956, Kirk made an album for RCA-Victor that recollected some of the recordings of the Clouds of Joy. It helped establish the band's reputation as an exemplar of Kansas City jazz but prevailing criticism of the band's populist repertoire otherwise assigned them to the margins of jazz history. This book argues, however, that it is precisely their problematic recorded repertoire and marginal situation that makes them illuminating of discourses about style and race associated with jazz.

Over the years, several great jazz virtuosi served short but significant stints within the ranks of the Clouds of Joy. These included the great saxophonists Lester Young, Ben Webster, and Charlie Parker. Although none of these luminaries made recordings with Kirk's band, many other fine musicians did. These included the brilliant but underappreciated tenor saxophonist Dick Wilson, the innovative trumpeters Howard McGhee and Theodore 'Fats' Navarro, and the pioneering guitarist Floyd Smith. Perhaps the most significant figure to be associated with the Clouds of Joy, however, aside from Kirk himself, was the pianist, composer, and arranger Mary Lou Williams. Williams, as much as anyone, served a productive apprenticeship with Kirk's band, and, as we will see, she helped to define its hot-jazz credentials when it came to record.

This study is not really concerned with charting the band's achievements or those of its leading players, nor does it investigate how they exemplified an influential style of regional jazz. Instead, it explores how the recordings of the Clouds of Joy illuminate a broader discussion about the ever-changing relationship between jazz music-making, its manifestation on records, and its underpinning in intersecting critical discourses about musical artistry and racial authenticity. Such discourses are still operating, and so the argument of this book has implications that extend way beyond the specific context of Andy Kirk and his Clouds of Joy. It casts new light on the way racial and musical values were and are entwined in understandings and evaluations of jazz music, and it raises fundamental questions about the basis for making aesthetic judgements about jazz. It pays particular attention to matters of style within jazz.

descending from there as far South as the Texan cities of Dallas and San Antonio ([1968] 1986: 280).

Save for a five-year gap between 1931 and 1936 and some breaks in the 1940s, Kirk's band recorded regularly from 1929 until 1949. Unfavourable economic conditions caused Kirk to disband the Clouds of Joy in 1949, but he returned to lead a recording band in 1956, albeit with only one of his former band members, to make a retrospective set of recordings. Although those 1950s' recordings did some important work in representing the band's jazz, the bulk of the band's records come from the 1930s and 1940s and involve a different representational agenda. That was a period in which jazz transformed into big-band swing and came to the forefront of American popular music. In the face of its increased commercialization, it was also a time of quite heated critical debate about jazz's artistry, but the war led to the eventual decline in the popularity of swing and a new style of jazz, bebop, developed. That led jazz away from popular big bands towards a more specialist audience and a different set of aesthetic values.

The recordings of the Clouds of Joy certainly chart the changing popularity and character of jazz over the course of that period. This book suggests, however, that Kirk's band also played its part in changing jazz by both confirming and confounding critical conceptions of the stylistic-racial character of the music. Although the book is not specifically focused on musical regionalism, it is undoubtedly because Kirk's band came from outside of the established centres for jazz (New Orleans, Chicago, and New York) that their records speak more loudly than most of the entwined concepts of jazz artistry and racial identity that had developed in those centres for the music and its recording. It is precisely the particularity of the regional or decentred position from which the Clouds of Joy came to record that allows this volume to open up such a discursive vein of stylistic-racial analysis in a way that no other text on this topic has done before now.

This book tells of how Kirk's band happened to be in the right place (Kansas City) at the right time (November 1929) with the right people (Jack Kapp, Mary Lou Williams, et al.) to start making jazz records. However, it also explains how the background and culture of the band and the character of its leader, Andy Kirk, meant that it had the enterprise, flexibility, and resources to adjust its repertoire to meet the requirements of record producers. They were seeking to make records for the specialist 'race' market that was aimed at African American consumers. Kirk's band was limited to that specialist market until 1936, when they found nationwide fame with vocal recordings that they made with their distinctive singer Pha (pronounced Fay) Terrell, a light-voiced baritone who was fond of breaking into falsetto.

Those vocal recordings of the later 1930s and early 1940s proved to be especially controversial with jazz critics for their style, which downplayed some of the cherished features of black jazz in favour of an apparent commercialism. I will show how this turn to commercialism was figured as inauthentic, white-sounding, and effeminate by influential critics like Gunther Schuller. It is precisely this disparity between critical expectations of black jazz and the apparently problematic musical style represented in the recordings of Kirk's band that forms the impetus for the argument of this book. In that respect, the recordings of the Clouds of Joy are considered in terms of what I see as formative interactions or contests between the enterprising culture and practices of Kirk's black band around stylistic expectations and the racist preconceptions that coloured the performance, recording, and criticism of their music.

In essence, this book proposes that Kirk's musicians appropriated racialized musical styles in their recordings in a subtle but effective way that was akin to black modes of expression that grew out of African American blackface performance practices. Such practices of masking or mask-play derived from the racist tropes of blackface minstrelsy but they were transformed during the early decades of the twentieth century by such black performers as Bert Williams, who always appeared in blackface but, it has been argued, turned it into a subtly subversive form of masking (cf. Sotiropoulos 2006: 46; Forbes 2008; Taylor & Austen 2012: 109–134). As with Williams's masked performances, the music of Kirk's band signified race as much as it undermined racist conceptions of apparently black styles, but, above all, it was always intended to be engaging and entertaining for contemporary audiences. This is the sort of practice that this book suggests can be heard in the play of styles in the recorded music of Andy Kirk and his Clouds of Joy.

Kirk himself, together with such band members as the much-lauded composer-pianist Mary Lou Williams and the much-criticized singer Pha Terrell, is reconceived within that context. Furthermore, the way the band manipulated musical styles and racial expectations of them in their recorded music will be explored for its significance in understanding how such black jazz musicians were instrumental in negotiations over what and how they performed and recorded. The practices and recordings of Kirk's band are, therefore, not just analysed for what they reflect of the jazz culture of their period but to illuminate the subtle but important influence that such musicians had upon it. It is precisely because the recorded music of Kirk's band proved troublesome for critics but was nevertheless highly regarded by audiences and record consumers that it has a special function in prevailing debates about race and jazz.

The band's agency in reconceiving racist notions of jazz styles is manifested in tensions that are evident between the music that is heard on their records and prevailing critical conceptions of the essential characteristics of black jazz. The book systematically considers the recordings of the Clouds of Joy for the way that interactions between the practices of the musicians, the concerns of audiences and the record industry, and underpinning critical ideologies of artistry, authenticity, and racial identity shaped and can be heard in them. The book is particularly concerned with the way that the Clouds of Joy confirmed and confounded critical expectations of a black band through the styles of music that they employed in their live performances and on records. To that end, it brings together analytical tools from musicology with critical perspectives drawn from literary theory and black studies that aim to show how intersecting discourses of racial and musical values are embedded in and expressed by the musical materials that are heard on the records.

Exploring the relationship between the band's live and recorded performances establishes the vital place of audiences, especially dancing ones, in shaping jazz as a conception and a practice in the swing era. That approach opens up new avenues for exploring the way that intersecting cultures of live performance and recording shaped our understanding of what jazz music is. Within that dynamic, the recorded music of Andy Kirk and his Clouds of Joy proves to be especially problematic for prevailing critical paradigms that tend to underpin aesthetic judgements with racist and sexualized notions of authenticity. So, this book will consider the distinctive output, character, and makeup of Kirk's band and its music in terms of the ways they trouble understandings of the cultures of jazz performance and recording in which the band operated.

The unpalatable commercialism and racial inauthenticity that critics like Schuller perceived in the output of Kirk's band is surely the reason that they are not as well-known today as other prominent black bands of the period. Had Kirk's band not made records that solicited the disdain of such influential critics, they might be better known, but we would not have the opportunity to hear what that special body of work might say about the critical values that underpin jazz. It is in that direction that this book shows how the band did not do what was expected of them in such a way as to shine a light on the critical values that conflate race with musical style. They thereby showed a way for black jazz musicians to challenge stereotyping based on racialized categories of style and envisioned a future for jazz beyond such racist essentialisms.

RIFFING ON THE EXISTING LITERATURE

Although this book is the first to be devoted to analysing the recordings of Andy Kirk and his Clouds of Joy, it follows in the wake of several books that have considered the band and its recordings more briefly within broader discussions of jazz. The most significant among these studies is Gunther Schuller's considerations contained in his two seminal volumes of jazz history and analysis, *Early Jazz* ([1968] 1986) and *The Swing Era* (1989).

Schuller's work stands out in the extant literature for articulating musical analysis of the band's recordings with broader historical and contextual research that position the music within a debate about the stylistic development of jazz. There are a number of problems with Schuller's approach that this book will address, however, and not the least is that he applies a set of tacit values that reinforce ideologies of musical artistry and racial authenticity in jazz criticism. This means that he is dismissive of the greater part of the recorded music of Kirk's band, even though their apparent commercialism and inauthenticity were very much a vital part of the jazz culture of their time. So, it is precisely by paying attention to the recordings of such musicians that we can challenge the dogmas underpinning jazz historiography and the canon of central figures and works of jazz to develop a fuller and more nuanced picture of jazz culture as a whole.

Before World War II, jazz was more often appreciated as a musical culture that embraced commercial forms than it was after the decline of swing and the rise of bebop and new forms of popular music in the postwar period. However, definitions of jazz that sought to separate what critics saw as authentic black artistic expression from seemingly inauthentic commercial forms certainly emerged during the swing era. For example, the adjectives 'hot' and 'sweet' were increasingly applied to jazz during the 1930s as a result of writing by European critics like the Belgian writer Robert Goffin ([1930] 1946) and the French commentator Hughes Panassié ([1934] 1936) in the first book-length considerations of the music.[2]

---

2 Panassié's two volumes, *Hot Jazz: The Guide to Swing Music* and *The Real Jazz* (1942) signify something of his agenda in their titles. Panassié's work followed in the wake Goffin's more anecdotal approach. Theodor Adorno's 1936 article 'On Jazz' used Panassié's terminology even

These writers deployed the terms 'hot' and 'sweet' precisely as a way to distinguish between what they saw as two distinct styles of music that should be valued differently. In essence, hot jazz was figured as a highly modernistic mode of an essentially improvised and authentic black musical expression, whereas sweet jazz was painted as a derivative commercial form, most often performed by white dance bands and featuring readily indulgent emotional and/or physical appeal rather than challenging artistry.

The trouble with such distinctions is that they struggle to cope with those figures and music that defy the division of the jazz field into discrete stylistic categories. The heightened commercialization of jazz during the 1930s meant that the period was actually rife with musicians and music, which, for one reason or another, did not sit comfortably within either of those racialized categories of musical style. Duke Ellington, for example, was later described (using his own words) as 'Beyond Category' precisely because much of his music appears to defy established stylistic conventions (Hasse 1993).

To my mind, Ellington's music, as much as that of Kirk's band, is problematic of categories precisely because of an imperative to get beyond the racist essentialism which underpinned musical categorizations. So, by casting light on the ways in which the music of Kirk's band defied the sorts of racialized understandings of jazz styles that developed with the writings of Goffin, Panassié, and Schuller, we are as much illuminating the efforts of other contemporary black musicians, like Ellington, for their part in redefining jazz.

Aside from Schuller's studies, there are several book-length surveys which consider Kirk's band within a discussion of the development and distinctiveness of jazz in and around Kansas City (Russell [1971] 1983; Pearson 1988; Driggs & Haddix 2005). These surveys apply a less musicologically critical mode than is in Schuller's work, but they place the band and their recordings within more detailed contexts of time and place, which is no less ideological. In that regard, Ross Russell considers Kirk's band within an agenda of explicating the specific and influential style of jazz that arose in Kansas City and the surrounding region. Frank Driggs and Chuck Haddix draw on an impressive array of informative sources to document the activities of the band within a similar sort of

---

while it challenges his sort of values. The American critic Winthrop Sargeant used similar terms in his *Jazz, Hot and Hybrid* (1938 [1975]), and H. Wilder Hobson presented similar values to Panassié's in *American Jazz Music* (1939), although he distinguished between 'natural' and 'commercial' jazz.

argument about regional specificity and influence. In contrast with these approaches, this book is more concerned with utilizing the unique situation of Kirk's band and their recorded music to critique thinking about categorizations in jazz that is founded on just such agendas of stylistic differentiation.

Nathan Pearson's 1988 book is notable for drawing on firsthand accounts transcribed from interviews conducted with several of Kirk's band members. That volume, along with Kirk's *Twenty Years on Wheels*, which contains his own recollections 'as told to' the journalist and critic Amy Lee, represents important primary source material that, along with others, informed this book. However, such reminiscences, collected long after the reported events, are not without problems, and the extent of the analysis in such volumes is strictly limited and tends towards hagiography. In contrast, this book suggests that if Kirk and his band deserve recovering from critical neglect or disparigment, it is because of what an analysis of their recorded music and their particularly off-centre position, as a marginalized band with distinctive regional origins, says about the mainstream of jazz and the racialized values that underpin it.

There are, of course, many shorter considerations of Kirk's band that can be found in specialist jazz journals and the standard reference works on jazz. Amongst the magazine articles are some important interviews with Kirk (1959, 1977, 1989) and with Mary Lou Williams ([1954] 1997: 887–116). The biographies of Williams (Dahl [1999] 2001; and Kernodle 2004) also explore her work with the Clouds of Joy within the broader context of her long musical career.

There are some fairly extensive appreciations of Kirk and his band penned by the likes of Albert McCarthy in *Jazz and Blues* (1971), Gene Fernett in *Swing Out: Great Negro Dance Bands* ([1971] 1993), and Chip Deffaa in *In the Mainstream* (1992). None of those studies, however, consider Andy Kirk and his Clouds of Joy in the way of this volume, which is much more concerned with how their recordings represent and contest connections between notions of musical style and race within the conditions of jazz culture of their time.

The approach that this book takes towards the recordings of the Clouds of Joy also fills a gap in the existing literature which considers relationships between conceptions of jazz music and race. In that regard, the subject of this book is situated between studies of the racial dynamics in early jazz culture, which have been explored by the likes of Tim Brooks (2005) and Charles Hersch (2009), and considerations of race associated with postwar black music, like that offered in *Race Music* by Guthrie P. Ramsey Jr. (2004).

Studies of the swing era are under-represented in this sort of literature, but it is not just that chronological gap that this book helps to address but also a methodological one. Nevertheless, the book's critical enterprise forms a passage between those approaches that discern formative musical-racial conceptions emerging in the cultures of early jazz and those accounts of music of the post-war period that more explicitly represented musical-racial discourse within the context of civil rights politics.

In his documenting of the 'struggle to bring black musical culture to America', Brooks suggests that black entrepreneurship was instrumental in establishing a culture of recording and consumption of jazz by black Americans in the face of a white-owned industry (2005: 3). That industry was otherwise preoccupied with offering stereotyped representations of the antebellum South and associated blackface-derived mediations of black identities. Brooks shows how early jazz culture demonstrates that 'race relations in the United States were not a simple matter of black versus white' (2005: 4) but a complex of interactions and negotiations about racial identities that were conditioned by the new recording industry.

It is this sort of idea of formative negotiations over racial identities within the racist cultures of recording and live performance of jazz that is developed in this study. The racial politics involved in the band's representations of black musical styles and their departure from them is a particular aspect of this book's argument that develops Brooks's observations. It also gives them greater theoretical weight because Brooks does not offer much in the way of theoretical analysis. In that regard, this book's argument also complements Hersch's thesis about the origins of such negotiations over race in early jazz culture.

In *Subversive Sounds* (2009), Hersch explored how the emergence of jazz in New Orleans involved inherently 'impure' concepts of race and music that were both enduring and powerfully transformative:

At a time when racial boundaries in America were rigidifying, jazz arose out of and encouraged racial boundary crossings by creating racially mixed spaces and racially impure music, both of which altered the racial identities of musicians and listeners. (2009: 5)

Hersch shows that this transformative understanding of early jazz music-making stems from its origins in New Orleans's complex and 'creolizing' entertainment industry, which effectively mixed up musical and racial markers as different music and musicians came into contact with one another.

That notion of creolization stands in contrast to prevailing but utopian understandings of jazz's origins in the 'melting pot' idea of America, which presented it rather as the resultant expression of a cosy sort of intermingling of different racial characteristics. Hersch proposes instead that a more dynamic concept of cultural circulation operated in early jazz that emerged from and was sustained by 'continuous interaction between the races' in the special musical spaces that arose in New Orleans's nighttime entertainment district (2009: 8). Hersch shows that the ready adaptability of New Orleans's musicians to their racialized circumstances was vital in this enterprise, and the argument of this book extends that sort of thesis into new musical territory of a later period.

In exploring the ways that Andy Kirk and his Clouds of Joy forged their musical identity relative to their ever-changing circumstances within the racialized performance and recording cultures that they experienced, the much wider circulation of ideas about race and jazz in the 1930s are implicated. There are some parallels between the sort of interactive and dynamic culture of New Orleans in the early jazz period of Hersch's study and that of Kansas City in the late 1920s and early 1930s, but, in many ways, Kirk's band was embroiled in a more established and racially segregated musical culture in which racist dogma around jazz styles had already crystallized.

The ever-wider distribution and consumption of jazz that occurred during the 1930s meant that the sort of circulations that Hersch describes increasingly moved from a localized to a national context. They also became about forging identities that were formed at least as much through radio broadcasts and recordings as in the spaces for live performances. In their transition from a local to a national profile as a result of recording, the Clouds of Joy are emblematic of changing modes of negotiation over racial identity politics in jazz that occurred during the 1930s and 1940s and the circulation of ideas about race and music that came with them. This book charts their flexibility and functionality in the face of that changing landscape for jazz.

A similar sort of conception of musical-racial identity formation, but one circulating within postwar black communities, is represented in Ramsey's *Race Music* (2004). Ramsey's study focuses on how 'an average audience of African Americans' has made sense of black music since the 1940s. He shows how subjective understandings of such music formed relative to prevailing notions of black identity that were continually and communally reshaped but especially at specific moments and in specific places.

Through a consideration of his own and his family's interactions with jazz since World War II, Ramsey shows that the racial meanings and functions of the music for a black community are contingent upon the historical moment and formative kinds of social interaction that occur in what he calls 'community theaters'. For Ramsey, these spaces include homes, churches, juke joints, dance halls, nightclubs, and theatres that act as 'public and private spaces [that] provide audiences with a place to negotiate with others—in a highly social way—what cultural expressions such as music mean' (Ramsey 2004: 77).

Many of the 'theaters' that Ramsey identifies functioned in the earlier period in which the Clouds of Joy were making records. In that regard, I want to consider their recorded music as powerfully theatrical in a related way that is both literal and figurative. However, in contrast to this study, Ramsey is predominantly concerned with an era in which issues of race, power, and identity were more readily and openly debated and, not least, by African Americans themselves. This does not mean that such formative discussions about music and black identities were not taking place in communities surrounding jazz before the war, but as this book will show, for black musicians especially, they took subtler but no less political forms than in the civil rights era.

So, this book extends some of Ramsey's observations backwards in time to consider those interactions surrounding the performance and recording situations of the Clouds of Joy and the critical discussions about the music that they involved. It considers these interactions as being just as significant in shaping understandings concerning jazz and race as Ramsey's later 'community theaters' were. In that respect, the band itself is as much a part of Ramsey's 'theatrical' community as any later black group—negotiating with its others (audiences, critics, producers, etc.) to form new understandings about what music means in terms of race.

STYLISH SIGNIFYIN(G): MANIPULATING MUSICAL-RACIAL MASKS

This book develops Ramsey's theatrical metaphor in a different way to suggest that the Clouds of Joy were engaged in a particular sort of musical 'theater' about race that was situated in an about the musical style of their recordings. In contrast to Ramsey's study, it was a theatre that drew on a similar sort of representational politics as that found in black forms of blackface minstrelsy, but it most often took a subtle musical form that involved Signifyin(g), to invoke Henry Louis Gates Jr.'s racially specific term, on prevailing racialized understandings of musical styles (Gates 1988).[3]

Gates's study of black storytelling traditions led him to propose the idea that the black-vernacular rhetorical practice of Signifyin(g) represents the 'trope of tropes' of African American expression within modernity (Gates 1988: 52). The trickster figure, like the Signifying Monkey in black folklore, is ubiquitous in black oratorical traditions and is symbolic for Gates of a mode of subversive language-use deployed to survive and challenge the racism experienced by blacks in urban modernity. Samuel A. Floyd Jr. sums up Gates's notion of Signifyin(g) succinctly in *The Power of Black Music* (1995):

> In the black vernacular, Signifyin(g) is figurative, implicative speech. It makes use of vernacular tropings such as 'marking, loud-talking, testifying, calling out, sounding, rapping, playing the dozens' (Gates 1988, 52), and other rhetorical devices. Signifyin(g) is a way of saying one thing and meaning another; it is reinterpretation, a metaphor for the revision of previous texts and figures; it is tropological thought, repetition with difference, the obscuring of meaning (33, 88)—all to achieve or reverse power, to improve situations, and to achieve pleasing results for the signifier. (Floyd 1995: 95)

Floyd conflates Gates's concept of Signifyin(g) with Houston Baker's observations about different sorts of performative rhetoric deployed by leading black political activists. Baker argued that such figures showed a 'mastery' of the minstrel's mask or else a 'deformation' of such masking that was achieved through the deliberate display of unsettlingly black characteristics. He further suggested that, whereas the likes of Booker T. Washington mastered minstrel-like rhetoric only to contest its racist basis, the likes of W. E. B. Du Bois and Paul Lawrence Dunbar deformed the enduring tropes of minstrelsy 'by displaying distinguishing and disturbing codes [of blackness], refusing and defusing the non-sense of the minstrel mask' (Floyd 1995: 88).

Whether it took the form of the mastery or the deformation of the mask of minstrelsy, this book shows that Signifyin(g) stylistic

---

3 Gates capitalizes the word and brackets the last letter to distinguish its African American vernacular usage and to demonstrate its rhetorical power, which derives from its subversion of standard language usage.

mask-play involving jazz styles functioned as an effective tool for addressing race within jazz of the period. It drew on a mode of performance/representation that was already understood by musicians, audiences, critics, and record producers alike, due to the long history and functionality of blackface minstrelsy within the entertainment industry. The shared understanding of this form of musical-racial 'theater' allowed for relatively safe negotiations about racial identities to take place in jazz in the period before the civil rights era when there were greater risks for blacks to speak openly about race.

In sum, this study of the recordings of Andy Kirk and his Clouds of Joy presents an opportunity to explore how Signifyin(g) mask-play involving jazz styles is deployed within a body of work that spans a period marked with the challenges that were faced by most, if not all, black jazz musicians as they operated within racist cultures of performance, recording, and criticism. In contrast to Floyd's focus on 'call-response' tropes found within black musical materials, the analysis in this book considers a wider range of markers of musical style. It aims to show how racialized styles were signifiers that were, in effect, worn as musical masks and manipulated by such black musicians as those in Kirk's band in a trickster-like manner to Signify on such conventions and their racist underpinning.

We will see that the Signifyin(g) manipulation of racialized stylistic markers allowed Kirk's musicians to function and survive within racist cultures of performance and recording. It also allowed them to thrive and subtly challenge racist dogmas surrounding jazz music while producing records that were always highly appealing, if not downright entertaining, for audiences. It is in that regard that the recordings of Kirk's band represent such black musicians as self-empowering trickster figures within jazz recording culture, playing with and on stylistic expectations of a black band. This book charts the manifestations of that stylistic mask-play from 1929 to 1949 and its reincarnation on records in 1957. In the process, it uncovers how connected notions of jazz styles and race were articulated and contested by such black jazz musicians when they recorded.

ANDY KIRK'S UPBRINGING AND EDUCATION IN MUSICAL-RACIAL MASKING

The Signifyin(g) stylistic mask-play of the Clouds of Joy derives at least in part from the upbringing and character of the band's leader, Andy Kirk. Kirk was born in 1898 in Newport, Kentucky.[4] His mother died before his fourth birthday, and, as his father had absconded, Kirk went to live with his mother's widowed half-sister, Mary Banion, and her three children. Kirk's 'Auntie' Mary was hard-working, protective, and above all, determined to secure a better situation (Kirk 1989: 6). So, in 1904, she moved her extended family to Denver, Colorado, where Kirk became part of a comparatively small black population in a community that was more racially integrated than most of the period.

Kirk recalled, 'My greatest advantage was to have lived in Denver. We [African Americans] were not recognized as equals, but we did have equal opportunity for education' (Kirk 1989: 33). So, Kirk received his early musical tuition alongside his white classmates and it was overseen by Wilberforce J. Whiteman, the father of the later famous bandleader Paul Whiteman. Kirk recalled that this early musical schooling did not extend much beyond tonic sol-fa and harmony singing, and it was not until after leaving school that he developed as an instrumentalist (Kirk 1989: 17). Nevertheless, it was his experience of music-making within the relatively integrated culture of the Denver school system that shaped his understanding of the musical representation of race.

At Denver's Gilpin School, Kirk sang as part of a mixed-race vocal quintet. The music they sang sometimes troubled him for its racist stereotyping. In 'Sleep, Kentucky Babe', for example, Kirk found the racist lyric 'Lay your kinky, woolly head on your Mammy's breast' deeply problematic, and so he resorted to wordless vowels for that line (Kirk 1989: 18). That led to his eighth-grade teacher, Miss Boyer, taking him aside to explain that singing those words did not reflect on him or his race. However, Kirk felt that she was wrong to presume the innocence of such racialized music. As he put it, 'I knew she didn't really know how the kids with "kinky, woolly hair" felt about that song. We were sensitive about these things' (Kirk 1989: 18).

This shows that because of the racial pride that was instilled in him by his aspirational Auntie, Kirk was already inclined to resist racial stereotyping, but his form of resistance was too blatant as he was ultimately forced to sing the song as it was written. The following Christmas, however, when he was required to deliver a recitation, Kirk found that he

---

4 Kirk's father, Charles, always maintained that Kirk was actually born in the house that he had shared with Kirk's mother in Cincinnati. However, Kirk learned that his mother had travelled the short distance across the river to Newport to give birth because she wanted him born in her home state of Kentucky. Chip Deffaa (1992: 77) has suggested that this narrative might be wishful thinking by Kirk, who felt closer to his late mother than his father.

could send up stereotypes through stylized (masked) performance without censure from the teachers and much to the delight of his classmates. He adopted what he called 'farmers' lingo' to perform his poem, and reported that 'it was so different from the usual angels' wings flapping, that the kids broke up' (Kirk 1989: 19). It was precisely that sort of undermining of stereotypes through such entertaining Signifyin(g) performance that stayed with him when he came to record with his band.

By Kirk's account, Denver was a city that offered plenty of opportunity for African Americans to engage with music and theatre and he took advantage of many of them. His autobiography makes it clear that his aspirational upbringing generally led him away from what were then considered lowly cultural forms towards higher ones that would better represent his race. This reflected a broader agenda of race pride that was current within the African American community at the time. Kirk recalled, 'There were minstrel shows at the Empress Theatre, but some of us looked down on them. We felt they weren't up-building' (Kirk 1989: 19). On the other hand, Kirk engaged with local bands that played light classics for dancing, and like many black kids from aspirational middle-class families, he took piano lessons. However, the feminized terrain of piano studies and the distraction of more overtly male-orientated team sports eventually put an end to them (Kirk 1989: 19–20).

Kirk left school at sixteen because he could see no point in over-schooling himself when Denver's most educated blacks could only aspire to become chauffeurs or butlers. His first jobs after leaving school, which included operating public elevators at the Denver Dry Goods store and shining shoes in a barber shop in Sterling, Colorado, taught him the art of show business, because, as he reported, it resulted in more generous tips (Kirk 1989: 35–36). His job in the barber shop also led him to take his musical studies more seriously.

As Sterling was some 130 miles away from Denver, Kirk lodged above the shop in which he worked and he filled the hours between his shifts practicing the tenor saxophone in his lodgings. That instrument was recommended to Kirk by one of his barber colleagues because it was still a relative novelty and was thus likely to lead to paid employment (Kirk 1989: 38–39). In fact, even before he was able and confident enough to play the instrument in public, Kirk got work that involved simply sitting on the bandstand with his saxophone, as the instrument's mere presence was enough to signal the band's black-jazz modernity (Kirk 1989: 41).

Kirk gradually became more capable and confident as a saxophonist, and when he returned to Denver to work as a postman, he began to take his musical studies even more seriously. He took saxophone lessons with Franz Rath, whom Kirk described as 'a former clarinetist with the Boston Symphony' (Kirk 1989: 40). He also studied arranging with Walter E. Light, a timpanist with the Denver Symphony Orchestra, and he took singing lessons (Kirk 1989: 43). He began playing the sousa-phone and string bass alongside his saxophone because he realized that the more doubling instruments that he could play, the more employable he would be as a musician.

In seeking out tuition from such distinguished Denver-based orches-tral musicians as Rath and Light, Kirk showed he was aspirational towards respectability in his musical education. That predisposition towards 'so-phisticated' musical culture carried over into his work in the dance-band field when, in 1919, he got a job playing with George Morrison's band that he held down alongside his post office duties. Morrison was a violinist and he directed the leading black band in Denver at the time. It was the resident orchestra at the fancy Albany Hotel and provided music for its white patrons and social dancers. Morrison also organized smaller combinations for private parties in the homes or gardens of well-to-do white-society figures.

Kirk recalled that Morrison's band 'had a sweetish style but also a beat. His orchestra was versatile. It could move easily from one-steps and two-steps into the schottisches and waltzes and light classics his society clientele demanded' (Kirk 1989: 43). The ability of Morrison to please white audiences with relatively classy sweet music, while still presenting some measure of a black musical identity, represented the sort of stylistic versatility that, as we will see, Kirk brought into his own work with the Clouds of Joy.

By this stage Kirk was, like the rest of Morrison's band, a capable music reader and he was often required to transpose cello parts of stock arrangements into a key to suit his saxophone because orchestrations did not yet carry sax parts as standard (Kirk 1989: 46). Furthermore, Morrison encouraged Kirk to develop his music-theory skills by making an arrangement of one of Kirk's waltzes as a means of teaching him about band orchestration (Kirk 1989: 45). In fact, Kirk found Morrison both encouraging and patient with anyone that he felt had musical talent.

Morrison's supportive, educative manner was another thing that clearly rubbed off on Kirk, because, as we will see, he adopted similar nurturing practices with members of the Clouds of Joy and, most no-tably, with Mary Lou Williams. This chimed with Kirk's genial and prac-tical manner. He was not a strict disciplinarian like Jimmy Lunceford, another Morrison musician who went on to become a famous band-leader, but encouraged a vital culture of mutual support and camaraderie in his band that helped the musicians to cope and develop within the racist cultures that they experienced. He preferred to exercise soft power and, even when he ceased to play in its ranks, he saw himself very much as a member of the band who happened to be its director, rather than as a detached leader.

To complement his musical education with Morrison, Kirk went to hear many of the musicians that came through Denver on tour. These were mostly white performers, but he did hear the likes of 'Happy' Gene Coy and His Black Aces and Ferdinand 'Jelly Roll' Morton (Kirk 1989: 46).[5] In his autobiography, Kirk recalled the stylistic distance between the music performed by these black figures and that which he experienced with Morrison's white-society band. Whereas the Black Aces played original music based on the blues, Morrison's band emphasized arrangements of popular tunes and utilized slower tempos, albeit with a definite beat that marked out their blackness. Morton introduced Kirk to the 'stomping' New Orleans style of jazz and the fact that it was apparently alien to him shows that Kirk was not really familiar with such jazz but was experienced in a different kind of dance music that was tailored to the tastes of white-society audiences.

We can get a flavour of Kirk's musical experiences with Morrison from a recording he made with Morrison's band. Kirk toured to New York with Morrison in the spring of 1920 and recorded for Columbia with them there in March and April of that year. The side that was released from those recording sessions was a medley of two popular tunes (A2945) that framed Jimmie Morgan's song 'I Know Why' with Frank Warshauer's 'My Cuban Dreams'.[6] These selections contrast in tempo and they show that Morrison's band emphasized a fairly indulgent style of melodic music. Underlying it, however, was a rhythmic bounce, heard in the banjo and percussion (woodblocks) in the central 'I Know Why' section of the track, which stops the music from becoming too sweetly melodic in its style and instead makes it highly danceable and somewhat 'hot' sounding.

Kirk's bass is all but inaudible on the record and this was something that he noticed at the time. On hearing the recording, he reflected that his training in the orchestral style of string-bass playing meant that his instrument did not record well and so he turned to the sousaphone

---

5 Morton came to Denver as a lone pianist but later performed with Kirk in one of Morrison's smaller function bands.

6 The track can be heard on YouTube (Morrison 1920): https://www.youtube.com/watch?v=DAzkJNozAoo

thereafter (Kirk 1989: 44). This willingness to change his practice following considered reflection was one of Kirk's great strengths, and it undoubtedly accounts for much of his lasting success as a bandleader with the Clouds of Joy within the ever-changing racist cultures of live performance and recording that they experienced.

In 1922 Kirk toured with Morrison's band again, this time to the West Coast of the United States as part of a circus-cum-cabaret package. Kirk is clear that 'we got the tour because of our showmanship talents', and this illustrates that Morrison's band was as capable as a vaudeville-type act as it was as a purveyor of relatively sophisticated dance music for white audiences. We will see in the next chapter that such theatrical showmanship was to come with Kirk into his work with the Clouds of Joy, and it no doubt helped Morrison's band secure their tour of the Pantages vaudeville circuit of venues in 1924.[7]

That tour ended in Kansas City in May 1925 and it was there that Kirk heard Bennie Moten's band for the first time. He wrote:

> I'll never forget the heat from Bennie Moten's five-piece band at a little after-hours club on 18th Street. It was the first time I'd ever heard a band like that. It was *swinging*—playing the blues, all kinds of blues. (Kirk 1989: 50)

The sort of hot jazz exhibited by Moten was clearly still new to Kirk, who was otherwise grounded in a differently styled repertoire of arrangements of popular tunes and light classics. That sweet-styled music was also in an entirely different category in terms of its representation of class and race dynamics. Although we will see that Kirk did absorb features of the sort of stomping hot jazz that both Morten and Moten had shown him, Kirk never strayed far from the racial-musical aspirations that he developed at school in Denver and with Morrison. Kirk's predisposition was always towards providing high-quality black popular music for polite white society, and this helps explain why Kirk did not feel he was in competition with Moten and his band when he moved the Clouds of Joy to Kansas City in the later 1920s.

Shortly after he returned from the tour with Morrison in 1925, Kirk married Mary Colson, a sometime pianist with Morrison's outfit.

---

7 The Greek-American Alexander Pantages built a chain of 15 theatres in various western cities of the United States that he ran until 1929 when increased competition from the film industry and a rape scandal caused him to give up his empire. See this Stanford web page about him: https://web.stanford.edu/~ichriss/Pantages.htm

The couple spent their honeymoon in northern Colorado, and that resulted in Kirk working away from the Morrison organization with a band that was run by a man named Frank Junior Jr. (Kirk 1989: 51). That group contained several former members of Morrison's band, including the talented young saxophonist Alvin 'Fats' Wall, whom Kirk had befriended during his Morrison days. An advertisement from a Chicago-based band looking for a tuba and a saxophone player caught their eye and Kirk and Wall decided to audition for the jobs and thus headed to the windy city (Kirk 1989: 53).

The opportunity in Chicago ultimately came to nothing but Wall secured work with a newly formed band that would ultimately become the Clouds of Joy. Knowing that Kirk was stranded in Chicago, Wall got the band's leader, the Texan trumpeter Terence 'T.' Holder, to invite Kirk to join that new band, and so began Kirk's long career with the Clouds of Joy (Kirk 1989: 54). Holder had a background playing with Alphonso Trent's band, which was somewhat like Morrison's, because it was the resident orchestra at the Adolphous Hotel in Dallas, Texas, and so Kirk found himself in a familiar environment in which capable black musicians provided relatively classy popular music for white patrons.

So, by the time Kirk joined the group that would become his band, he was well schooled as a musician and had experienced the stylistic versatility that was essential to survive in the racist music business of the period. Although he had experienced some of the prevailing styles and practices of leading black jazz musicians, Kirk also retained a predilection for the sort of tuneful and refined music that he had sung at school under Whiteman's instruction, hummed in the elevators at Denver Dry Goods, and played and recorded with Morrison's band for well-to-do white regional audiences. That sort of music chimed with the race pride that had been instilled in him as he grew up with his aspirational Auntie Mary in the relatively integrated environment of Denver.

Kirk remained as keen to provide a modern image of black popular music for audiences as he had been when he first sat with his new-fangled saxophone in a band in Denver. He was never comfortable, however, with presenting racist stereotypes of blackness of the sort he had experienced in music-making at school. In fact, his racial pride meant he always resisted such stereotypes by Signifyin(g) on them in stylized and entertaining ways, in much the same manner as he had in his Christmas recitation at school, most often by drawing on the mixture of sweet and hot styles he had experienced with Morrison's band.

In short, Kirk's upbringing and education meant that by the time he joined the Clouds of Joy, he was the embodiment of the critical enterprise of this book, because he was very much caught between the imperatives of the racist entertainment industry to conform to prevailing notions of black music and of representing a proud African American modernity. In that regard, he was always keen to show that black music could be classy and have a broad popular appeal, and he always sought to send up the racialized situation of his band and their music whilst retaining racial dignity and an easy-going affability. That meant that his band always remained entertaining and their racial politics stayed relatively subtle or low-key. However, when we listen for their stylistic mask-play, it can be heard to speak loudly of and to Signify on their particular racialized situation. Furthermore, it echoes a broader context of black musicians performing and recording within the racist structures of jazz culture of the 1930s and 1940s.

AIMS, METHOD, AND STRUCTURE: LISTENING FOR STYLISH MASK-PLAY

The recorded output of Andy Kirk and his Clouds of Joy involves some 170 tracks. This book does not attempt to discuss every single one of them and a couple of simple principles have been applied for their selection for study. The first of these principles involves focusing on those recordings most illustrative of the practices, contexts, and discourses that are germane to this study of the racial politics that are bound up with the styles of music heard on the records. This means that some tracks, which are more commonly analysed by jazz critics because of their apparent hot-jazz content, are not considered in much detail at all, whereas others, which are more often derided or ignored for their apparent commerciality or inauthenticity, are given fuller attention than in other studies.

In applying this form of stylistic inclusivity, in which the sweet music is given at least as much critical weight as the hot jazz, the aim is to signify a broader conception of musical style within the performing and recording cultures of prewar jazz than has hitherto prevailed. I aim to develop that perspective whilst illuminating a body of work that is rife with negotiations between perceptions of authentic black jazz artistry and critical notions of inauthentic musical commerciality.

Another of the principles applied in selecting recordings for analysis is that they should be easily obtainable on CD or by downloading or streaming from the Internet. Since the music of Andy Kirk and his Clouds of Joy was first recorded, there have been many releases of the recordings in various different formats and compilations. In writing this book, I sometimes listened to the original issues on 78 rpm discs, but I found the transfers on the CDs in *The Chronological Classics* series useful, despite their often hissy or muddy sound, not only for the music that they contain but also for the discography-styled listings in their accompanying liner notes.[8]

These CDs are now out of print and are getting harder and costlier to obtain. However, the Internet has made finding such obsolete releases far easier than it was in the past, and in fact, all of the tracks on *The Chronological Classics* series of discs are now readily available for download from online book and music stores at minimal cost, albeit without the liner notes. On such sites, the series is most often retitled as the *Complete Jazz Series*, and failing that, a search for the band by name and year usually brings up those recordings. Many of the tracks discussed in the book can also be heard for free on audio- and video-sharing sites such as YouTube, but I cannot vouch for the sound quality or legality of listening to the music through that medium. The 'Soundie' films referenced in chapter 3 of the book can also be viewed through that website.

Some of the recordings studied in chapter 3 are exceptions to the rule of ready availability on CD. They were not studio recordings made for commercial release but tracks that were 'transcribed' from remote radio broadcasts transmitted from Cleveland's Trianon Ballroom in early 1937. Their poor audio quality may well explain why they have not yet appeared on CD. Nevertheless, those tracks are considered in this book because they are still the most readily available of the band's 'live' recordings from the 1930s and they serve to reflect on the studio-made records from the perspective of the 'live' band as it broadcast on the radio.

The Trianon transcriptions were released on LP on the *Jazz Society* label (AA503) and also, in part, on the *Jazz Anthology* label ([F]30J5133). The *Jazz Society* LP, *Andy Kirk and his Clouds of Joy Orchestra "live" from the Trianon Ballroom in Cleveland*, regularly comes up for sale in online auctions and the music that it contains is now readily available for download from online retailers for only a small cost. On such download sites, the LP is most often retitled as *Sepia Jazz*, but don't let that put you off because it is identical in its content to the LP release.

---

8 The original 78 rpm releases are revealing of two particular things that are not always clear from other media or discographies: the surnames of the authors and or lyricists of the tunes that were recorded are indicated on labels (with varying degrees of accuracy) and the pairing of tracks that appeared on the records is represented.

These principles for selecting the recordings mean, of course, that certain tracks are not considered within the purview of this study. Some of those may well have been considered in previous studies of the band (mentioned earlier). Others, like some of the transcriptions of the band's broadcasts for the Armed Forces Radio Service, if they still exist at all, are collectors' items that have never been transferred to any medium beyond that on which they were originally recorded.[9] If this study helps in bringing more of such resources into the public domain, so much the better.

The principal aim of the analysis, however, is to highlight how we can hear the negotiation of stylistic-racial identities represented in and by the band's recorded music. That requires imparting some contextual information and especially an appreciation of critical values that have been applied to the music. If that contextual writing, which most often opens the chapters, represents a diversion from the music itself, it nevertheless helps attune ears to hear the distinctively troublesome or dissonant racial-stylistic features of the music on the records. Such features extend from rather general markers concerning genre, to really specific ones associated with rhythmic, melodic, and harmonic details of a given track or moment therein.

In keeping with the aspirations of this book series, the aim has been to keep the musical analysis accessible yet illuminating. In that respect, matrix numbers and track timings are included whenever possible to help direct listening and to overcome any difficulties that may be experienced in reading musical notation of transcriptions, which, in any case, can only approximate what is heard on the records. The material analysis of the music, however, is intended to function as an illuminating tool of critique that is as valuable as any of the other critical approaches that are deployed in the book. In this sense, this study aims to be interdisciplinary in its methodology.

The structure of the book proceeds in chronological fashion but it also develops thematically and methodologically. The first chapter explores the first group of recordings that were made by Andy Kirk and his Clouds of Joy in the period 1929–1931. It also provides an opportunity to explore where the band came from and to consider what sort of music they performed before they came to record and the contexts in

---

9 The Jubilee shows, made for the Armed Forces Radio Service during 1944, are not listed in the standard Kirk discographies but are referenced in the book on Theodor 'Fats' Navarro by Leif Bo Petersen and Theo Rehak (2009). Their source is the Andy Kirk Collection at the University of Michigan, which includes scripts to various shows. Two of the shows (numbered 68 and 70) have been released on CD. Most of the others have not yet surfaced on commercial recordings.

which it was produced. This helps to document the racist cultures in which the band operated, and it frames how the band effectively 'blacked up' their style when they recorded for Brunswick in Kansas City and how they began to manipulate and Signify on that stylistic maskery.

The very first recordings made in 1929 ranged from highly improvised 'head' arrangements, exemplified by 'Blue Clarinet Stomp', to more carefully crafted charts produced by Mary Lou Williams, such as 'Mess-a-Stomp'. The chapter shows how Williams, initially under the tutelage of Kirk, developed a style for the band's first recordings that was indebted to the stomping and riff-based jazz of Bennie Moten's Kansas City group, but it was nevertheless already individual and comparatively sophisticated. It married markers of Southwestern jazz with a classier dance-music sensibility that was the heritage of Kirk and the Clouds of Joy. In that sense, Kirk's band was as 'Sweet and Hot' in their hybrid musical style as they were in their 1930 recording of that tune, which is analysed in the chapter.

The 1930 and 1931 recording sessions show a less dogmatic adherence to an identifiably black style of hot jazz, as Kirk's band developed greater confidence that came with experience of recording more familiar repertoire. In those sessions, Kirk drew the highly theatrical 'Casey Jones Special' from the band's regular repertoire to record alongside Williams's specially composed pieces and stylized versions of stock arrangements. That track palpably demonstrates how a subversive form of stylistically based theatricality operated relative to the stereotypes of blackness and the evident urban black modernity of the band.

The second chapter considers the swing-styled records that the band made in the later 1930s and early 1940s for Decca. Mary Lou Williams's new arrangements and her re-arrangements of her outmoded stomping-jazz pieces serve to show how a smooth style of swing replaced the stomping jazz heard in the Brunswick sessions. Nevertheless, a stylistic blacking up for recording still prevailed and it was was the band's recording of the riff-based 'Christopher Columbus' that proved to be the biggest hit for the Clouds of Joy in the 'race records' market, despite it being uncharacteristic of the band's elegant swing music. In that regard, 'A Mellow Bit of Rhythm' is read as representing a sort of manifesto for the subtle style of bouncy swing that the Clouds of Joy played for dancers. This contrasted with the brasher styles developed in New York where energetic Lindy Hop dancing prevailed.

The band's elegant style of subtle swing also shows that the Clouds of Joy enjoyed a different sort of relationship with dancers than other black bands did at, say, New York's famous Savoy Ballroom, the long-acknowledged home of swing dancing. Through an exploration of the rhythmic features of swing and a consideration of their relationship to dancing bodies, the chapter seeks to extend the few considerations in this direction that have been made by André Hodeir, Charles Keil, and Howard Spring by invoking John Mowitt's consideration of drumming as a means of forming musical subjects. The proposal is that in a process of responding to one another's beat, a band and its social dancers develop a sort of communal beating out of swing rhythms between the parties that at once calls and identifies a particular kind of swing identity.

Williams's arrangement of 'The Count' is considered as her swan song swing number, and together with the boogie-woogie styled 'Little Joe from Chicago', it highlights how novelty portrait pieces featured in the band's swing repertory. The band's notorious manager, Joe Glaser, is depicted in a double-voiced way through Williams's application of hot and sweet styles, which can be read as both a celebration and a critique of Glaser. Such Signifyin(g) stylistic ambiguity becomes an out-and-out battle between styles in 'The Count' in which hot jazz is seen to triumph over any sweet commercial style.

The third chapter considers the numerous vocal recordings that followed Kirk's success in convincing Decca to record a special ballad: 'Until the Real Thing Comes Along'. For critics like Gunther Schuller, that ballad marked the beginning of a sort of rot that infected the recordings of the Clouds of Joy because it led to the replacement of hot jazz with what, for critics in Schuller's line, amounts to the worst excesses of sweet commercial pop music. In this sense, one might think that Adorno had a point when he suggested that the effect of the culture industry was to standardize music. However, Pha Terrell's apparently 'queer' falsetto performance of the ballad suggests that in whiting-up for these sweet vocal records, the Clouds of Joy never lost their subversive mask-play but employed it in ever more subtle and complex ways to decry their assumed racial-musical identity.

The chapter goes on to consider how Terrell's sweet ballads were replaced with more bluesy-theatrical vocals when June Richmond joined the band in 1939. The loss of Dick Wilson, Pha Terrell and Mary Lou Williams from the Clouds of Joy in the early 1940s marked a watershed for the band as suddenly Richmond's highly theatrical portrayal of blackness was foregrounded and helped propel the band to success in the newly formed 'race records' chart, the Harlem Hit Parade. 'Take It and Git', a decidedly black-styled novelty number was the first No. 1 in that chart, and then Richmond's bluesy 'Hey Lawdy Mama' reached the No. 4 spot in 1946.

Richmond's vocals marked a move toward rhythm and blues that was only intensified when the Clouds of Joy made recordings with the male gospel quartet The Jubalaires in 1945 and 1946. Stuart Goosman's reading of black and white resonances within gospel harmony singing indicates that, once again, the Clouds of Joy were playing out the tension between critical conceptions of black authenticity and mainstream commerciality in their recordings. This time, however, they were reduced to something of a backing band, most often hidden away behind the singing. Commercial pop music was changing rapidly and big bands of the likes of the Clouds of Joy were no longer sustainable in the way that they had been in the past. Thus, Kirk wound up the Clouds of Joy at the end of the 1940s after more than 20 years of touring and recording.

The fourth and final chapter focuses on a retrospective album that Kirk recorded with an RCA-Victor studio band in 1956. The resulting 1957 LP, *A Mellow Bit of Rhythm,* represents a 'greatest hits' compilation of twelve tracks. The selections were drawn from the hot-jazz output of the Clouds of Joy and the album thereby established a particular kind of black jazz legacy for Kirk and his band as much as it represented an updating of the style of the music to that of 1950s mainstream jazz. The bigger band, new arrangements, and more fulsome sound that were featured on the 1957 album together represent another hot-jazz mask through which the band's earlier music was reconceived as authentic black jazz. Exploring that approach serves to underline the place of the Clouds of Joy as a highly illuminating and fascinating band within broader understanding of jazz, race, and musical commerce.

In the end, this study of the recordings of Andy Kirk and his Clouds of Joy calls for a more all-embracing understanding of musical styles in interwar jazz than has often been represented in the critical literature. The band's recordings show us that limiting jazz to a definition that is based on prizing features of the supposedly black-authentic style of hot jazz and devaluing more popular or commercial sweet endeavours, not only misrepresents the fullness of jazz culture of the era and the musical efforts of such musicians, but it also perpetuates a sort of stylistically based racism.

The analysis in this book shows that this was the very thing that the Clouds of Joy undermined in their musical practices and recordings. However, precisely because of racial pride and the associated imperative for subtlety in racial politics of the period, the Signifyin(g) of their stylistic-racial mask-play might easily be missed when listening to their music. So, if this book can open ears to hear the musical-racial discourse in jazz of this period through analysis of the recordings of the Clouds of Joy, it does so in the spirit of amplifying resistance to seemingly innocent but racist conceptions and structures that underpin the music. It does this in an era when to speak loudly about such things is at least as urgent as ever it was.

CHAPTER 1

'SWEET AND HOT'
LEARNING TO SIGNIFY
WITH STYLE, 1929–1931

THIS CHAPTER EXPLORES the earliest recordings of Andy Kirk and his Clouds of Joy, which were made during the period 1929–1931. Those recordings fall into three distinguishable groups: the first group made in a makeshift recording studio at the KMBC radio station in Kansas City in November 1929; the follow-up recording sessions made in Brunswick's official studios in Chicago in 1930; and the vocal recordings made in New York City for Brunswick and in Camden, New Jersey, for Victor in December 1930 and March 1931, respectively. Although there are some clear differences in the types of music recorded in these various groupings, it makes sense to consider them together in this chapter because the 'stomping' style of jazz that they all represent forms a marked contrast with the swing music and sweet-styled ballads that the band recorded in the later 1930s.

Before we can analyse these early recordings for the ways in which Andy Kirk and his band negotiated racist expectations of jazz on records, it is important to establish the specific context of the racialized situation of the musicians and their approach to music making as an all-black band working in the Southwestern Territories of the United States. In that respect, even before they came to record, the Clouds of Joy were embedded in a somewhat different but equally racist culture of live performance. So, the first job of this chapter is to ask: What was the situation of the Clouds of Joy before the group came to record? Where did the band come from and what sort of music did they play? What was Kirk's role in the band, and how did the racist culture that surrounded them condition their music?

The second part of this chapter establishes the racist culture of recording that tended to confine black bands like Kirk's to specialist 'race records' or else to a decidedly hot-black style that differentiated their music from that of their white counterparts. It is in that context that the chapter analyses the music that was produced by Kirk and his pianist-arranger, Mary Lou Williams, for their first recording sessions in Kansas City. How did Kirk and Williams approach the task of ensuring that the Clouds of Joy sounded like a distinctly black band for recording, when their live music was suited to white dancers? To what extent did Kirk and Williams have to 'black up' the musical style of the band, and what were their models for doing so?

The third part of this chapter considers the recordings made in Chicago in 1930, and it suggests that they represent a diversification of musical styles in the recorded output of the band that contributed to the complexity of its stylistic masking. It poses such questions as: What did the introduction of more commercial vocals mean for Kirk's band and its stylistic-racial identity? How did that material relate to the more specialist hot-black jazz that the band continued to record, and what was Mary Lou Williams's role in the stylistic-racial mix that the Chicago recordings represent?

The final part of the chapter considers the New York and Camden recordings in terms of the theatricality of Kirk's band and the way that it was implicated in their masked representations of racialized jazz styles. The analysis in that section is focussed on a special version of 'The Ballad of Casey Jones' that was taken from the band's live repertoire and was one of very few pieces that they recorded twice. The two versions of the number effectively frame the early recording sessions and thus serve to show how the band's representation of stylistic blackness in their earliest records was ultimately as much about sending up such musical stereotypes through their caricatured performance as playing up to them.

In sum, the analysis within this chapter attempts to draw out the ways in which Kirk's band represented racialized jazz styles in their early recordings and, in donning stylistic masks, fashioned an always entertaining music that subtly pointed beyond racist stereotypes of hot (black) and sweet (white) categories. The aim is thus to look for those moments in the recordings in which the stylistic mask slips a little as the band performs hot blackness and the theatre of their mask-play is thereby revealed, as the more refined white-society dance band shines through.

DEVELOPING HOLDER'S BAND: JITNEY DANCES AND RACIALIZED STYLES

Kirk joined Terence 'T.' Holder's ten-piece band as a regular bandsman just after Holder had secured a contract to provide music at the Ozarks Club, a 'down-to-earth roadhouse' located on the outskirts of Dallas, Texas (Kirk 1989: 55). Holder's all-black band played for 'jitney dances' there, in which the men encouraged girls onto the dance floor by offering them a prepaid dance ticket. A 'floor director' or dance-master called the dances and tempos to ensure the tunes were kept short and that the men would buy more tickets (Williams, as cited in Pearson 1988: 56). This meant that jitney dances required a particularly short and flexible form of music, which Kirk described in his biography as follows:

> For the jitney dances we played—a nickel a dance and clear the floor—we used an introduction and two choruses of a tune, then an encore. The encore was the same tune with a slightly different sound. We used a modulation for the introduction [to the encore], then went into a special chorus or featured a solo, then out. Each dance set lasted about three minutes. (Kirk 1989: 56)

This shows that the music required for jitney dances was relatively simple in its structure: it involved a single repeated chorus of chord changes that was varied only on its third rendition or 'encore' by means of some change in key, instrumentation, and/or ensemble texture. Kirk goes on to note that because such music was founded upon the capable improvisations of the lead players, such as Alvin 'Fats' Wall, Holder's band had relatively little need for written arrangements. Instead they predominantly employed 'head' arrangements: music that was worked out in rehearsal based on memorized melodies and their underpinning chord changes.

Holder's band did not make any recordings before Kirk became its leader, but 'Blue Clarinet Stomp' (KC-592-A) was recorded just a few months after Kirk took over leadership of the Clouds of Joy, when several of Holder's musicians were still with the band.[1] The track shows the qualities of their jitney dance music: it is entirely carried by the efforts of the various soloists, rather than an ensemble arrangement, and the whole thing is based on repeated 12-bar blues changes in A-flat major. The solos are generally a little stiffly executed, and they are accompanied only by a rhythm section consisting of guitar (Claude 'Fiddler' Williams), baritone saxophone (Andy Kirk or John Williams), and drums (Edward 'Crackshot' McNeil).[2] The absence of accompanying horn lines and ensemble passages indicates that written arrangements were not used at all to create this track. Instead, the small band that is heard on the record followed the tried-and-tested 'head' arrangement formula to offer a simply formed piece that is based upon a straightforward set of blues chord changes.

The first blues chorus (0'07"–0'23") befits the track's title because it features a solo for John Harrington's earthy-sounding clarinet. Pairs of blues-based solo choruses follow for Williams Dirvin on banjo (0'23"–0'55"), Kirk on baritone saxophone (0'55"–1'26"), Harrington on his clarinet again (1'26"–1'58"), and then Claude Williams on his violin (1'58"–2'30"). The final 'encore' chorus (2'30"–2'49") is of the 'featured solo' type used to close jitney dances, as it introduces Harry 'Big Jim' Lawson's scat-singing. The novelty of Lawson's singing was clearly enough to obviate need for the modulation that, as Kirk mentioned, often differentiated such a closing chorus. Lawson's scatting forms a sort of call-and-response dialogue with solo breaks for Williams's violin (with Harrington's clarinet heard in counterpoint). This dialogue brings the piece to a wonderfully bluesy-jazzy conclusion.

---

1 Mary Lou Williams recalled that Holder did not play trumpet with his band by the time her husband joined it in 1928 but conducted it on the bandstand (Williams [1954] 1997: 96).

2 The discographies disagree about the personnel used on this track. Rye's discography names seven players, including John Williams on baritone sax in addition to Kirk on bass sax. Lord's discography lists just six players: John Harrington (clarinet), Andy Kirk (bass sax), Claude Williams (violin), William Dirvin (banjo, guitar), Edward McNeil (drums), and Harry Lawson (vocal). I can only hear one saxophone on the recording, however, and it is a baritone.

In sum, what we get with 'Blue Clarinet Stomp' is the very simplest form of a 'head' arrangement of the jitney-dance sort. This is not really dance-band music, however, but a decidedly 'country' sounding blues. When compared with the other 1929 recordings of the Clouds of Joy, the materials, instrumentation, and playing style are the most evocative of the sort of blues-based jazz that was most often played by black musicians of the Southwest on race records of the period. Indeed, the bluesy qualities are precisely those which Gunther Schuller noted as being typical of contemporary black Southwestern jazz (Schuller [1968] 1986: 284).[3] However, alongside these qualities are features like the scat singing and the bouncy swing of the rhythm section that suggest a voguish and dancey jazz character.

It is as if the black mask of the Southwestern blues cannot quite contain the band's true identity as a white-society band, and that means that it slips out at the edges of the stylistic mask. Given the squeak in Harrington's solo (1'27"), the band was evidently trying just that bit too hard to sound like a low-down blues band in this track. So, this is the Clouds of Joy using their jitney-dance formula to appear on recordings as a somewhat blacker-sounding band than they normally were. By adopting the characteristic changes, instrumentation, and sonorities of other regional black bands on recordings of the period, they effectively donned a mask of Southwestern blues, but features like the too-stiff soloing, the supple swing feel, and scat singing give the band away as an altogether different one beneath this bluesy black-jazz mask.

If Kirk was deliberately trying to pander to the racist stylistic expectations of record companies by offering the sort of small-ensemble bluesy music that was most commonly heard on race records of the period, such stylistic 'blacking up' through the jitney-dance formula was short-lived. Furthermore, 'Blue Clarinet Stomp' was something of an anomaly in the first Kansas City recording sessions, because it featured just a small group of the band's players when most of the contemporary tracks feature the full band.[4] Furthermore, the lack of ensemble passages

---

3 Although 'Blue Clarinet Stomp' was released in Brunswick's 'Popular Music' series rather than amongst their race records, the other similar small-band recordings of the 1929 sessions were released in Vocalion's race-records series. When Vocalion decided to release an alternate take of 'Blue Clarinet Stomp' (KC592) in the later 1930s, they issued it on a record (3255) in their race-records series (numbered from 2500). So, this is obviously race-records material that was judged to have a broader appeal by Brunswick.

4 If Brunswick's matrix numbers are correct, and there is some doubt about the chronology of the Kansas City recording sessions, this track was recorded between 'Mess-a-Stomp' and

within the arrangement was something that simply didn't fit with the backgrounds of Kirk and Holder.

Holder, like Kirk, had a background in playing dance music for relatively classy white audiences because he had been lead trumpet with Alphonse Trent's band. Around 1924, Trent's group secured an 18-month residency in the Adolphus Hotel in Dallas, a glamorous whites-only establishment (Schuller [1968] 1986: 300). Through broadcasts from the hotel they quickly became one of the most venerated and high-earning black bands in the Southwest, but record companies overlooked them until 1928, when they recorded a few sides for the Gennett label of Richmond, Indiana (Russell 1971: 63).

By that time Holder had left Trent's group, but the few sides they recorded show them as an accomplished and versatile band. Their speciality was well-rehearsed and neatly executed ensemble numbers that were so polished that, as Schuller puts it, they 'tended to smother the soloists' (Schuller [1968] 1986: 301). That indicates that the sort of style which Holder's band aspired to emulate was rather different from that of 'Blue Clarinet Stomp,' and it helps explain why Kirk, as much as being a vital player in the band, was employed to help with arrangements and painstaking rehearsals to develop the ensemble capabilities of Holder's group.

Kirk had been well trained in music theory and thus he did what little music writing was required for Holder's band, in addition to providing the bass line on sousaphone or baritone saxophone.[5] Kirk was particularly impressed by Alvin 'Fats' Wall's alto saxophone playing, and he took to transcribing Wall's more exceptional solos and arranging them so that they could be reproduced night-after-night in such forms as a harmonized chorus for all three of the saxophones in Holder's band (Kirk 1989: 56). In this way (and others), Kirk gradually influenced the music of Holder's band away from a dependence on 'head' formulas of the jitney-dance sort towards more calculated and structured written arrangements that emphasized ensemble playing from the band, at least as much as improvised solos.

Kirk was clearly aspirational for the Clouds of Joy, even before he became its leader, and he was as keen to help in its musical development

---

'Cloudy'. That suggests that the use of a small combo to record the track was a deliberate decision rather than some sort of contingency.

5 Buddy Tate suggested that before Kirk joined the band, their pianist, Lloyd Glenn, was the writer for the band, but he concedes, 'we were doing heads [arrangements] too' (Tate, as cited in Pearson 1988: 57).

by mentoring band members as he was in rehearsing and arranging for the band. He recalled his mentoring of one of the weaker music readers as follows:

I was growing more and more interested in the band as a whole, and was willing to give any help I could to make it better. Our trombone player [Allen Durham], for instance, had a beautiful tone and could memorize easily, but he was a little slow on reading—he could spell. When something came along that he had trouble with, I'd pick up my bass sax and play the trombone part so he could hear it and that way get it in his mind. (Kirk 1989: 55–56)

Kirk enjoyed this supporting of the band as a teacher-facilitator. His coaching was not all self-serving though, because it allowed for greater earning potential for the Clouds of Joy as a dance band: better reading broadened the range of repertoire and styles of music that the band could offer their dancing audiences. If the band could read well, they could more readily make use of 'stock' arrangements of popular tunes that were a must for any really commercial dance band.[6] Furthermore, an accomplished and distinctive sound could be developed through original arrangements penned by Kirk and others in the band. Kirk was thus a creative and entrepreneurial force as much as an educative one within Holder's band because he encouraged its greater versatility and commerciality as much as its better musicianship. Such things also allowed the band to escape the typical confinement of a black group to a particular style of music. In that regard, in discussing his impression of the trombonist Jack Teagarden, Kirk recalled the way that musical styles were racially stereotyped as follows:

I want to say here that any time people saw a colored band they immediately expected it to play jazz and jazz only. And by the same token, white bands were expected to play 'pretty' in conventional styles à la Guy Lombardo. (Kirk 1989: 57)

---

6 Stock arrangements were flexible orchestrations in a standardized form that were commissioned by sheet music publishers to help sell the songs in their catalogues through live performances and recordings by bands. Amongst the preeminent stock arrangers of the late 1920s were Mel Stitzel and Archie Bleyer; several of their arrangements were featured by Kirk's band in their 1929–1931 recordings (Clark 2009: 139).

Lombardo formed his highly successful and long-lasting band, The Royal Canadians, around 1917. By the late 1920s, Lombardo's band had found fame through radio broadcasts from Cleveland, Ohio, and then they cemented it with a record contract with Columbia and a long-standing engagement at the Roosevelt Grill in New York. As the jazz scholar Mark Tucker has written, 'Lombardo aimed for, and reached, the broadest possible audience' with a style that was the epitome of sweet music (Tucker 2001: 88).

Lombardo's band offered music that emphasized melody, good dancing tempi, and an easy-listening sound that came 'from the saxophone section's heavy vibrato, the rippling two-piano accompaniment, and the unobtrusive rhythm section' (Tucker 2001: 89). The easily digestible repertoire and the indulgent but unobtrusive quality of the playing of Lombardo's band stood in marked contrast to the pseudo-primitivism, free-formed ebullient music, and unusual playing techniques featured in hot-black jazz of the period.

In the face of this demarcation of stereotypically white (sweet) and black (hot) musics and their associated playing styles, Kirk admired Teagarden, because the white trombonist sounded hotter and thereby blacker than many of his black contemporaries. In the black-sounding style of his music he seemed to Kirk to undermine prevailing racist expectations about musical styles (Kirk 1989: 57). Kirk was ultimately inspired by the likes of Teagarden to avoid being confined to a stereotypical black style and thereby to challenge racist expectations of what a black band should sound like.

A greater use of written arrangements was instrumental in that enterprise because it allowed for a broadening of the repertoire beyond the black stylistic 'ghetto' to embrace sweet music that was more usually considered the territory of white bands like that of Lombardo. Kirk's development of the Holder band's repertoire and style in that direction meant that there was much truth in his assertion that the Clouds of Joy 'played more white' than Teagarden's band, especially in the later 1930s (Kirk 1989: 57).

A short time before Kirk took over the leadership of Holder's band, Holder secured a new contract with a management company that operated multiple dance venues in Tulsa and Oklahoma City.[7] The company had expanded its operations and thus needed a new band

---

7 In his interview with Frank Driggs, Kirk named the company as 'the Southwest Amusement Corporation' (Kirk 1959: 13), but in his interview with Kent Hazen (Kirk 1977: 6) and in his autobiography, he called it the 'Northeast Amusement Company' (Kirk 1989: 56). A Storyville article names it as the 'Amusement Service Corporation' and the abbreviation 'MCA' is referenced by Kirk's contemporaries (Zwicky 1971: 170).

to play for the increased number of dances on its books. Under their new contract, Holder's band was required to shuttle between two venues in Tulsa and two in Oklahoma City, playing at each for as long as three months at a stretch (Williams, as cited in Pearson 1988: 56). Landing this relatively steady contract marked a step up from piecemeal roadhouse work for Holder's band. It was also something of a coup, because the band's new employers had hitherto hired only white bands. In a bid to avoid alienating its white customers, the management company followed the advice of a consultant and requested that Holder's band adopt the name 'The Dark Clouds of Joy' to avoid any doubt about their blackness.

One of Kirk's first resistive acts, when he became the band's leader, was to drop the word 'Dark' so that its negative racial connotations would not be any impediment to the band or its commerciality (Kirk 1989: 59). This is how the band came to be known as the Clouds of Joy and the name change shows both the racist culture in which Holder's band operated and Kirk's awareness and responsiveness to their racialized position. Such small acts of resistance to racism were, therefore, very much a part of his work with the Clouds of Joy and they indicate that subtle racial politics were at the heart of the band's culture and practices.

The relative stability provided by the new contract represented an opportunity for Holder's band to work together in regular rehearsals under Kirk's leadership to consolidate their style and broaden their repertoire to include new ensemble arrangements of tunes that were popular with white audiences. The music of Holder's band was generally worked out in a collaborative creative process during rehearsals that embraced the musical ideas of the players and crystallized them into an arrangement. Kirk's music writing, coaching, and rehearsing were thus part of a collaborative mode of working that made the most of the strengths of the band. Kirk put it as follows:

> With our four steady locations, we could rehearse regularly and build up our book. Many of the tunes we played were head arrangements. By putting our talents and ideas together at rehearsals, we developed a style that dancers liked to dance and listen to. We were pulling in crowds and pleasing our bookers, and we soon became Northeast's [sic] No. 1 band. (Kirk 1989: 57–58)

Kirk is clear here that Holder's band was concerned with developing their repertoire of arrangements for white dancers, but this did not mean that their music was no longer bluesy or jazzy. As Kirk noted, 'within the context of those times Holder's band was a swinging group' (Kirk

1989: 56) and it most likely had to be, for to seem too white within such a racist culture was dangerous for a black band. It was precisely to avoid racial antagonism that Kirk always strove to meet his white audiences' expectations. He wrote, 'If you played the kind of music they liked to dance to, that's what mattered' (Kirk 1989: 62).

'Cloudy' (KC493) was most likely recorded in the same session as 'Blue Clarinet Stomp' in early November 1929 and was probably an early theme tune for the band. The piece is credited to Andy Kirk on the original Brunswick record (4653), and it shows something of his work with Holder's band.[8] Like 'Blue Clarinet Stomp', 'Cloudy' is a blues-based number that relies on a succession of solos, but it utilizes the full band and the music is less stylized and arranged. It incorporates much more ensemble arrangement, albeit still most likely in a 'head' arrangement that was more memorised than written down.

The four-bar introduction (0'00"–0'11") features the reeds in portamento-filled close harmony, interspersed with choked cymbal strikes. The musical texture in the subsequent choruses is altogether richer and more varied than in 'Blue Clarinet Stomp' as a result of Kirk's work to finesse the ensemble playing. Listen out, for example, for the sustained chords that are scored for the reeds behind the trumpet solo (Harry 'Big Jim' Lawson) in the first chorus (0'11"–0'35") and the characterful background riffs in the brass that accompany Freeman's tenor sax solo chorus (1'05"–1'29").[9]

When compared with 'Blue Clarinet Stomp', Harrington's clarinet style, heard when he dialogues with solo breaks for Kirk's sousaphone in the second chorus (0'39"–1'02"), is altogether more fluid and less earthy-sounding. It is, however, the strikingly orchestrated 'encore' chorus (2'25"–2'52") that really shows the impact of Kirk's work with the band to develop its ensemble capabilities. The chorus is prefaced by a sudden, loud, and sustained chord that is scored for the whole band (2'22"–2'25"), and then it features Harrrington's 'shrieking' clarinet set against stomping brassy riffs. Kirk must have carefully rehearsed the closing coda-tag (2'52"–2'58"), because its beat-defying syncopation

---

8 The collaborative mode of the Holder band's creative practice suggests Kirk may have been more of a compiler of ideas from various members of the band rather than the sole originator of the music.

9 The early recording sessions may well have featured cornets rather than trumpets but the discographies invariably list trumpets. As it is hard to hear the difference in the early records I have opted to reference trumpets consistently.

demands really confident and secure ensemble playing, especially in a 'head' arrangement.

The result might be music that is a little less characterful in a stereotypical hot-black sense than in 'Blue Clarinet Stomp', but it shows less pretention towards country-styled Southwestern blues. Instead, it points to the sort of tight-but-swinging ensemble that the Clouds of Joy became under Kirk's sustained leadership. This is not to say that the bluesy quality is entirely absent, only that it is more constrained, or, put another way, it plays second fiddle to a greater dance-band sensibility. In this track, then, we get music that is more typical of the dance-band style of Holder's band but it still shows a gloss of hot-styled blackness, despite Kirk's ensemble work.

So, Kirk's work with Holder's band was not about moving it entirely away from Southwestern jazz practices towards more arranged dance music, but it was about supporting the development of a style that met the expectations of white audiences and promoters by giving them music that mixed the arranged qualities of dance music with the supposedly blacker qualities of Southwestern jazz. In other words, they aimed to appropriate a style of dance music for white audiences, while still remaining apparently 'true' to their evident identity as a black Southwestern jazz musicians.

According to John Williams, when Holder left his band to head back home to Dallas with the band's pay, apparently in the wake of his absconded wife, Kirk was elected its leader because 'he was the oldest in age and most settled' (Williams cited in Klein 1997: 35). No doubt his role in developing the band through his rehearsing, arranging, and mentoring was also uppermost in the band's decision. However, the transition in leadership from Holder to Kirk was not altogether straightforward because three members of the band left after Holder. Perhaps the most notable loss, aside from Holder himself, was Holder's star saxophonist Fats Wall.[10]

According to Kirk, Wall left the band because he felt that he should have been made leader on account of the ideas he had contributed to the band in his solos. To replace the likes of Wall, Kirk took on two new reed players, John Harrington and John Williams, and the trumpeter Gene Prince, and he reappointed the former Holder-band trombonist, Allen Durham, who had left some time before. By appointing four players in

10 The other players to leave the band were the alto saxophonist Theodore Ross and trombonist Flip Benson (Kirk 1989: 59).

the place of three, Kirk developed what was by then Holder's eleven-piece outfit into the band that became known most often thereafter as 'Andy Kirk and His Twelve Clouds of Joy'.

Although Kirk was now officially the leader of the Clouds of Joy, he continued to play sousaphone or sax on the bandstand and left the fronting of the band to their vocalist Billy Massey.[11] Kirk was happy to take a back seat because, as he explained, in those days it was a band's reputation and not that of its leader that was the appeal for dancing audiences (Kirk 1989: 61). By continuing his development of the band's musicianship and repertoire as its backstage leader, Kirk ensured the band's popularity in Oklahoma City and Tulsa and the continued development of its hybrid sweet-and-hot repertoire.

Soon a second black group, George E. Lee's Kansas City band, was hired by the ballrooms' management to meet the demand that Kirk's band had generated. Ironically, it was Lee who gave Kirk the tip-off that there was a job going in Kansas City, which led to the Clouds of Joy leaving the Oklahoma City–Tulsa circuit in the summer of 1929 to take up a residency at the whites-only Pla-Mor Ballroom (Kirk 1989: 60).[12] When Lee returned to Kansas City, Kirk agreed a matched scale of fees with him, as Lee's band was their only real competition in the city and this avoided any undercutting (Kirk 1959: 14). This arrangement cemented an important and long-standing connection with Kansas City for the Clouds of Joy, and it led to them first recording there when producers came looking for new bands to record.

MESS-A-STOMP: REPRESENTING A HOT-BLACK STYLE FOR 'RACE' RECORDS

Record company executives Jack Kapp and Dick Voynow travelled from Chicago to Kansas City in the autumn of 1929 (Kirk 1989: 70). Kapp and Voynow worked for the Brunswick record label and its subsidiary Vocalion. Vocalion had marketed a line of so-called race records (its 1000 series) since 1926, and Brunswick had launched its own line (its 7000 series), featuring a distinctive 'lightning strike' label design, in 1927 (Laird 2001: xiv). Rival companies such as Okeh had been profiting from

---

11 John Williams recalled that after Massey, Pha Terrell took to 'conducting' the band but it was only showmanship as he could not read music, let alone direct it. He recalled that Kirk did not appear in front of the band until they were managed by Joe Glaser. (Williams cited in Klein 1997: 1)

12 Pla-Mor is pronounced 'Play-more'.

race records since the early 1920s, so Brunswick were comparatively late in getting into that market (Gronow & Saunio 1999: 47–48). Kapp and Voynow were, therefore, trying to make up for lost time and revenues by seeking out new talent that they felt was suited to the race market.

An article of June 1926 in the trade magazine *Talking Machine World* explained the record company's apparent benevolence with their new line of race records as follows:

> In issuing the race records the Brunswick company stated that the main purpose of its plan is to give the colored people records made by artists of their own race which are absolutely above reproach insofar as the theme and manner of presentation are concerned. . . . Jack Kapp, who heads the Vocalion race records division[,] is combing the country to secure the services of prominent colored artists and no effort will be spared to give the race the type of music that is most appealing. (Cited in Laird 2001: 9)

The patronizing tone of Brunswick's apparent ambition indicates that the music recorded for race records was selected according to white producers' understandings of what black audiences wanted to hear. Producers such as Kapp and Voynow could also influence the style of the music to ensure that it fitted with their conception of what appealed to the race market.[13] By the later 1920s, such stylistic expectations were so well known to black musicians that they would self-select repertoire and tailor their style even before they auditioned to record. So, despite the stated race-appropriate agenda of race records, the music issued on such discs actually represented white-determined stereotypes of black musical tastes rather than wholly authentic expressions of black musical culture. In other words, the structures that supported the making of such records were inherently racist and most often required black musicians to play up to white producers' notions of what black music should sound like.

By 1929, if a black band was deemed by Brunswick executives to have an appeal beyond the confines of the specialist race market, their music would be issued in the broader 'Popular' series of recordings. In fact, by 1932 Brunswick had abandoned its specialist line of race records altogether in favour of subcategorizing race records within its 'Popular

---

13 Jay McShann, for example, described how Dave Kapp (Jack's brother) insisted that the McShann band record blues tracks even though McShann had prepared upbeat instrumentals (see McShann, as cited in Pearson 1988: 176).

Records' catalogue. This helps explain why Kirk's band made only two records that were released on specialist race records (Vocalion 1453 and Brunswick 7180). Those recordings, like 'Blue Clarinet Stomp', all feature a smaller band in more overtly hot or bluesy repertoire.[14] The rest of their output of 1929 and 1930, although classed by Kirk as race music, was issued within Brunswick's 'Popular Records' (catalogued in the range 2000–7000). They appeared alongside recordings made by the likes of Duke Ellington, George E. Lee, James P. Johnson, and numerous white musicians such as Red Nichols and the Louisiana Rhythm Kings.

Kirk's escape from the specialist line of race records may in itself be seen as remarkable, but the institutionalized racism of the recording industry meant that there was still pressure on musicians such as Kirk and Ellington to differentiate their music from that of the white artists listed in Brunswick's catalogue. That catalogue billed Ellington's orchestra as a 'Jungle Band', and the titles of the tracks that were listed for Kirk and his black contemporaries most often include terms like 'stomp' and 'blues' to signal their black difference. Furthermore, the music heard on the records is most often in a decidedly black-sounding hot style that further differentiates the recordings from those of their white contemporaries, which most often featured more melodious and less bluesy or frenetically syncopated fare.

When Kirk put his band forward to audition for Kapp and Voynow, he faced the problem that the repertoire he had developed with the Clouds of Joy for their live work was only partly suited to prevailing expectations of what a black jazz band should put out on race records. In that respect, Kirk explained that the music that his band provided for white dancers at the Pla-Mor Ballroom and elsewhere was not overtly jazzy or stereo typically black-sounding, stating,

> our band didn't stress jazz, though we played it. We emphasized dance music—romantic ballads and pop tunes and waltzes—Viennese as well as standard popular waltzes like *Kiss me again* and *Alice Blue Gown*. I love to play waltzes. We were first and last a dance orchestra, because people were dancing. I was 'brought up' in the dance music field, and that influenced me. We were also great on entertainment.

14 The Vocalion sides ('Sumpin' Slow and Low' and 'Lotta Sax Appeal') were attributed to 'John Williams and his Memphis Stompers'. The Brunswick sides ('Gettin' off a Mess' and 'You Rascal, You') came out of the later Chicago sessions and were attributed to the 'Seven Little Clouds of Joy' (Rye cited in Kirk 1989: 124–126).

We put on a ten-minute show every night with loud, fast stuff and it used to break everybody up. (Kirk 1989: 62)

Kirk suggests in this that his band was concerned primarily with providing relatively sweet (melodic, smooth, and sedate) music for close-partner dancing, and their hotter jazz numbers were novelties that most often functioned as floor-show type entertainment during breaks in the dancing. It was that sort of balance in their live repertoire that made the band appear whiter than most of their black counterparts. In fact, the whiteness of Kirk's band was apparent enough that he felt the need to underline the fact that his band played for black dances as well as white ones in Kansas City. He explained this in his autobiography as follows:

As our popularity grew we played both white ballrooms, the Pla-Mor and the El Torreon, and other spots. We were popular with all those white audiences. In fact, we were often thought of as a white band because of our smooth style and our emphasis on ballads and waltzes. But—and this is important—we were also playing our share of black dances, along with native Kansas City black bands, at the two black ballrooms—Labor Temple and '15th and Paseo'. (Kirk 1989: 65–66)

Kirk placed such emphasis on performing for black audiences to counter any sense that he and his band sold out on their black authenticity or stylistic integrity in the apparent whiteness of their music. In that respect, it is interesting that Kirk does not suggest that they adopted a different repertoire or style for black dances. The irony in that is that the requirement of an assuredly black-sounding musical style for recording was at odds with the music that the band's black audiences consumed in Kansas City. Nevertheless, Kirk had to find ways to meet that racist stylistic requirement, and he did that both by selecting the hotter parts of his band's existing repertoire and by working with Mary Lou Williams to develop new music for the band to record.

One of the numbers that Kirk most certainly drew from his band's live work for recording was 'Casey Jones Special', which we will consider later in this chapter because it was recorded both in 1929 and in 1931. The other number that seems likely to have been in the band's regular repertoire was 'Cloudy', which was issued on the reverse of 'Casey Jones Special' on Brunswick (4653) and was most likely the band's theme tune. Aside from those and 'Blue Clarinet Stomp' the rest of the 1929 recordings were new numbers that were fashioned by Williams under

Kirk's supervision. Those new numbers drew on the hot-black style of a rival band in Kansas City, that of Bennie Moten.

The music of Moten's band provided a model because it had featured on numerous race records produced for the Okeh and Victor labels during the earlier 1920s. From September 1923, Moten's band recorded sides that were indebted to the ragtime-derived style of the Southwest and the style of jazz stemming from New Orleans that was recorded by the likes of Joe 'King' Oliver, Louis Armstrong, and Ferdinand 'Jelly Roll' Morton. But Moten gradually developed a more riff-based style of his own that, especially in its increasingly distinctive two-beat feel, departed from the New Orleans style and pointed toward the four-beat feel of swing. Todd Bryant Weeks put it this way:

> Moten's idiosyncratic style was most evident in a characteristic rhythmical approach. On many of the band's recordings from this period, there is a tendency for the rhythm section to emphasize beats one and three rather than two and four, or to 'swing' on both sides of this relationship, moving emphasis around in a way atypical for the period. This rhythmic flexibility prefigures a later, more even emphasis on all four beats. (Bryant Weeks 2008: 75)

By the time Kirk came to record with the Clouds of Joy in early November 1929, Moten's style of hot jazz was synonymous with the sort of music required for race records. Kirk recalled the record companies' expectation that his band would record music like Moten's and that they did not have much of that kind of music in its repertoire as follows:

> Remember, Moten had been *the* band on Okeh. What he was doing was what Brunswick and Vocalion wanted us to do. So we continued to do a lot of that [after the 1929 Kansas City sessions]—things like *Snag It, Mary's Idea* and *Dallas Blues*. That type of number was the smaller part of our library. The bigger part we could play only in person. (Kirk 1989: 71)

So, while Kirk claimed that the Clouds of Joy did not compete with Moten in their live work in Kansas City, it was a different matter when it came to making records (Kirk 1959: 14). In live performances, the music of the Clouds of Joy displayed a different style and could be mistaken for that of a white band because their repertoire stressed the smoothly melodic sort of instrumentals and vocals that were popular with white social dancers. That set them apart from the likes of Moten, but that sweet style would not do for recording: Kirk's band might have gotten away with sounding white when they appeared in person, but as the physical bodies of the black performers were not visible on records, their recordings were required to more clearly emphasize aural markers of hot blackness to differentiate them from the white bands in Brunswick's 'Popular Music' catalogue. To that end, they felt pressure to model the music for their first recordings on Moten's hot style precisely because they were expected to present jazz that was blacker-sounding or hotter than most of the repertoire that they played in their ballroom work.

If we leave aside pop-song numbers, which as Schuller noted were not really Moten's territory, by the later 1920s Moten was recording an almost equal mixture of blues-based tracks and upbeat jazz numbers that featured voguish titles that included such characteristic black-modernistic dance terms as 'shuffle', 'stomp', 'wobble', and 'squabble' (Schuller [1968] 1986: 285). Such tracks generally include a short introduction that leads to an ensemble chorus in either a repeated 12-bar blues structure or a 32-bar AABA song form. The cornet (or trumpet) invariably takes the lead with the melody while the other horns offer improvised counterpoint. Most often a bridging fill or secondary introduction then follows to introduce a succession of solo choruses (perhaps including a vocal) that are based on the same chord structure as the opening chorus. After the solos, a final chorus for the whole band closes the arrangement with either a straightforward reprise of the blues or AABA chorus or, most often, a more energized recapitulation of that 'head' as a 'shout' chorus.

Moten's upbeat numbers of the later 1920s still tended to follow the character of jazz pieces derived from the New Orleans tradition in being quite busy and even cacophonous in the improvised counterpoint of their opening and closing choruses. For instance, 'Moten Stomp' (38674-3), which was recorded by Moten's band for a Victor disc (20955) in June 1927, features an opening chorus (0'04"–0'35") with a texture that is fairly typical of New Orleans polyphony, but it also shows Moten's development of it. In typical style, it features a lead-cornet melody (played by Ed Lewis and/or Paul Webster) backed by fills and counterpoint from the trombone (Thamon Hayes). However, in the New Orleans tradition one would also expect to hear clarinet counterpoint here, but it is replaced in Moten's track by the saxophone ensemble (Harlan Leonard, Jack Washington, Woody Walder, and Laforest Dent) playing in close harmony. This shows how the East coast style of jazz, exemplified by the more tightly arranged music of Fletcher Henderson's band, was already influencing the polyphony of the traditional 'front row' line up of cornet, clarinet, and trombone in the direction of more sectional instrumentation and cleaner homophonic textures.[15]

The saxophones' soft riffs, which are set against the cornet melody and the counterpointing trombone, are quite difficult to hear on the Moten band's record, partly because the rhythm section of banjo (Leroy 'Buster' Berry), piano (Bennie Moten), sousaphone (Vernon Page), and drums (Willie McWashington) is so forward in the mix. However, the overall effect of this sort of clamorous ensemble texture is to immediately convey the lively spirit of a dance party (a 'stomp-down') that is in full swing. This energy represents a great deal of the apparent hot-jazz quality that was no doubt considered essential for race records of the time.

All of the AABA choruses in 'Moten Stomp' feature solo 'breaks' in their B sections that show the characteristic styling of hot-black jazz. In the first chorus we hear Hayes's plunger-muted trombone (0'20"–0'28") in the 'talking' style of playing that was so beloved of Duke Ellington's band in their so-called 'Jungle Band' recordings. Washington's baritone sax is heard in the B-section of the second chorus (0'51"–1'21"), which otherwise features Walder's tenor sax. The third chorus (1'21"–1'53") features Lewis's tinny-sounding muted cornet, which yields to Thamon's equally idiomatic raspy trombone. Berry's banjo solo with Moten's piano backing (1'53"–2'23") follows it in the fourth chorus and it inevitably evokes sonorities of minstrel-show blackness. This leads to the final 'shout' chorus (2'23"–2'55"), which features high-note wails from Webster's cornet (rather than the clarinet, which usually assumed that role in jazz of the New Orleans tradition), and a return of ensemble riffs and 'talking' breaks in the B section (2'39"–2'47"). This time the 'talking' is done by a muted cornet (probably Lewis). All in all, there is much in the instrumentation and its distinctive deployment to signify stereotypical black-sounding hot jazz.

The more bluesy numbers that were recorded by Moten's band in the later 1920s are no less characteristic of black-sounding jazz of the period, albeit with somewhat less emphasis on the sort of energy-imparting polyphonic clamour that is found in upbeat numbers like 'Moten Stomp.' 'Sad Man Blues' (42928-2), recorded by Moten's band for a Victor race record (V-38048) in September 1928, for instance, opens with back-to-back blues-based ensemble choruses (0'00"–0'37") that feature a riff-based melody

---

15 Todd Bryant Weeks has suggested that the visit of Henderson's band to Kansas City in February 1927 had a transformative effect on Moten's music. (Bryant Weeks 2008: 74).

for harmonized cornets (Booker Washington replaced Paul Webster by 1928).

The Latin-sounding riffs of the head, highly evocative of Jelly Roll Morton's notion of jazz's 'Spanish tinge', are notable for some stylish articulation of the rhythm by the cornets (cited in Lomax [1950] 2001: 62). In the first chorus, the cornets opt for a clipped (staccato) articulation of their melodic riffs before they adopt a smoother (legato) approach in the second one. However, the players bring a hot-black styling to the melody by varying the note lengths and accenting some notes within the syncopated riffs (notably those that fall on the first beat of the second bar of each riff) to give the music a distinctively swinging quality. This is not the sort of stylistic feature that would have been notated, but rather a performance convention developed in rehearsal and based on whatever notation (if any) was supplied by Moten.

The saxophone riffs, which back the cornets in the opening and closing ensemble choruses, feature soft and sustained chords that then drop down the scale in a more rapid succession of notes set in a dotted rhythm. These subtle but characterful accompaniment riffs not only offer a more translucent texture for the opening chorus than the polyphony in 'Moten Stomp', but they also immediately impart the appropriately mournful character of the blues. There is also evident hotness in such features as the high-note opening call of Leonard's soprano saxophone solo (0'37"–0'56"), especially as it is backed by what might be heard as African tom-tom beats.

These drum beats emphasize beats one and three in contrast to the emphasis on beats two and four in the other choruses and thus show Moten's band playing with metrical accentuation. The little pitch bends and inflections in the open and muted cornet solos (0'56"–1'14" and 1'34"–1'54") and the hot glissandi in the trombone solo (1'14"–1'34") add to the hot-black styling of the track. Furthermore, the baritone sax solo (2'31"–2'51"), which follows James Taylor's dialect-filled vocal chorus (1'54"–2'31"), is coloured by keyed tremolos that are characteristic of hot-black jazz performance practices.

The final chorus of Moten's 'Sad Man Blues' (2'51"–3'10") offers a faithful return of the blues head, rather than the more energized sort of 'shouting' recapitulation that is heard in Moten's upbeat numbers, but the cornets are now tightly muted, the music more subdued, and the texture is all the clearer for it. A short retarding coda for the saxes is added to the end of the chorus before the piece closes with a swelling dissonant (dominant seventh) chord for the whole ensemble, which is silenced by a voguish choked hi-hat strike from Berry. All of this stereotypical instrumentation and characteristic performance of the musical materials is emblematic of the sort of distinctively hot-black jazz that was heard on Moten's race records in the later 1920s and expected of Kirk's band.

In mentioning Moten as a model, Kirk highlights two of the early recordings of the Clouds of Joy that had direct roots in the black jazz tradition that came out of New Orleans: 'Snag It' (C4470) was originally recorded by King Oliver's band in 1926 for one of Vocalion's first race records, and 'Dallas Blues' (C6178) is another classic of hot jazz that Louis Armstrong covered for Okeh in 1929. It is highly suggestive that Kirk groups these established race-record pieces with one of Mary Lou Williams's compositions, 'Mary's Idea' (C4473), because that was one of a number of pieces that she wrote for the Clouds of Joy to record for Brunswick. Its grouping with 'Snag It' and 'Dallas Blues' suggests that Williams's compositions were employed precisely because they met the requirement for black-sounding hot jazz for Brunswick's race records in a way that the greater part of the band's live repertoire did not.

'Mess-a-Stomp' was not only the first track recorded by Kirk's band but it was also Williams's first composition for the Clouds of Joy and, indeed, her first arrangement for any band. It was issued on the A side of the Brunswick record (4694) that included 'Blue Clarinet Stomp', and, although both tracks use blues chord changes, 'Mess-a-Stomp' is an altogether more tightly arranged piece of black-sounding jazz for Kirk's band. It is somewhat more ambitious in form than Moten's music of the period, as it is more in line with the multi-strain stomps recorded by the likes of Jelly Roll Morton. However, in most other respects there are notable similarities in the hot-ensemble styling of 'Mess-a-Stomp' and Moten's recordings of the later 1920s.

In that regard, Kirk recalled that Williams had ambitions to write original music based on her harmonic ideas and the style of jazz that she experienced in Kansas City:

> From the start she wanted to write arrangements. She would have certain chords in her mind but she didn't at first know how to voice them. She had a good ear and tried to write down what she heard. If she wasn't out all night at the jazz clubs in Kansas City, listening and getting ideas, she'd be sitting up at the foot of the bed, legs crossed like an Indian, just writing and writing, while [her saxophonist husband] John [Williams] was sleeping. Sometimes she'd stay up all night working at her arrangements. She'd try one thing, then another, get mad, and start over. (Kirk 1989: 73)

In this account, Kirk emphasizes Williams's remarkable determination to emulate the musical styles that she heard and the hard work that she put in to developing her own ideas in such styles and to getting them down on paper. 'Mess-a-Stomp' represents the first fruit of those labours and, as she always acknowledged, she got help and support in writing the piece from Kirk and his bandsmen:

> He would sit up as long as twelve hours at a stretch, taking down my ideas for arrangements, and I got so sick of the method that I began putting them down myself. I hadn't studied theory, but asked Kirk about chords and the voicing register. In about 15 minutes I had memorized what I wanted. That's how I started writing. My first attempt, "Messa Stomp," [sic] was beyond the range of half the instruments. But the boys gave me a chance and each time I did better, until I found I was doing five or six arrangements per week. (Williams [1954] 1997: 98)

There is no doubt that Williams had amazing aural abilities that helped her learn quickly, but she may well have understated Kirk's influence because we will see that 'Mess-a-Stomp' shows in its ensemble writing that Kirk imparted much of his experience as an ensemble arranger. Williams certainly worked closely with Kirk around the time of the band's first recordings, when she acted as the band's pianist as well as its arranger. In fact, the pair produced 'Corky Stomp' (KC-618-A), a piece named after a new character in the popular *Gasoline Alley* comic strip, by putting together a section composed by Williams in the major key with another composed by Kirk in the relative minor (Kirk 1989: 73). In that respect, a photo from the later 1930s appears to show the sort of relaxed and collaborative working relationship that Kirk established with Williams as an extension of his work with the band (see Figure 1.1).

As he did with Holder's bandsmen, Kirk mentored Williams to help her develop her musicianship, and, in the process, he further developed the musical style and repertoire of his band. This time, however, his coaching helped to meet expectations of an appropriate style of black music for recording. The fact that the 'boys' in the band also played their part shows that the band's collaborative creative process, which Kirk had nurtured, was also a help to Williams in developing a music suitable for recording. The availability of a band that could play her music and offer her immediate feedback and a stylistic gloss in performance was

FIGURE 1.1   Andy Kirk and Mary Lou Williams working together.

surely instrumental in Williams's development as a composer of hot-jazz arrangements for the Clouds of Joy and other big bands.

To my mind, these sorts of influences have been understated in the recent writing about Williams, perhaps in a bid to establish her as a composer in the traditional sense of an author figure, in the line of Beethoven, that shows masterful control of musical materials without the interference of others. In general, the accounts of Williams's time with Kirk tend to emphasize what she contributed to the band over what she got from them, and the sense of an ongoing collaborative and supportive culture in which she thrived is underplayed. That is coupled with a tendency to overestimate the number of arrangements that Williams contributed

FIGURE 1.2   The brass-ensemble riff that backs the clarinet solo is the first blues chorus of 'Mess-a-Stomp'.

to the band. For example, even Theodore Buehrer in his otherwise authoritative edition of Williams's compositions credits 'Loose Ankles' to Williams when it is clearly a stock arrangement by Archie Bleyer (Buehrer 2013: xxi). Nevertheless, Williams was certainly an amazing creative musician who was vital to the success of Kirk's band, and that is apparent in the ambition of her very first arrangement for the group.

In its multi-strain structure, 'Mess-a-Stomp' far exceeded tracks like 'Blue Clarinet Stomp' in its structural ambition. For a start, the piece is not composed of a single strain, as in the jitney-dance numbers of Holder's band or Moten's typical pieces, but it contains three different structural strains that are each made up of a pair of repeated choruses. These strains are arranged to form an overarching rondo pattern that might be represented as ABACA. The A strains bind the piece together and are all based on repeated 12-bar blues sections, but the other strains form an important contrast with that material because they are not based on blues changes.

'Mess-a-Stomp' opens with a four-bar introduction (0'00"–0'06") that, like in the 'Moten Stomp', is split between two distinctive timbres: a motif for the brass followed by one for Kirk's sousaphone. John Harrington's clarinet is featured in the first of the A strains, which is made up of a pair of blues-based choruses in B-flat major (0'06"–0'35"). Harrington's use of a relatively low register, a reedy tone, and an on-the-beat 'stomping' emphasis imparts a Southwestern hot-jazz quality. Williams backs Harrington's earthy-sounding solo with a distinctively hot-styled riff for the brass (see Figure 1.2).

The riff is actually a more syncopated form of a motif that is first heard in the brass in the opening two bars of the introduction (see Figure 1.3). In contrast, however, it features a distinctively 'talking' motif of three repeated quavers followed by an accented note on the third beat of the bar. This motif has a quality of plunger muting in the accentuation of the quavers, in which the third note in each grouping is hardly audible

FIGURE 1.3   The brass-ensemble motif from the opening of 'Mess-a-Stomp'.

on the record between the more accented ones.[16] Such riffs and their stylised performance are characteristic of the hot-styled materials heard in Moten's recordings, and not least because they contrast material that is set against the meter with their on-the-beat emphasis.

Another feature of 'Mess-a-Stomp' that is heard in Moten's records is the four-bar fill that serves as a secondary introduction (0'37"–0'42") and features William Dirvin's banjo. It introduces the B strain of repeated eight-bar phrases (0'42"–1'01") that are set in the relative minor key (G minor). This section features harmony that simply alternates tonic chords with especially jazzy-sounding dominant-seventh chords with an added flattened ninth. In the first of the eight-bar choruses (0'42"–0'51") the three saxes are featured in close-harmony writing that is performed with fairly tidy articulation by the ensemble. Kirk's influence on this material is obvious, because this is exactly the sort of ensemble passage that he developed from Wall's solos for Holder's dance band and wrote in 'Cloudy' and 'Corky Stomp'.

Within the B strain of the second chorus (0'51"–1'01"), the saxes drop in volume to provide the backing riffs for a characteristically swinging trumpet solo from Harry 'Big Jim' Lawson. The way Lawson bends the pitch of the long note in the second bar of his solo reminds us that we are in the territory of hot riff-based jazz of Moten's sort rather than that of melodic dance music. An even more hot-stylized piano solo from Williams (1'01"–1'32") follows Lawson's chorus and serves to bring back the repeated 12-bar blues changes of the A section, albeit with a cessation of the rhythm section. The hotness in Williams's solo comes from a combination of rhythmic drive, syncopation and accentuation.

16 Buehrer consistently notates these groupings of quavers as a single quaver followed by a dotted crotchet in his transcription of 'Mess-a-Stomp' (see Buehrer 2013: 4–5). His notation obscures the origins of the riff in the musical material of the introduction but it highlights the importance of the bandsmen's articulation of Williams's writing which doubtless accounts for the inconsistency.

FIGURE 1.4 The opening bars of Mary Lou Williams's piano solo in 'Mess-a-Stomp' showing the emerging stomping motif (brackets).

Williams's solo features prominent off-beat accentuation of a sort common to the playing of the great 'stride' pianist James P. Johnson.[17] This syncopation is especially obvious when it upsets the driving 'oom-pah' figures of the accompaniment in Williams's left hand. In the way of Moten's varying of metrical emphasis, Williams's solo contrasts emphatically syncopated playing with what gradually emerges as an on-the-beat 'stomping' figure. The first half of Williams's solo (1'02"–1'17"), transcribed in Figure 1.4, demonstrates this emerging metrical contrast in the way her right hand features off-beat accentuation of quavers until halfway through the fourth bar, when an on-the-beat emphasis of accented crotchets (marked with brackets) implies the idea of a stereotypical 'stomp-down' motif. This motif is only fully realized in the following section (C) which is scored for the full band.[18]

The rest of William's solo is basically an elaboration of this sort of contrast of metrical accentuation with syncopation, but she incorporates ever more surprising accents that further upset metrical regularity. In her second 12-bar chorus (1'17"–1'32"), for example, an especially prominent accent is heard in her left hand (e.g., 1'19"–1'20"). Such features

---

17 In a 1972 interview (published in 1974), Williams stated, 'My favorite piano players were, Jelly Roll Morton, Earl Hines, Fats Waller and James P. Johnson' (Williams cited in Baggenaes 1974: 2).

18 The difference here is that the three on-the-beat crotchets do not sound as accented as in the C strain because of the heavy accentuation that Williams gives to the off-beat quaver accentuation in the first four bars.

destabilise the otherwise predictable stride-piano style of her accompaniment playing. The solo even ends with a decidedly off-beat 'call' to the rest of the band to re-enter (1'30"–1'32"), as if to say, 'now show me your 'hot' syncopation. There is nothing smooth or easy-sounding about Williams's solo, and it can be heard as an extension of Moten's playing with rhythmic emphasis within the bar. In that respect, it is undoubtedly a hot-styled solo that would certainly defeat close-partner dancing.

The stomping in Williams's solo prepares for the new musical strain (C) that follows it (1'32"–2'02"). That features a repeated 12-bar ensemble chorus arranged by Williams for the brass. It does not utilise the blues changes of the rest of the piece but features the brass in a distinctive riff that contains harmonized and syncopated broken chords set in a descending sequence (see Figure 1.5). These decidedly hot figures are interspersed with cymbal strikes and followed by on-the-beat 'stomping' motifs of a character that Williams hinted at in her solo. The defining function of this section, which undoubtedly puts the hot-black stomping into 'Mess-a-Stomp', is underlined by the fact that it is the only strain in the piece in which a constituent chorus is strictly repeated without any

FIGURE 1.5   The brass-ensemble phrase following Williams's solo in 'Mess-a-Stomp' showing syncopated broken-chord motifs (bb.1-8) contrasting on-the-beat 'stomping' figures (bb.9-12).

variation. The choruses are here split between the syncopated riff material (bars 1–8) and the on-the-beat stomping (bars 9-12) from the ensemble. Williams underlines this split by contrasting dissonant, hot-modernistic harmony with a more traditional chord progression.

In that respect, the C strain moves away from B-flat major more than any other section in the piece by passing through some jazzy-sounding seventh chords in this progression: Bb–Gb7–F7–G7–C7–F7–Bb.[19] The most dissonant (hot) movement is heard in the first half of this sequence, which is also the most syncopated part. The fact that the plunge through the flattened submediant chord (Gb7) and the following lift to the G7 chord sounds so smooth and seamless only goes to show the deftness of Williams's part writing for the brass, which no doubt was a result of Kirk's guidance or else Henderson's example (see below).

The subsequent 'stomping' material is founded on standard harmony for jazz; a circle-of-fifths progression embracing a perfect cadence: G7–C7–F7–Bb (VI7–II7–V7—I). The effect of this harmony is, like the rhythmical effect of the on-the-beat stomping, to return us to familiarity after the dalliance in dissonant syncopated music. To reinforce the feeling of returning to safe ground, the perfect cadence is immediately reiterated at the half bar to emphasize that we have definitively arrived back in the 'home' key of Bb-major.

The reappearance of blues-based choruses thereafter signals the arrival of the final A strain (2'04"–2'37"). The first of its two constituent choruses features a banjo solo from Dirvin before four loud off-beat 'stabs' and a sustained chord for the whole band (as in Kirk's 'Cloudy') herald the final 'shout' chorus with an impressive crescendo that extends the subsection by an extra bar. The closing chorus shows the effects that the earlier play with metrical accentuation has had on the blues-based material, as the trumpets lead in riffs featuring loud syncopated chords which give way to quaver-filled figures that, like the broken-chord riffs in the C section, are grouped in threes across the beat. It is clear from this that hot syncopation has won the day and a final set of off beats are echoed by the saxes before a sustained chord extends the chorus by four bars to bring the piece to its close with hi-hat cymbal strikes.

It is interesting to note the differences as well as the similarities between 'Mess-a-Stomp' and the contemporary hot tracks of Moten's

19 Buehrer spells the second chord in this sequence as F#7 but the transcription by Jeff Sultanof uses Gb7 (Buehrer 2013: 14; Sultanof 2010: 9). The latter is the more likely spelling used by Williams because of the flat-key brass instruments used in that passage.

band. There is notably less of the clamorous polyphony derived from the New Orleans tradition and a greater emphasis on homophonic ensemble textures. High-register 'wails' are absent, but the final 'shout' chorus is nevertheless busier in its texture for the overlaying of different syncopated ensemble passages. While the 'talking' qualities of muted brass and hot-styled solos for clarinet, trumpet, piano, and banjo are evident, the neatly articulated ensemble passages have a greater importance in Williams's piece, not least because they offer the definitive 'stomping' material at its heart. The clamorous excitement of Moten's tracks, which imparts a sort of hot vitality, is replaced by a more muted and refined hot energy that presents more of a bouncy swing than a 'dance-party' abandon. Once again, the sweeter dance-band identity of the Clouds of Joy slips out from behind the mask of hot blackness.

The other arrangement by Williams that was recorded by the full band in 1929 is similarly styled as a hot number but of a more bluesy kind. 'Froggy Bottom' (KC-619-A) is a lowdown blues in B-flat minor that features a string of idiomatic solo choruses until about two-thirds of the way through the track, when the ensemble arrangement finally kicks in (from 2'09"). This suggests that the piece is a 'head' arrangement, and there is ultimately little ensemble writing in it. The ensemble section (2'09"–2'41") is notable for its contrasting form of two eight-bar phrases, and the melancholic riffs, which are much like those in 'Sad Mad Blues', soon give way, after a short break, to improvised polyphony in a more typical New Orleans style (from 2'41"–3'09"). This closes the piece in the characteristically black-jazz vein that is closer to the Moten style than any of the strains in 'Mess-a-Stomp'.

The earlier solos in 'Froggy Bottom' also show hot-black qualities in such features as the 'wailing' calls and pitch bends in Lawson's trumpet chorus (1'18"–1'43"), Dirvin's finger picked banjo solo (1'43"–2'09), and the backing of all the solos by a decided four-to-the-bar 'stomping' feel from the rhythm section. By comparison, 'Mess-a-Stomp' shows that Williams was helped by Kirk and his bandsmen to finesse an idiosyncratic but stereotypically black-sounding piece of hot jazz in her arrangement. It was somewhat indebted to music of the sort recorded by Moten but combined with the multi-strain models of Jelly Roll Morton, a figure whom both Kirk and Williams had met, and ensemble writing that drew on the dance-band background of Kirk and Holder's band. Furthermore, the greater emphasis of ensemble material within the hot aesthetic that they finessed for recording may well have come from the example of Fletcher Henderson's band.

Henderson's New York band visited Kansas City in September 1929, just a couple of months before Kirk's band made its first recordings (Kirk 1989: 66). The *Kansas City Call* announced that on 13 September 1929, the bands of Kirk, 'The Best in the West', and Henderson, 'King of Jazz', would 'engage in a battle of the bands' (Dance Gossip 1929a: 8). At that time, it was a standard practice to have such a 'battle' when one band replaced another for a run at a ballroom, but this particular skirmish represented a battle of prevailing styles: slick Eastern ensemble arrangements pitted against the solo-led bluesy or else melodic style of Kansas City's leading dance band.

Kirk is clear in his autobiography that Henderson's band differed from the Clouds of Joy in its more driving two-beat metrical emphasis, its bigger sound, and a repertoire that embraced more show tunes, which Kirk felt 'was natural for a New York band' (Kirk 1989: 67). The 20 September 1929 edition of the *Kansas City Call* reported on the 'battle' and judged that 'the huge crowd seemed in its applause to give an edge to the novelty numbers, melody and blues of Kirk although an appreciable group obviously preferred the masterly arrangements of Henderson' (Dance Gossip 1929b: 2).

This shows how, by 1929, Kirk had successfully fashioned a repertoire and musical style that was tailored to the musical tastes of his Kansas City audience, but it also indicates what was still lacking in the music of the Clouds of Joy, if they were to enjoy broader success: really slick arrangements that offered greater ensemble impressiveness. This was obvious to Kirk because he remembered that Henderson's band 'really opened our ears' (Kirk 1989: 66). The opportunity to record allowed Kirk to work with Williams to fashion new arrangements that addressed the shortcomings of the band's repertoire while continuing the move away from solo-led 'head' arrangements toward more ensemble-led written ones.

In a way, then, Kirk's band developed a new hot-black style to record that did not just draw on Southwestern models like Moten's music but also on the more current and arranged style that was exemplified by Henderson's band. So, the masking of the Clouds of Joy as a hot-black band for race records is complex in terms of the hybrid black identities it represented: it was as much a hot jazz band offering bluesy solo-led stomps as a swinging dance band featuring characteristic ensemble writing (riffs) and an underlying four-to-the-bar bounce. That mixture was also a strength when it came to resisting racist politics, which like to stress racial absolutisms, because the band could mix up or slip between styles and expectations.

In sum, the first set of recordings made by Kirk's band in Kansas City shows a concerted effort to represent a hot kind of black musical character through a combination of selecting pieces in the band's ballroom repertoire that utilised a hot-jazz style and presenting new pieces developed by Kirk and Williams that mixed qualities of hot Southwestern jazz with the sort of slick ensemble arrangements that Fletcher Henderson's band exemplified. Such stylistic hybridity not only won the Clouds of Joy a two-year contract with Brunswick but also formed the basis for their subsequent manipulation of styles relative to racist expectations of them and their music. If the band 'blacked up' their style to record then, like the most adroit of black blackface performers, they were soon Signifyin(g) on their masked representation of blackness by contrasting it with music that was truer to their origins and experience as a white-society dance band. The seeds of that approach were sown in the band's next recording sessions, which were held in Brunswick's proper studios in Chicago.

THE RECORDINGS OF 1930: GOING BEYOND STEREOTYPED HOT-BLACK JAZZ

In the spring of 1930 the Clouds of Joy followed up on their Kansas City recording sessions with a visit to Brunswick's proper studio in Chicago. Over the course of three days (29 April to 1 May) they recorded a total of twelve different numbers of which eleven were released: nine of them were issued in Brunswick's 'Popular Records' series and two of them in Brunswick's '7000' series of race records. The latter featured a small combo named 'Seven Little Clouds of Joy', rather than the full band.[20] Whereas the Kansas City recordings were almost all blues-based stomp numbers, the Chicago recordings introduced a decidedly more commercial type of swinging jazz that befitted Brunswick's popular catalogue and better suited Kirk's band because it was closer to the style of their ballroom repertoire.

More than half of the 1930 Chicago releases were songs. These vocals were of a particular sort that contrasted with the romantic ballads that the band would go on to record in the later 1930s. Like most vocal-jazz recordings of the period, the singing represents but one of several solo elements in the tracks. In other words, these tracks are not wholly songs, like the later ballads, but rather hot-jazz numbers that reference their

---

20 Rye lists the following players in the Seven Little Clouds of Joy: Harry 'Big Jim' Lawson (trumpet), Floyd 'Stumpy' Brady (trombone), John Williams (alto sax), Mary Lou Williams (piano), Wiliam Dirvin (banjo), Andy Kirk (baritone sax and leader), Ben Thigpen (drums) (Rye in Kirk 1989: 125).

basis in pop-song material through a vocal chorus. Furthermore, the racism that conditioned what could be recorded at the time meant that only certain types of song were considered appropriate for a black band, especially one that was marketed beyond the confines of specialist race records.

An enduring patronizing attitude toward African Americans and fears of racial integration meant that black singers were confined to certain sorts of songs that did not extend to expressing the supposedly higher poetics of serious love. This was because, from a racist perspective, blacks were either considered incapable of such serious romantic intentions or else their expression by blacks suggested the unholy idea of interracial unions. For those sorts of reasons, as Will Friedwald has put it, 'no black man dared attempt a "straight" love song' until later in the century (Friedwald 1990: 225). From that perspective, the important thing was that any romantic expression should not be taken too seriously or else it should be distanced from the here-and-now by association with minstrel-type stereotypes of Southern-black otherness. In that regard, it is no surprise to find that the vocals in the 1930 recordings are either vernacular and bluesy evocations of lost love, located in an imagined South (e.g., 'I Lost My Gal from Memphis'), or else lightweight, bouncy, and voguish dance numbers with a decidedly comedic gloss (e.g., 'Loose Ankles').

All but one of the songs are sung by the band's regular vocalist of the period, Billy Massey.[21] His voice is somewhat nasal and pinched in its tone, and he is often a little wayward in his intonation. His issues with tuning meant that Massey was better suited to the clipped style of singing needed for upbeat vocals than the long-breathed phrases of slower blues numbers. However, his distinctive vocal character certainly brings an audible black-vernacular quality to the 1930 recordings and transforms what are often fairly typical pop songs into recognizably black-sounding music. In this way, Massey's vocality, as much as the hot-jazz sensibility of the band, facilitates the black stylistic masking of the band in these sessions.

The 1930 recordings of the Clouds of Joy differ from those of 1929 in terms of the more fully orchestrated quality of the arrangements. In fact,

21 Rye's discography, in the back of Kirk's autobiography, lists Massey as the vocalist on 'You Rascal, You' (C-6435) but to my ears it doesn't sound like Massey on the record (Brunswick 7180), despite the fact it was recorded in the same session as the released take of 'Dallas Blues' (C-6430-A), which does sound like Massey (Kirk 1989: 126). The drummer-singer, Ben Thigpen, could be the vocalist on 'You Rascal, You'.

they are generally much more fully arranged dance-band tunes than the likes of 'Blue Clarinet Stomp' or 'Froggy Bottom', and they are performed with a tightness of ensemble and a bouncy finesse that were missing or only hinted at in 1929. Furthermore, the solos are less stilted, hesitant, and error-filled, and the music displays a greater fluidity and sense of confidence from the band. They seem to have gotten over any nervousness about recording, and, in engaging in repertoire that was somewhat closer to that employed in their live work, they sound like they are in their element in several of the songs. This might be because the 1930s recordings make use of stock arrangements, no doubt a staple feature of the band's live music, for the first time.

'I Lost My Gal From Memphis' (C4460-A) was the first track that Kirk's band recorded in Chicago, and it is a good example of a Massey vocal that was based on an arrangement by Archie Bleyer, one of the pre-eminent stock arrangers of the period (see Clark 2009). The original song was written by the all-white songwriting team of lyricist Charlie Tobias and composer Peter DeRose. The song's chorus is in the typical AABA form of Tin Pan Alley pop tunes, but it displays much of the character and sentiment of the blues despite its contrary structure and bouncy rhythmic character. The song is for the most part in the key of E minor, and the sense of loss conveyed in the lyrics is as much underscored with such devices as it is with the 'sighing' articulation of the band in the B section of the opening chorus (0'24"–0'33").

The lyrics of the song mention both Memphis and Carolina, which immediately positions the track, and by extension, the band as Southern or at least Southwestern. Vogish, vernacular expressions such as 'I ought to hop a choo-choo' in Massey's singing help convey both a sense of hip modernity and the notion that this is a song of the black South, even if it was written by two white songwriters. So, the song is a piece of white-composed pop music with a bluesy sensibility which is presented in a hottish dance-band character. That hybrid styling represents a masked, double-voiced racial character that is as much in the musical materials as in the lyrics: hot jazz solos are intercut with orchestrated sections of typical dance-band-styled writing that are drawn from Bleyer's arrangement.

'Loose Ankles' (C4462–A) was paired with 'I Lost My Gal From Memphis' on the record that Brunswick released (Brunswick 4803). The song was composed by another team of white songwriters, the composer Pete Wendling and the lyricist Jack Meskill, for the 1930 movie of the same name. This AABA-structured pop song was relatively unproblematic material for a black band to record as it simply extols the virtues of loose ankles for fashionable modern dancing to hot music.

That sentiment played up to the dance-band work of the Clouds of Joy and that helps explain why the band rose to the challenge to produce one of the very best-performed tracks of their early recording sessions.

Any racial mask-play in 'Loose Ankles' is strictly limited to the way the band turns this stock arrangement, again by Bleyer, into hot-sounding Southwestern jazz. In the first chorus (0'08"–0'39"), for instance, after the eight-bar introduction for the band (0'00"–0'08"), Massey's distinctive voice is shadowed by Claude Williams's country-sounding fiddle. Harrington's highly characteristic, if rather shrill, clarinet solo follows in the second chorus (0'39"–1'11"), with Williams's violin resurfacing for a solo break in the B section (0'54"–1'03"). The arrangement then modulates in a transitory passage (1'11"–1'16") that moves the number from G to F major for a rendition of the song's verse section (1'16"–1'33"). That section follows the stock arrangement closely and is performed by the full band in a neat and tidy way with quite clipped but bouncy articulation. That shows just how well rehearsed the band had been by Kirk.

Another solo chorus (1'33"–2'03") follows the verse section, and it features some agile tenor sax playing from Lawrence 'Slim' Freeman. This time the ensemble arrangement returns to provide the B section of the chorus (1'48"–1'56"). A second modulatory passage then lifts the music to A-flat major for a repeated ensemble 'shout' chorus (it is not repeated in the stock arrangement). The arrangement here features the song's melody, but it is set in syncopated stab-chords for the band. The syncopated pushing on of the tempo in the arrangement and the tight ensemble playing of this voguish material bring renewed energy to the piece and allow us to forgive John Williams's rather out-of-tune alto sax solo, heard in the B sections (2'24"–2'32" and 2'56"–3'03") of these choruses.

A few bars are tagged on to the end of the second rendition of the repeated closing chorus (2'40"–3'09") to present an ensemble motif that is immediately reiterated an octave lower, over Ben Thigpen's tom-toms. Those drums serve to bring the number to its conclusion in what is ultimately an accomplished rendition of a popular song arrangement, the likes of which Kirk's band had not hitherto presented on records. It marries neatly played dance-band style orchestrations with some lively jazz, and the precision and characterful rendition of the arranged parts for the band are matched with some great solo work. In all of that, the band exudes confidence in a way that is unmatched in any of the 1929 recordings. This confidence most likely came from the better balance that these numbers represented between the band's sweet-styled ballroom music and the hot-jazz style they had developed for recording.

On 30 April 1930, the day after the first Chicago session, the Clouds of Joy were back in the Brunswick studio to record the sort of identifiably black-sounding, stomping jazz that they had recorded in Kansas City. However, this time they used a stock arrangement by Mel Stitzel of 'Snag It' (C-4470), already a classic hot-jazz number credited to Joe 'King' Oliver, which he had recorded with his band for a Vocalion race record in 1926. The stomping character of 'Snag It' marks quite a contrast from the bouncy vocals that Kirk's band had recorded the day before, and the song contains many of the clichés of the hot style of jazz that we examined elsewhere in this chapter, with the notable addition of a soli chorus for a trio of clarinets (1'29"–1'51"). The trio is heard again, utilising the bottom of the clarinet range, in the final chorus of the arrangement (2'17"–2'41"). Kirk has his band repeat that chorus (2'41"–3'09") but with the clarinets transposed up the octave to bring a greater hot-stomping energy to the close of the track and fill up a side of the 78 rpm record.

Recorded alongside that cover of an established hot instrumental and released on the same Brunswick disc (4878) was an original composition, 'Sweet and Hot'. The track is credited to the band's tenor saxophonist, Lawrence 'Slim' Freeman, but it was almost certainly not written by him alone, if at all.[22] As with 'Corky Stomp', the track seems to be the result of a collaborative effort in which distinct sections of the piece, most probably written by different people, were put together to form the number. The most interesting thing about 'Sweet and Hot', though, is that it is a piece that reflects the stylistic-racialized situation of the Clouds of Joy, just as their 1930 recordings were increasingly mixing up the sweet-white dance-band style of their live work with the hotter black-sounding one that was required of them on records.

Like many other arrangements of the period, 'Sweet and Hot' has an introduction that features a syncopated and harmonized melody line scored for unaccompanied reeds and brasses and punctuated by just a few hi-hat strikes (0'00"–0'10"). The following 32-bar AABA chorus (0'10"–0'57") is led by the saxophones. Their harmonized ensemble melody is coloured with fast vibrato, some portamento, and a distinctive rhythmic laxity that together are intended to represent the stereotypically 'sweet' style of playing that one can hear on recordings by the likes of Guy Lombardo's band. After a brief fill of four bars (0'57"–1'03"),

22 In fact, at least part of the number may well have been based on the contemporary Harold Arlen song of the same name which was published in a stock arrangement by Archie Bleyer in 1930.

which serves as the secondary introduction, a more nimble ensemble passage is heard in a 16-bar section (1'03"–1'27") consisting of two eight-bar phrases that are drawn from the first chorus but varied somewhat in their harmony.

The first of these phrases has a distinctly stop-time quality; in the second phrase the more nimble saxophone ensemble comes to the fore, reinforced now and then by the brasses. The original chord changes of the opening chorus return for a solo 32 bars (1'27"–2'16") for John Harrington's clarinet, with Floyd 'Stumpy' Brady's trombone taking over for the B section (1'50"–2'04") of the chorus. The solos are not especially hot in their style—they feature none of the mute work or unconventional playing techniques that are heard in other Moten-like tracks—but they nevertheless mark a move away from the sweet-styled ensemble writing that opened the arrangement towards hot jazz.

The full band caps off this solo chorus with a modulation to B-flat major ahead of a completely different section of new material (2'16"–3'06") that is clearly meant to represent the upbeat, hot character in 'Sweet and Hot'. This new chorus features dialogue between mordant-laden saxophone riffs and solo trumpet breaks (probably Lawson). A solo for John Williams's rough-hewn baritone sax forms the B section (2'41"–2'53"), and the final A section is adjusted somewhat to become a 'shouting' coda (2'53"–3'06") of riffs for the saxophones that are punctuated by interjections from the brass. By this point, the arrangement has moved well away from the sweet style of the opening to a much less melodious and more rhythmical and clamorous hot sonority.

In this recording, then, the Clouds of Joy offer a journey in their stylistic masking from a representation of a stereotypically syrupy and white-sounding style of sweet jazz to a decidedly hot- and black-sounding one. In showing how they can don different musical masks by indulging in contrasting stereotypical markers of sweet and hot styles, they show how they can effectively draw attention to the falsity of racialized stylistic categories, whether they are black (hot) or white (sweet), because the stylistic mask is all too apparent. They do that, however, in a highly engaging and entertaining way that belies the underlying racialized discourse and thereby protects the band. This seems to me to be key to understanding the mode and power of the Signifyin(g) mask-play or stylistic black minstrelsy that is represented by the band's sweet *and* hot style. That hybrid style becomes increasingly apparent from this point on in their recording career.

Most of the other tracks recorded in Chicago during 1930 were vocals of the bouncy kind recorded with Massey (e.g., 'Once or Twice') or else decidedly black-sounding hot jazz in the manner of 'Snag It' (e.g., 'Dallas Blues'). However, amongst the 1930 tracks were two new compositions by Mary Lou Williams, 'Mary's Idea' and 'Gettin' Off a Mess', that show Williams's part in the sort of stylistic theatre of Kirk's band. What makes Williams's critical role in the recordings of the Clouds of Joy all the more remarkable is that she was only involved in the recordings through an apparent accident of fate.

In a much-quoted anecdote Kirk relates how, when the band arrived to audition to record in Kansas City, their regular pianist, Marion Jackson, did not show up. Kirk recalled that 'he was somewhat of a ladies' man and must have had something on that day' (Kirk 1959: 14). Because it looked as though the Clouds of Joy would have to pass up the audition, Kirk suggested that the band's saxophonist, John Williams, call up his pianist wife, Mary Lou Williams, to fill in for Jackson. Whatever it was that prevented Jackson from attending the audition, it ultimately did him out of a job with the Clouds of Joy, because he was soon replaced by Williams: she sat in as the band's pianist for the recording sessions in Kansas City and for the follow-up ones in Chicago. When Jackson was incapacitated by a car accident in 1931, Williams assumed the role of the band's regular jobbing pianist, and that marked the end of Jackson's tenure with the Clouds of Joy and the start of an important and long-standing relationship with Williams.[23]

Kirk reports that Williams only replaced Jackson to record in Chicago when the recording company executives were heard to say, 'Where's the girl? We liked her style' (Kirk 1989: 72).[24] Kirk's band actually recorded in Chicago in the wake of Williams, who made two solo sides for a Brunswick disc (7178) five days before Kirk's band arrived at Brunswick's studio. So, no doubt, it was the producers' familiarity with Williams and her style that led them to request that she sit in with the band in place of their regular pianist when they came to record in Chicago.

Leaving aside her obvious novelty as a young female performer in the very male-dominated territory of 1930s jazz, the reference to her style was surely as much about the hot-black character of the music that came with her. As stomps and blues numbers dominated the race records catalogues and as Williams arrived at the band's Kansas City sessions

23 Claude Williams recalled that Jackson was replaced after he broke both his legs when he fell asleep at the wheel of the car in which they were travelling (Pearson 1988: 61).

24 Williams remembered that a similar comment was made by a theatre owner in Philadelphia who, on noting the absence of Jackson, remarked, 'You don't need that man, just take the girl' (Williams, as cited in Pearson 1988: 62).

with such pieces fashioned in the Moten-Henderson mould, it was no wonder that the executives wanted her involved.

Whereas all but one of Williams's 1929 compositions were blues-based pieces, the first of her pieces recorded in 1930, 'Mary's Idea' (C-4473), utilized the 32-bar AABA chorus form that was so common in show tunes performed by dance bands of the time. This apparent reflection of the band's shift in style, away from its hot-jazz mask, is matched by a much greater reliance on ensemble writing than in 1929. Such writing also tends to be more assured and sophisticated as a result of her studies of arrangements made by some of the leading arrangers of the period. As Kirk explained, Williams learned to arrange not just from his tutelage and Henderson's example but also from some materials he had purchased from a band that the Clouds of Joy had encountered during their stint appearing at New York City's Roseland Ballroom in the first few weeks of 1930. Kirk recalled it this way:

> She learned voicing for the different horns from things I showed her from some arrangements I'd bought. I'd been fortunate enough to pick up 40 professional arrangements from Hank Biagini, who had led the Casa Loma band when it was a [Jean] Goldkette unit called the Orange Blossoms, but had pulled out of Casa Loma when we played opposite them at the Roseland. Some were by Don Redman, some by Gene Gifford. We sounded like a new band. (Kirk 1989: 73)

In a 1964 interview in the *New Yorker*, Williams acknowledged the importance of these arrangements when she stated that 'Redman was my model'. Theodor Buehrer has since pointed to such features as the harmonized introduction to *Mary's Idea* to highlight the influence of Redman's voicings and rhythmic style on her writing (Buehrer 2013: xxiii). He also follows the examples of Max Harrison and Linda Dahl in comparing Redman's arrangement of 'Rocky Road' with the October 1930 recording of 'Traveling That Rocky Road' (C-6431) by the Clouds of Joy to show Redman's influence. But my research has found no evidence that the arrangement of 'Traveling That Rocky Road' was written by Williams. Moreover, the similarities between the arrangements that are noted by Harrison, Dahl, and Buehrer are passing, at best, and might as much be due to the presence of features that were common to many similar arrangements of the period. To my mind, however, the most likely feature of 'Mary's Idea' to have come from Williams's study of the Redman-Gifford arrangements is the much greater presence and variance of ensemble writing in the arrangement.

The introduction of *Mary's Idea* (0'00"–0'11") is set by Williams for unaccompanied horns (save for the usual cymbal strikes) in a harmonized and syncopated descending line that is taken at a surprisingly brisk tempo (ca. 208 bpm). The first chorus of the number (0'11–0'47") then features a trumpet solo (probably Lawson) in the A sections of the AABA 32-bar form, which is accompanied by a distinctively agile stomping-styled riff from the other horns. The trumpet solo gives way to a passage for harmonized saxes in the B section (0'28" –0'38"), which makes great use of a rhythmic cell featuring a quaver followed by a dotted crotchet. In the second chorus (0'47"–1'23"), neatly executed riffs for the ensemble trade with baritone sax solo breaks (probably John Williams) in the A sections. This material is contrasted in the B section (1'05"–1'15") with a passage for harmonized brass, which again makes use of the ear-catching rhythmic cell of a quaver followed by the dotted crotchet but now moved to the middle of the bar.

A secondary introduction of six bars (1'23"–1'31"), which is led by the lead trumpet, proceeds to an interlude (1'31"–1'49") of two eight-bar phrases in which the solo trumpet continues to lead in a call-and-response dialogue between saxophones and the rest of the ensemble. The third chorus (1'49" –2'26") then contrasts long-breathed chordal accompaniment figures beneath Harrington's clarinet solo in the A sections with harmonized and crisply articulated ensemble riffs that are marked by syncopation. Long-note accompaniment chords return under John Williams's alto sax solo in the B section (2'07"–2'17") of the third chorus before the syncopated riffs return in a reversal of the two four-bar subphrases that made up the A section, but this time the clarinet remains silent throughout.

The final chorus (2'26"–3'06") takes the call-and-response ensemble dialogue further, but by this point in Williams's piece, solo material is reduced to just a few two-note statements from the solo trumpet that are eventually passed to the saxes and then the brass section. From the B section (2'44"–2'54") onwards, the final chorus is a show piece of ensemble writing with a soli run of semiquavers from the saxes leading to the final A section. This section is extended by a short coda (3'01"-3'06") in which Kirk's sousaphone makes one last plea on behalf of the soloists but is symbolically beaten into submission by the ensemble statements.

In sum, it seems that Williams's idea with 'Mary's Idea' was to go even further with the sort of hybrid hot-and-sweet style that was beginning to emerge with 'Mess-a-Stomp'. In that respect, 'Mary's Idea' contains all the essential ingredients of a stomping hot-jazz arrangement (such as a characteristic introduction, solos for the front line instruments, and an invigorating ending) but they are made to adjust, as never before, to a decidedly faster and more bouncy dance-band sensibility. That sensibility shows off much more involved and intricate soli ensembles, requiring music reading and careful rehearsal for neat articulation and execution in performance.

That writing of impressive ensemble features ultimately comes to dominate the arrangement by its close, and that represents the effective retirement of the old Southwestern-style 'head' arrangements for Williams. In that change we can see how Williams was already moving away from the stomping style of hot jazz that dominated the first recordings of Kirk's band toward a more bouncy swing that would get realized in her arrangements of the later 1930s. At the same time, and perhaps unwittingly, she was disrupting stylistic expectations of 'race' music and thereby confounding their racist underpinning.

'CASEY JONES SPECIAL': HOT-BLACK JAZZ AS RACIALIZED THEATRE

On 15 December 1930, Kirk's band recorded for the first and only time with a white vocalist, Dick Robertson, in Brunswick's New York City studios. Robertson made numerous recordings for various different record companies during a long recording career. Laird's Brunswick discography indicates that he fronted almost every band on their books during the early 1930s, including those of Duke Ellington, Luis Russell, and Red Nichols (Laird 2001). In other words, Brunswick employed Robertson regularly to bring jazz-styled commercial songs of their choosing to the bands that were contracted to record for them. This shows something of the obligation that bands like Kirk's were under to record commercial material like the songs in the 1930 recordings.

The record that Kirk's band made with Robertson (Brunswick 4893) was thus an example of Brunswick's practice of imposing commercial songs upon bands through their in-house singer. The irony of that commerciality, of course, was that this pushed the Clouds of Joy someway further back towards the sort of repertoire and style that they played live for white audiences of social dancers. Thus 'Saturday' (E35750), a song lifted from the revue *Snapshots of 1921*, presents a decidedly sweet style in, for example, the dialogue between the saxophones and vibrato-laden trumpet in its opening chorus (0'06"–0'56"). In fact, there is comparatively little jazz in this number and, in the way of commercial dance-band music, the emphasis is on the arranged material for the band rather than improvised solos.

'Sophomore' (E35751), the song on the other side of the Robertson disc, gives more room to improvisation than 'Saturday', but the solos, featuring John Williams's baritone sax and Floyd 'Stumpy' Brady's trombone in the second chorus (1'04"–1'40") display some lax intonation. Mary Lou Williams's solo in the third chorus (1'40"–2'16") is more accomplished and driving, but the following chorus (2'20"–2'58"), a final one for the full band that follows a short modulatory passage (2'16"–2'20), is when the track really gets into its stride and this shows two things: the greater rhythmic swing and precision brought to the band by its new drummer, Ben Thigpen, and the way the ensemble playing had been finessed under Kirk's leadership. These elements helped produce a really neat and nimble sounding band in the 1930 recordings that was not so evident in 1929.

The Clouds of Joy returned to the recording studio on 2 March 1931. This time they recorded for Victor, but, presumably, to avoid breaking their contract with Brunswick, they recorded under the pseudonym of 'Blanche Calloway and Her Joy Boys'. This also made sense because, at that time, Kirk's band was working with Calloway at the Pearl Theatre in Philadelphia. Sam Steiffel, who managed both the theatre and Calloway, tried to lure Kirk's band away from him to become Calloway's permanent backing group (Shipton 2010: 63). But Steiffel and Calloway hadn't reckoned with the loyalty of Kirk's musicians.

By 1931 Kirk had invested a great deal of time in supporting and coaching his band members and in generally developing the Clouds of Joy towards a secure future. He had won contracts with the Pla-Mor Ballroom and with Brunswick and had extended their touring out of the Southwestern Territories to encompass big-time venues on the East coast, like the Roseland Ballroom in New York City. All of this bred understandable loyalty from the band, which meant they let Kirk know about the takeover attempt. In the end, only two trumpeters, Edgar Battle and Clarence Smith, left Kirk to join Calloway and that was actually a relatively small loss, when one considers that six players (including Ben Webster and Clyde Hart) were later lured away from Jap Allen's band to play for Calloway (Shipton 2010: 64).

Blanche was the older sister of Cab Calloway, and by all accounts, had an act that was as flamboyant in its black-urban modernity as her brother's mode of performance.[25] Blanche got Cab into show business

25 In a 1932 review *Billboard* described Calloway as having an act that keeps 'strictly to the family tradition' (Sampson [1980] 2013: 542).

and performed with him for a time, so it was actually Blanche's style of performance that Cab developed into his own famously idiosyncratic band-leading, posturing and vocalizing at New York's famous Cotton Club. As Earl Hines recalled, 'Blanche Calloway had a very good way of entertaining. She was wild and wiry in certain things and very sensitive in others... Although Cab may not say this to himself, all of his style was from her. His sister taught him everything he knew about performing' (Hines, as cited in Dance 1983: 49).

Blanche Calloway's act may well have been more varied than her brother's, precisely because of her greater capacity for representing sensitivity, but she nevertheless offered a similar form of highly stylized black performance. If Cab's better documented style is anything to go by, she took racist stereotypes of blackness and mixed them up with hip urban modernity and ironic exaggeration to the point that such old-time minstrelsy was, as Middleton puts it, 'returned under new management' (Middleton 2006: 84). Her highly energetic performances were most often accompanied by orchestrations that *Billboard* described as 'Loud and wild and furious' (Sampson [1980] 2013: 542). This hot-black style, of course, was not the typical musical territory of the Clouds of Joy, but it chimed with the interval entertainment part of their live repertoire and the hot qualities that they developed for recording. In other words, their stint as a backing band for Calloway represented an extension of their stylistic blacking up to record and it re-engaged the showmanship and theatricality that featured in a small way in their ballroom sets.

Blanche Calloway most often operated within the white male gaze, and, unlike her brother, she had her ever-apparent femininity as much as her racial difference to contend with in the mask-play of her performance. In that respect, the song 'I Need Lovin'' (64070-2) can be read as double voiced in its representation of her, both as a black figure of heterosexual male fantasy—the supposedly virginal but readily available sex object—and as a black proto-feminist, assuming the power from that stereotyping to demand sexual satisfaction on her own terms. Thus, several times in the song, she revels in the lyrics that extend the plea of the title line, 'I need lovin'', into the demand, 'I need lovin', now!'

In fact, the musical architecture of the song suggests a journey towards fulfilment of her demands as she and the music become ever more desperate and/or determined as the track progresses towards its close. The last chorus of the track begins with a driving brassy rendition of the song's melody from the band (from 1'48") but ends with a section of 'patter' for Calloway (from 2'13"). This patter moves from fully-formed words through lyrical contractions towards a series of four wordless pseudo-orgasmic moans that are heard over the coda (from 2'38"):

> Now, I'm sweet sixteen and never been kissed,
> Come on, show me what I've missed,
> I need some lovin';
> Do you think I'm made of wood?
> [It's] too darn lonesome when you're good,
> I gotta have some lovin';
> I'm a rag, a bone, a hank of hair,
> Uh, forget it baby, I don't care,
> I need some lovin';
> Oh, boys, let's go back; can't stand,
> Ah . . . Ah . . . Ah . . . Ah . . .

Calloway certainly doesn't sound like a sweet sixteen-year-old here but presents herself as very much more worldly and sexually experienced: she knows precisely what she wants and how to get it. Her vocal performance certainly evokes stereotypes of black primitivism, physicality, and promiscuity, but she turns these into an act of black-feminine self-determination. It is precisely Calloway's black mask-play in the song that allows for her apparently bodily-rooted and highly sexualized vocal performance of femininity. It is hard to imagine a contemporary white female playing this highly sexualized role in quite the same self-determining way.

The orchestration of the song for Kirk's band is bold, brassy, and bouncy and this underscoring of feminine sexual gratification underlines that 'I Need Lovin'' is a song about black-feminine empowerment rather than merely a stereotypical representation of a patriarchal fantasy of female sexual availability.[26] There are characteristic solos from Brady's trombone and Williams's piano in the song's third chorus (1'15"–1'48"), and a freewheeling, if brief, tenor sax solo from Freeman forms the second phrase (1'56"–2'05") of the closing chorus. These solos help to give the song a jazz quality and thereby bring a crucial stylistic blackness to this musical representation of subversive femininity.

26 The original record label mistitles the track as 'All I Need is Lovin'' and credits Charlie Brown as arranger. Interestingly, the tempo of Kirk's recording is twenty bpm slower than Calloway's 1934 recording of the song with her own band. A comparison of the Clouds of Joy's three different takes of the song suggests that Kirk's band struggled to settle on an agreeable tempo with Calloway.

'There's Rhythm in the River' (64069-2) was released on the reverse of 'I Need Lovin'', and it represents the typical contrast of an upbeat number paired with a slower bluesy one that was presented on records of the period. A double-voiced representation of black femininity is again evident in this song: Calloway assumes the stereotypical role of a woman pining after a lost love. She has the blues, however, because she has stood up to patriarchal hegemony by throwing her man overboard to drown for lying and cheating on her. The tension between this self-determined act and her stereotyped position as a bereft black female constitutes much of the resistive mask-play of the theatre in this track.

There are no jazz solos to speak of in this bluesy number, which is based on another stock arrangement by Archie Bleyer, but the Southern-gospel allusions, the orchestration and the stomping quality of the music signify a hot-black character. The orchestration for Kirk's band sends up the whole scenario through such details as Harrington's limpid clarinet counterpoint at the opening (which is not in Bleyer's arrangement) and the emphatically accented 'comments' from the ensemble that are inserted between Calloway's vocal phrases. We are clearly not meant to take Calloway's capacity for murder or her feminine pining or the hot blackness too seriously as this is, after all, just good-fun entertainment, isn't it? Such questions are raised by the double-voiced theatricality of the Signifyin(g) of the song's performance on the record: this is both hot-black expression and its caricature in theatricalized exaggeration.

Amongst the recordings that the Clouds of Joy made as a backing group for Calloway on Victor is 'Casey Jones Blues' (64068-1), which shows how the theatrical sort of double-voiced masked performance in Calloway's songs also operated in the band's instrumentals. This track revisited one of the numbers that the Clouds of Joy had recorded in Kansas City in November 1929. Brunswick originally issued the number as 'Casey Jones Special' (4653), which is a title that speaks of the piece's special role in the band's live repertoire, as it was one of the novelty numbers that the band played in the breaks between dance sets in their ballroom work when they could assert a hot-jazz blackness. The fact that the Clouds of Joy recorded two different versions of the famous 'Ballad of Casey Jones' for two different releases shows that their 'hot' treatment of it was considered as highly appropriate material for recording.[27]

27 'The Ballad of Casey Jones' is listed as No. 3247 in the Roud Folk Song Index.

Offering such entertainment numbers in the live work for white audiences was a risky business for a black band, and thus the piece benefitted from some distancing and disarming humour that drew on the conventions of minstrel-like showmanship, if only for the band's protection. In both of the band's versions of 'Casey Jones', the musicians thus play various characters that, as we will see, are stereotyped representations of blackness, but they are rendered relative to the prevailing black-theatrical practices of blackface minstrelsy so as to recover them from the pernicious racism of such stereotypes.

Kirk recalled his band's special version of the 'Ballad of Casey Jones' in his autobiography in terms of its overt theatricality and its effect on white audiences:

> We dressed up in engineers' black caps and tied red bandanas around our necks. Just before going into our routine I would borrow a cigarette from one of the smokers—I didn't smoke myself—take the mouthpiece off the sousaphone and blow a lot of smoke into the tubing. [Billy] Massey sang the verse, then the whole band would come in on 'Casey Jones, mounted to the cabin, Casey Jones, with the throttle in his hand . . .' By the time I got out front, smoke was pouring out of the bell of my horn. Allen Durham was imitating the drive shaft of a train engine with his trombone, and Big Jim Lawson was dancing a jig as he 'oiled' the 'drive shaft' with his trumpet. The crowds loved it, especially white audiences. They'd gather around the bandstand and clap and yell, 'Let's get hot. Come on, get hot'. Whites used expressions like that to egg us on. (Kirk 1989: 62)

So, contemporary white audiences loved the evident hot theatricality of this routine and found in its performance what they took to be a particularly authentic kind of black expression by Kirk's band. In such routines, the band was very much framed as stage entertainment and tellingly donned items of costume as a physical mask to perform an act that involved an important measure of disarming humour. As can be heard in the recordings, the piece evokes a discourse about rural Southern life—always a setting for blackface minstrelsy—in the face of the modernity that is otherwise represented by the engineer Casey Jones and his famous steam locomotive.

The piece opens with the reeds imitating the locomotive's whistle. The train's departure bell is then heard before we are treated to the following exchange over it:

ENGINEER: Hey down there! Get that cow off that track so we can get outta here.

COWMAN: Uh-what?!

ENGINEER: Bongbell, dongbell, bongbell [all indistinct] and Hicksville [very distinct].

COWMAN: Uh-what?!

This comedic exchange sets the tone for the rest of the treatment of Casey Jones by the Clouds of Joy: happy-go-lucky country hicks who are at odds with and oblivious to progressive modernity that is represented by the railroad. In this scenario, the band offers a caricature or a stereotype of the Deep South as laid back and backward. For the band's white audiences this would have been a familiar representational trope of blackness, as a result of its repetitious depiction in the 'plantation' settings of minstrel shows and their vaudeville derivatives. It was, no doubt, the band's evident black-jazz modernity within the apparently backward Southern depiction that spoke to their audiences of hot blackness.

The markers of this Southern territory are especially apparent in the arrangement of 'Casey Jones' in which John Harrington's reedy clarinet, Claude Williams's country-sounding fiddle, and Dirvin's evocative finger-picked banjo are especially prominent. However, around the contributions from these figures are more urbane solos by Lawson (trumpet), Mary Lou Williams (piano), and Freeman (tenor sax). It is the stylistic tension between the Southern-styled hootenanny, offered by the likes of Harrington and Claude Williams, and the urbane modernity found in the solos of Mary Lou Williams and Freeman that the track gains its hot comedic energy.

At the heart of the piece is a vocal ensemble section that represents a much-shortened version of the famous 'Ballad of Casey Jones'. It is rendered in a call-and-response manner between Billy Massey and a trio of others in the band. This rendition with its gospel-like references to 'the promised land' gives the piece a decidedly black gloss but the references to the great Southern Pacific and Santa Fe railroads immediately place the performance within the context of relatively modern industrial American society. Furthermore, the emphasis is clearly more on the notion of Casey Jones wanting to ride these great modern railroads than on his impending journey to the Promised Land. Thus, the song becomes a decidedly secular vehicle for representing stereotyped Southern blackness within a decidedly contemporary American modernity than a sacred one about the passage to the afterlife.

At the end of both versions of 'Casey Jones', the spoken dialogue returns when the Engineer character is heard to shout, 'All out for Hicksville!' and the musical representation of the train gradually comes to a halt with the slowing of Dirvin's banjo strums. It seems then that this journey has been a round trip that ultimately took us nowhere else but back to where we started: to the stereotyped lazy, hick-filled plantation territory of an imagined South. In this circularity, though, we are left in no doubt that it has been a highly entertaining Southern indulgence: this black-fantasy reimagining of 'Casey Jones' was one well worth taking for the fun it offered en route through its depiction of stereotypical blackness in the face of contemporary modernity.

Here, then, is a black band playing up to stereotypes of Southern-black identity but in a theatrical form which represents an excess in the blackness of the caricature within a context of their own situation as a modern-sounding jazzy dance band. Within that context, the final 'All out for Hicksville!' is double-voiced: it is not only an exhortation for everyone to get off the train of modernity to indulge in the caricature of backward 'Hicksville' for a while, but it is also a ironic statement of wholehearted ('all out') dismissal to the underlying false-ideal of black naturalism. In contrasting a grotesquely 'happy-go-lucky' black Southern cowman with the modernity of the railroad hero, Casey Jones, the band leaves us in no doubt that industrial progress has or should have left such rural and primitivistic stereotypes far behind, even if it is still fun to indulge in them with reedy clarinet, fiddle, and banjo from time to time. In this lies much of the theatricality represented by the stylistic mask-play and Signifyin(g) representation of blackness that Kirk's band engaged with in their earliest recordings.

By the time the band were heard again on records, in March 1936, the whole character of their music had changed to embrace swing. As we will see, however, the way the band negotiated their racialized position was no less complicated, nor was it any less influenced by the subversively hybrid performances of hot (black) and sweet (white) styles of jazz presented by Kirk and his musicians on their records. Although their later 1930s recordings helped the Clouds of Joy find a wide audience for the first time, many of their early recordings reappeared in swing versions. That only goes to show what a formative phase 1929–1931 was for the Clouds of Joy and how and why a hybrid sweet-and-hot style was at the heart of their identity and stylistic racial politics as a recording band for years to come.

CHAPTER 2

'WALKIN' AND SWINGIN''
SIGNIFYIN(G) IN ELEGANT
HOT SWING, 1936–1941

THE DOWNTURN IN record consumption and recording activity during the Great Depression that followed the 1929 Wall Street crash meant that Andy Kirk and his Clouds of Joy did not record for exactly five years after their Victor session with Blanche Calloway of 2 March 1931. By the time they began recording again, on 2 March 1936, stomping jazz had been replaced by a new hot style; swing music. This chapter focuses on the hot-swing instrumentals that the Clouds of Joy recorded in the five-year period between March 1936 and July 1941 and it leaves discussion of the more numerous sweet ballads that also appeared during that timeframe to the next chapter. The recording session of 17 July 1941 marks a sensible end point for this five-year period in the band's recordings, because shortly after that, Mary Lou Williams, who had been so instrumental in forging their musical-racial identity, left the band.

As the next chapter shows, with Williams's departure, the music of the Clouds of Joy turned in a different stylistic direction.

When Kirk's band began recording for Decca in March 1936, they once again worked with Jack Kapp to record music that was intended for the race market, albeit in the new style of swing. In the earlier 1930s they had spent nearly two years playing in the ballrooms of New York and other cities along the Eastern seaboard where they experienced the development of swing. They had also established their base in Kansas City and it was from there that the band toured the ballrooms of the Southwest. When they were not touring, Kirk's band members participated in the vibrant nightlife that thrived in Kansas City despite the Depression. The main jobs of this chapter are to establish how these sorts of experiences produced a distinctive style of swing music that features in the post-1936 recordings of the Clouds of Joy and to consider what that style might mean in terms of the racial-musical identity of the band and its records.

This chapter shows that despite qualities of the hot-jazz styles of New York and Kansas City that are evident in the 1936–1941 swing recordings, there is also a distinctively elegant if restrained quality in the comparatively understated swing of Kirk's band. Unlike many other black bands of the period, the Clouds of Joy do not impress with rhythmic drive, unusual sonorities, or sheer volume of sound. Their swing music is more subtle, unobtrusive, and refined in its character. So, this chapter asks, how can we account for the comparatively restrained quality in the swing recordings of the Clouds of Joy? This central question for the chapter is as much about race as style as we will see how Kirk's band continued to draw on Bennie Moten's hot style and the riff-based swing of Eastern bands like Fletcher Henderson's to develop a black-jazz identity that ensured their music appealed to Decca's race-records market.

Despite scoring a hit in that market with 'Christopher Columbus', a tune that subsequently became Henderson's theme, the Clouds of Joy simply don't sound like the bands of their black contemporaries. The comparatively understated style of their swing, which is heard in their late-1930s recordings, was unusual for a black band and even proved white-sounding for radio listeners and inauthentic for jazz critics like Gunther Schuller. So, this chapter aims to illuminate and account for that distinctive musical-racial character of their swing music in terms of where it came from. It also asks what it might mean for audiences, critics, and the musicians themselves, and what it might say about conceptions of jazz artistry and race that have been used to understand swing culture of the 1930s.

This chapter explores such questions by first establishing a Kansas City context for the musical development of the Clouds of Joy as a swing band. After its return from the East, Kirk's band continued to secure ballroom residencies in Kansas City and toured from that base. In all of that work, they predominantly, but not exclusively, played for white social dancers of a regional kind that demanded a particular sort of dance music. They also took part in the rich and gregarious cabaret culture that flourished in the entertainment district when they were resident in the Kansas City. That, together with their exposure to New York ballroom culture, helps account for the development of the Clouds of Joy as a rather special sort of swing band with its own particular style of swing music.

Like other great swing bands, Kirk's group offered movement-motivating pieces of dance music built out of rhythmically juxtaposed riffs, but it more often presented a comparatively melodic, smooth, and non-showy style of swing. However, the band's swing always contained a characteristic 'little bounce-beat', as Kirk put it, and there is quiet accomplishment in the clarity, modesty, and refinement of their swing recordings (Kirk 1989: 67). Such subtle qualities are often lacking in the swing music of their contemporaries, and, perhaps because of the apparent inauthenticity of their understated style, Kirk's band are most often marginalized and undervalued by jazz critics. Nevertheless, it is precisely such characteristics that help to account for the band's popular appeal and they have a great deal to do with their work as a white-society dance band.

As Albert Murray bemoaned in 1976, jazz critics have too often overlooked the fact that swing was fundamentally conceived as a type of music for dancing rather than for consumption in a jazz club or concert hall setting (Murray [1976] 1997: 992–996). In that regard, this chapter asks how we might use the later 1930s recordings of the Clouds of Joy to illuminate the complex relationship between swing music and social dancing which conditioned it. This is a more difficult enterprise than it may sound because the musical qualities of swing, as much as the musical requirements of social dancing of the period, have not been much codified or related in really searching analysis. Nevertheless, the chapter draws on a small but significant body of literature that has sought to establish such details and it uses that to develop the concept of a two-way formative relationship between social dancing and music-making in swing culture of the later 1930s.

This begs the question, if the highly racialized culture of social dancing was as vital in shaping the musical qualities of swing as the music was in

influencing the movements of dancers, what might that mean for understanding the musical-racial identity of the Clouds of Joy and other black
swing bands of the period? A significant problem for addressing that sort
of question through the swing recordings of Kirk's band is that most of
those records represent something of a distortion of their style and practice as a live band, because in that live context they specialized in sweeter
styled dance music. It is that distortion, however, which represents the
black-swing mask that was donned by Kirk's band to record swing in
1936, and which, after the success of their first sweet-ballad recording,
'Until the Real Thing Comes Along', became increasingly coloured by the
whiter-sounding style of their live work as a dance band.

It is in the context of such stylistic hybridity that the last section of
this chapter considers the musical portraits that featured in the band's
repertoire for what the swing style might say about their subjects. The
band's manager, Joe Glaser, is thus read from the perspective of his depiction in sweet-and-hot swing in 'Little Joe From Chicago' to show
how his portrait is double-voiced as both a celebratory and critical reflection. The portrait of Count Basie in 'The Count', on the other hand,
shows the balance of styles slipping towards a hot-black character that
won't be contained behind the sweeter side of the band's style of swing.
However, that feature might be as much about the piece's arranger, Mary
Lou Williams, who was tiring of the culture of the band and left it just a
year or so after the piece was recorded partly because she was bored with
its sweet commercial style.

In short, the chapter considers how the sort of racial mask-play in the
band's earlier Brunswick and Victor recordings was transformed into a
swing aesthetic when they came to record for Decca in 1936. In the context of an ever more popular jazz culture, in which swing facilitated the
widespread consumption of jazz by Americans as never before, the evident hybridity of musical-racial styles in the band's subtle brand of swing
raises questions about the function of such music in relation to critical
notions of stylistic-racial authenticity and artistry in jazz. In that respect, what does the complex interplay between the band's experiences,
audiences, and recorded music mean for their mask-play and its
Signifyin(g) discourse on racialized musical identities of the period?

A KANSAS CITY SCHOOLING: DEVELOPING ELEGANT
HOT SWING

When the Clouds of Joy arrived in Kansas City in the late 1920s, Andy
Kirk was impressed to discover that although the city was highly

segregated, its African American population had forged a thriving culture and economy that was unlike any that he had experienced before. He recalled, 'It was a revelation to me. Kansas City was a regular Mecca for young blacks from other parts of the country aspiring to higher things than janitor or chauffeur' (Kirk 1989: 69). The racial pride and aspiration that had been instilled by Kirk's upbringing within the much smaller black community of Denver meant that Kirk immediately identified with the atmosphere of confidence, enterprise, and opportunity that emanated from Kansas City's black culture. By adopting Kansas City as his band's home, Kirk positioned himself and the Clouds of Joy within its confidence-giving creative ferment, which was right at the beating heart of the culture of the Southwestern Territories.

During the 1920s, Chicago and New York replaced New Orleans as centres for jazz, but Kansas City's bands were somewhat removed from the musical developments that took place in those cities. As Driggs and Haddix point out, although Chicago was easily reached by road and rail, 'Kansas City bands played only short stays in that city' because the Chicago branch of the musicians' union protected opportunities for local bands by imposing short-term residency rules on visiting ones (Driggs and Haddix 2005: 4). As much as for reasons of distance, New York was also relatively inaccessible to Kansas City bands. Ross Russell suggests that this relative isolation allowed for the development of a distinctive style of jazz in Kansas City. He argues that it ultimately came to revitalize the mainstream of jazz during the 1930s because the city proved comparatively free of the economic pressures that negatively impacted on jazz cultures elsewhere (Russell [1971] 1983: 3).

The development and influence of Kansas City jazz undoubtedly owed a great deal to the vibrant nightlife that developed in that 'wide open' town during the 1920s. Tom Pendergast, the notorious political 'Boss' and sometime mayor of the city, helped sustain an unusually buoyant nighttime economy in Kansas City during the depression by effectively allowing clubs and cabarets to flout prohibition laws. Pendergast had inherited his family's business interests and political influence from his father in 1911. After the National Prohibition Act was passed in 1919, Pendergast hid his family's wholesale liquor concerns beneath a whole raft of legitimate businesses. He also developed what Russell called an 'invisible government' by gaining influence over a clutch of leading city officials (Russell [1971] 1983: 7).

In 1925, a new City Manager role was proposed, in part to undermine Pendergast's control of city governance. As Russell puts it, 'Pendergast's masterstroke was to support the plan, see it made into law, and then appoint his own creature, [Judge] Henry F. McElroy, to the post' (Russell [1971] 1983: 7). Pendergast's cronies, like McElroy, supported a culture in which the city authorities turned a blind eye to the many saloons, dance halls, and nightclubs that supported such illegal activities as liquor consumption, gambling, and prostitution. They thereby protected both Pendergast's business interests and the city's nighttime musical culture that thrived in the black district, which was situated around 18th and Vine streets and which accommodated quite a number of clubs and speakeasies.

According to Driggs and Haddix, the result was that Kansas City became known as the 'Paris of the Plains', more because of its licentious nightlife than its wide boulevards and fountains (Driggs and Haddix 2005: 6). The nighttime economy supported a thriving jazz scene, and musicians from elsewhere increasingly arrived in the city seeking work within that lucrative prospect. It was not just musicians that were attracted to Pendergast's Kansas City but also the record companies that, towards the end of the 1920s, sought (somewhat belatedly) to bolster their catalogues with the untapped jazz talent that could be found there. This meant that records as well as performers increasingly travelled out from that Southwestern cultural hub and they helped spread the influence of the distinctive riff-based style of ragtime and blues derived jazz that emerged within the creative ferment of Kansas City.

Driggs and Haddix offer a suitably colourful account of the wide range of vice that was provided by the many and varied cabarets and dance halls in the entertainment district. They also note, however, that it was always accompanied by music. According to their research, the clubs around 18th and Vine, 'ranged from rough, bucket-of-blood joints with sawdust on the floor and a stomp-down piano player, to elegant nightclubs presenting elaborate floor shows accompanied by full bands' (Driggs and Haddix 2005: 8). Kirk's band most often worked in the bigger and classier venues of the city, like the whites-only Pla-Mor Ballroom, but members of Kirk's band—along with most other musicians in Kansas City—attended and participated in the after-hours jam sessions that were accommodated by the numerous smaller clubs that proliferated during the Pendergast regimen.

Mary Lou Williams estimated there to be 'fifty or more cabarets rocking on 12th and 18th streets' in Kansas City (Williams, as cited in Jones 1988: 187). The jam sessions at these small clubs provided an important forum for musicians to exchange ideas and to show off and learn in apparently friendly cutting-contests of virtuosic musicianship that would often last late into the night. Such opportunities helped individual musicians develop their confidence and capabilities as improvisers; the jam sessions allowed them to try out ideas and challenge their creativity while experiencing the ideas, styles, and practices of others. Kirk recalled, 'It was in those little clubs [in Kansas City] where musicians from bands like mine got "educated" in jazz and blues. They were our school. That's where we learned improvising and got ideas' (Kirk 1989: 25). If Kirk's dance band did not know too much about jazz before they arrived in Kansas City, it was in that city's nightclubs that they gained experience which had a profound influenced on the music that they recorded in the 1930s.

A legacy of ragtime, boogie-woogie, and blues music prevailed in the Southwest that the likes of Russell and Schuller credit with influencing the distinctive style of jazz that arose in and around Kansas City. One important venue in that regard was The Sunset, a club which Mary Lou Williams visited regularly with others in Kirk's band (Williams [1954] 1997: 102). It became a particular centre for Kansas City's jazz musicians because Walter 'Piney' Brown, who managed the club for a local politician, was renowned for his generosity towards musicians who were down on their luck.[1]

While Piney saw to the gambling upstairs, downstairs the club featured 'Big' Joe Turner, one of the bartenders who would 'shout' the blues, accompanied by Pete Johnson's boogie-woogie piano playing. However, many differently schooled musicians would show up there after hours to jam together in a friendly but competitive atmosphere. As many as fifteen at a time would crowd on to the bandstand to be involved in the sessions and many more would listen in (Driggs and Haddix 2005: 8). In this way, the indigenous musical styles of the city and region came into contact with those of visiting musicians and no doubt influences and learning flowed both ways.

The richness of the black culture of Kansas City and its dissemination was aided by the fact that it marked the most westerly stop on the touring circuit operated by the Theatre Owners Booking Association (TOBA). The TOBA network developed during the 1910s and 1920s as an organization for coordinating tours of vaudeville acts around a network of 80 or so mostly white-owned theatres (Russell 1983: 12). TOBA was a

---

1 According to John Williams, for broke musicians The Sunset represented one of '2 places you automatically had a job, it was $2 a night and all you could drink.' He goes on to mention the ready availability of prostitutes and that 'they would take care of you all night for sure' (Williams cited in Klein 1996: 4).

major employer of black performers, especially during the Depression years when long-term contracts in ballrooms tended to be rare.

Some musicians, including Mary Lou Williams, re-ascribed the TOBA acronym as 'Tough on Black Asses' because of the hard work and harsh conditions that black performers endured on their tours in return for relatively little money. Russell explains that Kansas City marked 'a turnaround point' for TOBA where 'acts and shows were re-routed, disbanded, and re-formed, so that there was always a pool of talent at liberty in Kansas City to give tone to its night life and show business status' (Russell [1971] 1983: 12–13). Russell also suggests that 'TOBA served a useful purpose in giving . . . a sense of unity to Afro-American culture. It also helped circulate musical ideas throughout the country' (Russell [1971] 1983: 14).

Kansas City thus represented something of a hub for a whole range of black performers and the styles, modes and politics of black performance that came with them. Much of that talent was musical-theatrical in nature because of vaudeville and it produced new acts, approaches, and conceptions that were subsequently carried elsewhere on tour. Thus, the Clouds of Joy did not just get a musical education in Kansas City, but they were immersed in the circulation of a whole range of ideas about black styles and performance practices that, no doubt, included forms of Signifyin(g) performance that drew on the legacies of blackface minstrelsy that were shaped by black performers that worked in vaudeville.

The musical-theatrical culture of Kansas City gave Kirk's band something of a show-business sensibility, which chimed with Kirk's inclination towards showmanship. As we saw in the consideration of 'Casey Jones Special' in chapter 1, this proved useful when it came to engaging with the racist expectations of a black band within the mainstream of the music industry. In short, it was not just a jazz schooling that the Clouds of Joy got in Kansas City but a raft of important experiences and exchanges involving a whole range of black (and white) performers and ideas. This not only helped them develop their musical style as a band but also shaped their understanding of how to continue to Signify on modern, urban blackness through their swing music and its recording.

Although members of Kirk's band were immersed in Kansas City's culture of cabarets and jam sessions, Kirk himself was somewhat removed from them:

> I heard all the little jazz groups from time to time, but not as a regular diet. [After work] I went home to be with Mary. We were expecting

our first child. That to me was more exciting than all the blues and jazz in Kansas City. (Kirk 1989: 68)

He goes on to explain that the new African American social life that he and Mary discovered in Kansas City was so engaging that it also prevented him from visiting the clubs. When he moved to an apartment close to The Sunset club, Kirk could hear Turner and Johnson 'rolling out the blues till four and five in the morning' without venturing to the club, but it often annoyed him by keeping him awake (Kirk 1989: 68). Despite the difficulties that Kirk had in attending the clubs, he is clear that he did visit them when he could, and it was enough for him to experience all the most prominent performers in the city and their musical styles. In that regard, he was always adamant that the Kansas City music scene had a profound influence on him and his band and it provided a crucial education:

Kansas City music was different from music that we played in Denver. When I went to Kansas City, I learned more than I learned in those sixth, seventh and eighth grades of music. I learned how to express my own ideas, and I also learned how to express the ideas of those I had listened to. Those in the Southwest. (Kirk 1977: 6)

If only for commercial reasons, Kirk was concerned to stay ahead of rival bands in Kansas City, like those of George E. Lee and Bennie Moten, and it was as much from hearing the likes of these that the Kansas City style of riff-based jazz, with its Southwestern inflections from ragtime and blues music, came to his attention.

Although the Clouds of Joy occasionally played for black dances, Kirk's band generally needed to please a white audience of social dancers at ballrooms like the Pla-Mor. White dancers in Kansas City had been well served by bands like the Coon-Sanders Original Night Hawk Orchestra, a white ensemble that was very popular in the earlier 1920s. According to Driggs and Haddix, they 'specialized in novelty tunes, popular songs, and hot jazz', but the band's saxophonist, Floyd Estep, described their repertoire as 'dance music with a little jazz mixed in' (Driggs and Haddix 2005: 19). It was that sort of balance, in which hot jazz played a small but significant part amongst more danceable sweet music, which Kirk emulated in his own band's repertoire. Moten's band was the exemplar of the Kansas City style of black jazz for Kirk, and we have seen that he looked to their style for the hot-jazz character of his band's recorded music but otherwise married it with a smooth and supple sweet style of a sort that appealed to his regular audience of white dancers.

Gunther Schuller has written that the roots of the Moten band's jazz were in ragtime, a style indigenous to the region and one of such lasting popularity that Schuller claims it held back the development of jazz in the Southwest (Schuller [1968] 1986: 281). Russell also considers ragtime to be at the basis of the riff-based style of band jazz that was distinctive to Kansas City. Russell suggests that the riff, a short but characterful musical statement that is ripe for catchy repetition, emerged as a building block for band music in the region because it solved the problem of how the pianist-leaders of ragtime bands, like Moten in his early days, could create relatively complex musical structures with players that generally could not read music. Russell writes, 'Simple, practical, readily understood by everyone, the riff became for early Kansas City bands a kind of musical ground rule for the real business at hand, improvisation' (Russell [1971] 1983: 49).

Russell differentiates between the riffing of Kansas City bands and the similar sorts of approaches and structures that were employed by bands in New York and elsewhere in terms of affect. This leads him to suggest what riffs gave to Kansas City's black bands and the individual musicians within them:

> The ground rules implied in the riff gave Kansas City bands, and their sidemen, great confidence. At their best Kansas City bands were possessed of an unassailable esprit de corps, an astonishing, concentrated ensemble power, together with an ability to play easy, foot-tapping dance music in the pianissimo range. Their best soloists possessed a fierce self-assurance, bred in innumerable battles of bands and jam sessions, so that tackling one of these Kansas City bands in home territory became an uncomfortable and often disastrous chore for the name bands of the North and East. (Russell [1971] 1983: 50)

This notion of quiet confidence and self-assurance being engendered in jazz musicians by the special musical culture of Kansas City fits with the style of Kirk's band and his understanding of the benefits that the city afforded its highly segregated African American population. In that respect, the riff-based jazz of Kansas City represents the musical equivalent of the rich and confidence-giving subculture that Kirk noticed the black community had forged within that segregated city. The sense of collective effort towards social advancement within that community is represented in the *esprit de corps* of its bands and the finessing of such a range of expression by those bands is as much a musical measure of the cultural pride that the community instilled. From that perspective, it was no wonder that Kirk found the city to be so remarkable, chose to make his band's home there and adopted characteristics of its distinctive style of jazz with his band.

In a 1977 interview, Kirk states that the music of the Clouds of Joy was a little different from that of other black bands that came from Kansas City because his band generally 'played a lot of tunes and stressed the melody first' (Kirk 1977: 8). In the main, improvisation and driving riff-based arrangements were a secondary concern for Kirk and his musicians because they primarily played for social dancing which required clear melody and phrasing and a regular meter that would be undermined by extemporized solos and brash ensemble textures. Thus, they did not often extemporize swing arrangements based on hot riffs, as bands like Moten's did. Instead, improvisation and riff-based music, when it did feature, tended only to follow smooth melodic material in order to avoid alienating the band's dancing audience. As Kirk explained, 'We'd identify the tune we were playing by playing the melody that the people knew, and then we'd play the same thing with improvised solos' (Kirk 1977: 7). Kirk is clear that even when shifting to hotter music with solos, 'we didn't change the tempo so much, but the style' (Kirk 1977: 7).

So, at the heart of the musical character that Kirk and his band developed in Kansas City were three general features that gave his band a particular take on the swing style of jazz that came to prominence by 1935. The first feature was a concern to always please white social dancers of the regional sort that attended Kansas City's Pla-Mor Ballroom with rhythmically bouncy but mostly melodic, smooth, and unobtrusive music that was always played at danceable rather than frenetic tempos. The second feature involved the marriage of that with riff-based structures, derived from the blues, boogie-woogie, and ragtime traditions of the region, which were more typically employed by Kansas City's hot-jazz bands and thereby appeared as authentic for a black band. The third feature was that when room was given in arrangements to solos, they reflected the experience and quiet confidence of Kirk's musicians that was derived from the jam sessions staged in the cabarets of Kansas City.

The importance of retaining populist features, like danceable tempos and obvious melody, was only reinforced by the band's experiences on the road during the early 1930s when pleasing regional audiences proved more important than ever for the financial survival of the band. The Great Depression did not effect the business of Andy Kirk and his band until a few years after the 1929 Wall Street Crash. They enjoyed nearly two years of relative stability at the start of the early 1930s due to a string of residencies that they secured in New York and other towns and cities in the East. However, on their way back to Kansas City, the Depression finally hit home and they only survived the downturn by enduring gruelling tours of back-to-back one-night engagements to regional dance halls.[2]

These tours were vital for sustaining the income of Kirk's band and often involved them travelling quite some distance by road from Kansas City. Despite the inconvenience and discomforts of such touring, it mitigated risk for Kirk and his band during an especially uncertain period. As Kirk put it, 'Playing one-nighters in those Depression years of the early 1930s was all part of making a living in music. We didn't have to depend on one location' (Kirk 1989: 74). Within that context, it is no wonder that Kirk developed a style that would appeal to regional social dancers and thereby not risk their income.

The Clouds of Joy only played for relatively short stints in New York City during the early 1930s because, as Kirk explained, 'We were still classified as a territory band and we had no big records out, just the race records that reached only Blacks' (Kirk 1989: 77). However, at the Roseland and Savoy ballrooms, Kirk's band experienced the new style of big band swing and the more energetic style of dancing that it accompanied. Furthermore, Kirk acquired arrangements by Don Redman and Gene Gifford that, he reported, made the Clouds of Joy sound 'like a new band' (Kirk 1989: 73). Kirk complained, however, that despite their updated popular style and their ability to increasingly cross the race line with college-dance dates, 'the record companies *still* didn't know what our band was like' (Kirk 1989: 77). He became increasingly frustrated by the institutionalized racism that required them to constantly black up their style and repertoire to make race records. This not only misrepresented their capacity as a band but it also limited their ability to reach a broader audience and thereby restricted their reputation and earning potential.

Racial segregation was commonplace in Southwestern towns and cities of the early 1930s and Kirk recalled that 'there weren't facilities and sleeping accommodations for us in most towns as there were for other white bands' (Kirk 1989: 76). That only exacerbated the driving that was involved in getting between gigs and so the band engaged in softball and other sports to 'get the kinks out after driving miles and miles cramped

---

2 In addition to residencies in Kansas City ballrooms, the band performed at leisure resorts in the summers that included Winnwood Beach (a summer resort located north of Kansas City), Wild Wood Lakes (a more modest resort just outside the city), and Fairland Park (the main outdoor location for summer seasons).

up with our instruments, baggage, bats and balls and boxing gloves' (Kirk 1989: 76).

Kirk's ad-hoc softball team not only allowed the musicians to unwind, but on several occasions, it also helped to win the support of communities that otherwise would not have engaged with the black band. In the town of Weldon, Iowa, for instance, Kirk convinced the local populace to come to their dance date by organizing a charity match against the town's resident team to help raise money for new lights for their playing field (Kirk 1989: 75). The Depression required such efforts to survive the hardships that came with being a black touring band in a highly segregated society during especially tough times.

Although Kansas City remained a famously 'wide-open' town into the 1930s and thus escaped the worst effects of the Depression, the towns and cities that featured on the band's tour itineraries were not so lucky. Kirk recalled how many of the band's regular venues closed down and how dance dates became so scarce and the band's pay so often withheld by dance promoters that some of Kirk's bandsmen lost patience and left the band (Kirk 1989: 77). On top of the turnover of players in the band, Kirk himself became demoralized and considered giving up his band until he was talked out of it by his drummer, Ben Thigpen, and trumpeter, Earl Thompson (Driggs & Haddix 2005: 139).

It was the enduring culture of camaraderie and mutual support within the Clouds of Joy that helped Kirk and his band to get through the trying Depression years. For example, when a tour in March 1933 fell afoul of enforced bank holidays that closed the dance halls in which they were due to play, John Williams found work for the band in Memphis and St. Louis, which paid for them to get back to Kansas City (Kirk 1989: 77–78).

A turning point in the fortunes of the Clouds of Joy came in 1934 when they played at the Blossom Heath dance hall in Oklahoma City (Kirk 1989: 82). This relatively classy whites-only ballroom was wired into the Columbia Broadcasting System (CBS), which brought live dance music to radios across several neighbouring states. This radio exposure led to a tour of the Southwest to meet requests from promoters who, as Kirk noted, could not tell from the radio that the Clouds of Joy were a black band. This confirms that because of their relatively elegant, melodic, and sweet swing music, the band sounded white to contemporary listeners. However, their tour manager at the time, Harold Duncan, made it very clear that he was acutely aware of their blackness.

On hearing the salaries that Kirk proposed for his band for the tour, Duncan questioned, 'Ain't you afraid you'll spoil them?' (Kirk 1989: 83).

Kirk was inclined to like Duncan, but the racism in that comment, which for Kirk suggested 'that the Clouds of Joy were not grown up, not adults', but naïve folk to be exploited, led to Kirk turning to Louis Armstrong's manager, Joe Glaser, to manage the Clouds of Joy after the tour (Kirk 1989: 83). Glaser immediately engineered an Eastern tour for the band that took them back in to New York and back into the recording studio to make their first swing-styled records with Jack Kapp at Decca in the spring of 1936 (Kirk 1989: 84).

Mary Lou Williams's 'Walkin' and Swingin'' (Decca 60852-A) was the first piece that the Clouds of Joy recorded for Decca on 2 March 1936. Even a cursory comparison of the 1936 recording of the band's earlier records indicates that the so-called Swing Era had arrived during their five-year period away from recording: the band's music had clearly shifted from the stomping style of jazz that was heard in the 1929–1931 recordings to a much more fluid and lilting style of swing music. The two-to-the-bar rhythmical emphasis that pervaded the recordings made for Brunswick is entirely replaced in 1936 by a more supple four-to-the-bar bounce on the Decca records. The band otherwise sounds completely transformed as a smoothly swinging outfit with much greater confidence and refinement in both its tight ensemble playing and the less patchy solo work of its leading players.

The band's shift to a swing style was greatly aided by changes in personnel in the rhythm section: Kirk's sousaphone had been replaced by Booker Collins's double bass, and William Dirvin's banjo was superseded by Ted Brinson's guitar.[3] In many ways, these new players complemented Ben Thigpen, whose drumming had already shown signs of a remarkably swinging style in the band's 1930–1931 recordings. The ensemble otherwise sounds brassier than the band that recorded for Brunswick. That is because the brass section was expanded, through the addition of a third trumpet and a second trombone, and the 1936 arrangements generally feature less muting of the brass than was common in the 1929–1931 sessions.[4] Although Kirk was no longer audibly present as a player in the band by 1936, his vital influence as its rehearsal director can still be heard in the well-finessed ensemble playing.

---

3 Kirk did not perform or record as an instrumentalist with the band after surrendering his place to Collins.

4 By 1936 Paul King and Earl Thompson had joined the trumpets in place of Edgar 'Puddin' Head' Battle and Clarence Smith. Ted Donnelly and Henry Wells were in the trombones in place of Floyd Brady, and Dick Wilson replaced Lawrence Freeman on tenor sax. The only remnants of the Brunswick/Victor band, aside from Kirk himself, were Harry Lawson in the

'Walkin' and Swingin'' is based on AABA-structured choruses. Each of the A sections is eight bars long and built from a two-bar progression that is founded on the so-called 'rhythm changes' (I^6–vi^7–ii^7–V^7). This set of chord changes featured in George Gershwin's 1930 song 'I Got Rhythm', and it became common in many jazz standards and arrangements thereafter. Theodor Buehrer has argued that 'Walkin' and Swingin'' should not strictly be included in the family of rhythm changes pieces in jazz because,

> although it shares the repeated I–VI–II–V progression in the first four measures of each eight-bar *a* section, a standard trait of 'rhythm changes' tunes, it diverges harmonically in each *a* section's second phrase, and also in the bridge. (Buehrer 2013: 55, n.2)

However, the rhythm changes are so prevalent in the arrangement that they are certainly a defining feature of its audible character. To my ear, the diversions from them are not as marked as Buehrer implies, and when they do occur, they are really only there to achieve the change of key in the transition to the bridge sections or to allow for a harmonic rounding off of the final A section of each chorus.

The scheme of Williams's piece runs as follows: the two-bar rhythm-changes progression is repeated four times to make an eight-bar phrase (A). This phrase is then itself repeated before a slight alteration is made in its harmony at its close to shift the music to the flattened submediant key for the contrasting eight-bar bridge phrase (B).[5] The bridge simply alternates tonic (I^6) and dominant chords (V^7) for four bars before two bars of tonic harmony lead to a final couple of bars that are founded on the dominant seventh chord of the original key. That chord signals the return of tonic key and the reprise of the rhythm-changes phrase (A), which is, again, only adjusted at its close in order to lead on to the next chorus, or else, in the final chorus, to finish the piece.

With respect to the band's idiosyncratic style of swing, this harmonic structure of the choruses, although emblematic of Williams's harmonic

---

trumpets, John Harrington and John Williams in the reeds, Claude Williams on violin, and Mary Lou Williams and Ben Thigpen in the rhythm section.

5 The first chorus 'Walkin' and Swingin'' is written in A-flat major. The manuscript of the piece in the Mary Lou Williams Collections shows that, probably for music-reading convenience, Williams writes the B section in E major, which is the enharmonic equivalent of the flattened submediant key of F-flat major. When the key shifts to F major for the second chorus, she writes the B section is written in D-flat, which is the flattened submediant of F.

inventiveness, is a less important feature than the contrast between the syncopated accompaniment riffs in the brass and the sweet styled smooth melody that is introduced by the saxophones in the first chorus on the Decca record (0'00"–0'42"). While the brass riffs are phrased in a highly rhythmical style, which is fairly typical of hot swing bands of the period, they are not the immediate focus of the arrangement but function as counterpoint to the saxes' smooth melodic line. That line is more in keeping with the dance-band background and sweet-jazz sensibility of the Clouds of Joy. A choppier rhythmic style provides contrast in the B section (0'20"–0'30")but, as the chorus closes with the reappearance of Williams's smooth theme, melody rather than riff-based energy is framed as the prime feature of the first chorus. So, even in this rather idiosyncratic piece, we can see in this what Kirk meant when he said his band generally emphasized elegant melodic music over riff-based jazz.

'Walkin' and Swingin'' shows that Williams had not only absorbed the stock devices of swing-styled band arrangement, like characteristic riff-based melodies and structures, but she was prepared to innovate upon them as circumstances demanded. Thus, in the second of the four AABA-structured choruses (0'42"–1'21"), Williams adds a trumpet (playing into a hat) to complement the saxophone section in a passage of particularly inventive but highly practical orchestration. This unusual instrumentation was required to fill out the harmonies because the band did not yet carry four saxophones, but it makes for a distinctive sound, especially in the well-blended and tightly executed combination that is heard on the recording. It also produces an impressive chorus of close harmony, which covers nearly the full compass of the instruments as they negotiate melodic twists and turns at a fair pace and bring out the unexpected syncopated accents that colour the hot phrasing.

To make this unconventional instrumentation work, Williams shifts from the opening key of A-flat major to F major for this second chorus and that key is retained for the remainder of her piece. Despite the change of key and orchestration, the second chorus features ensemble material that is really just a variation on the melody that was heard in the opening chorus. The saxophones and trumpet wind their way through the exact same chord changes and structural sections as were used in the first chorus, albeit in the different key. However, the melodic style is much more improvisatory, and that makes the chorus appear to be in the tradition that Kirk established with Holder's band, when he harmonized Fats Wall's improvised solo lines to become ensemble choruses of this nature.

The quasi-improvised style of the second chorus helps prepare for the third one (1'21"–2'01"), which features properly extemporized solos, first for Williams on piano (in the A sections) and then for Dick Wilson on his tenor saxophone (in the B section). Williams's solo, while not especially remarkable, is much more swinging and less rhythmically disrupting than those heard from her on most of the band's earlier recordings and, unlike in most of the Brunswick sessions, it is accompanied by the rhythm section rather than Williams being left alone to improvise. Williams's solo frames Wilson's more liquid eight-bar phrase (1'40"–1'51") that immediately conveys his engagingly light and fluid style of solo playing.

Wilson was an important new addition to Kirk's band because he brought with him top-rank solo virtuosity coupled with a good deal of musical inventiveness, which he always wears lightly in his playing. Wilson's fluent soloing is often said to be akin to that of Chu Berry, Fletcher Henderson's tenor player, but to my ears, his style is also related to that of Lester Young, a consummate swing soloist and former Kirk bandsman. In its most harmonically adventurous moments, Wilson's improvising also points towards that of the great innovator-saxophonist, Coleman Hawkins. It is such modernistic characteristics in Wilson's solos that complement Williams's innovative soloing and arranging. Together they help the late 1930s records of the Clouds of Joy to sound as stylistically up-to-date in the solos as they do in their new swing-styled ensemble arrangements.

Two different takes of 'Walkin' and Swingin'' (60852-A and 60582-C) were issued on different records (Columbia [E] DB5023 and Decca 809).[6] They show something of the character and variance in the soloing of Wilson. Wilson's solo on the first take (issued on English Columbia label), for example, shows a concern for ever-increasing momentum, as note lengths tend to diminish as his solo progresses. In the alternative take (issued on Decca), he retains the idea of rhythmic diminution but utilizes a higher pitched and more energetic tessitura together with greater formal rigour: the lead-in to the sixth bar of his solo mimics its second bar, the solo's first proper statement, before he goes on to follow that phrase's general thrust to direct the solo to its close (see Figure 2.1). This gives Wilson's brief solo a palpable sense of form and direction, and it supplies an aural geography for listeners even within what is just

6 The track featured on the CD in the 'Classics' series, *Andy Kirk and His Twelve Clouds of Joy, 1936–1937*, which most often uses transcriptions of the Decca discs, is actually the Columbia issue. The Decca issue can be heard on *Mary Lou Williams: 1930–1941* (ACRCD 345).

FIGURE 2.1   Wilson's solo in the Decca issue of 'Walkin' and Swingin''.

an eight-bar phrase. If he can achieve this structural sense within such confines, just imagine his capability in longer solos.

The solo chorus eventually gives way to a final, brassy 'shout' chorus (2'01"–2'41") for the whole band, which is summoned up by a call from Williams's piano and a unison response from the brass that features ear-catching repeated notes (1'58"–2'01") In the typical fashion of swing pieces, the last chorus is the high point of the arrangement and Williams sets the accompaniment riffs from the piece's opening against a string of offbeat brass stabs before offering a call-and-response dialogue of riffs between the brass and the saxophones. The smooth saxophone melody of the piece's opening is here entirely replaced by hot riff-based writing as there was evidently no need to please the audience with smooth melody by this point in the arrangement.

The B section of the shout chorus (2'18"–2'29") features two-bar riffs that quote from Moisés Simons's 'El Manisero' ('The Peanut Vendor'), this time deploying a solo trombone with the saxophones to form a close-harmony quartet.[7] The tongue-in-cheek quote from a tune that must have been familiar to the band's audiences in another context, is followed by more call-and-response dialogue in the closing A section. This rounds off what is ultimately a very stylish, bouncy, and witty piece that is so brilliantly conceived and executed that one never suffers the oft-repeated 'rhythm changes' or the reiterated AABA form. Despite quite fulsome orchestration, the piece never gets heavy or hurried but the band maintains a light and elegant bounce throughout, even in the intricate passages, almost as if they were being light on their feet themselves.

In 'Walkin' and Swingin'', we get a piece that represents precisely what Kirk described of the 'somewhat different' style of Kansas City swing that

7 'The Peanut Vendor' had become a standard by 1936, mostly through the aegis of Louis Armstrong's recording (Okeh 41478) of December 1930. Armstrong had become a Decca artist in 1935 and Vocalion had reissued Armstrong's recording (Vocalion 3194) in early 1936. This probably explains its quotation by the Clouds of Joy on their rival label.

was played by the Clouds of Joy: the piece uses riffs and develops a hot vibe, but it is firstly melodic and danceable in its intentions. Only later do improvised solos and riff-based ensemble exchanges come to the fore. The tempo is brisk but not too fast for partner dancing, and even in the final chorus the band is not too loud but light hued and well enough balanced to bring great clarity and poise to the ensemble texture.

It is also telling that the title of the piece references walking steps in contrast to the more energetic movements like jumping that were typically employed in the Lindy Hop dancing developing in New York. Social dances involving walking steps, like the two-step and the cakewalk, were famously refined by Vernon and Irene Castle in the 1910s, and that made them highly accessible and acceptable for social dancers (Giordano 2007: 19). It is important to note that such 'walking' dances cannot be taken at breakneck speed without risking undignified awkwardness that results from the breaking of the smooth horizontal movement that is the ideal in swing dance. Such smoothness is essential in the context of close-partner dancing, which was the norm in regional dancehalls. Thus, the very title of the piece represents the genteel restraint and elegant refinement that is in the band's swing music and which comes from their classy dance-band sensibilities: the sweet-and-hot jazz style of the 1929–1931 records is thus effectively translated into a walking-and-swinging one in 1936.

'MOTEN SWING' AND 'CHRISTOPHER COLUMBUS': BLACKING UP IN HOT SWING

The Clouds of Joy recorded 'Moten Swing' (60853-A) alongside 'Walkin' and Swingin'' in their first session for Decca on 2 March 1936. The decision to record this Moten piece shows that despite their developing idiosyncratic style of swing music, the Clouds of Joy were still drawing on the hot-jazz of Kansas City to bring the expected racial colour to the music that they recorded. As we saw in chapter 1, in 1929 Kirk had looked to the music of Bennie Moten's band as the model for hot-black jazz to record for the race records market. In recording 'Moten Swing' in 1936 the Clouds of Joy returned to the style of their Kansas City rivals in order to court that same market for Decca (853). Moten had died unexpectedly in 1935, so 'Moten Swing' also marked a fitting tribute to their fellow Kansas City musician.

Despite the fact that the piece had become something of a standard around Kansas City by 1936, its recording by the Clouds of Joy was actually the first to be made since Moten had recorded it with his own band in December 1932, under the slightly different title of *Moten's Swing*

(74847-1) on Victor (23384). Moten's recording marked his latest attempt to reignite the success that he had enjoyed with 'Moten Stomp', a 1927 record that had sold well in the race market. He had already followed that with 'New Moten Stomp' in 1930, but with the dawning of the Swing Era, the manager of the Pearl Theatre in Philadelphia, Sam Steiffel (who had tried to lure Kirk's band away from him), convinced Moten to turn away from stomping jazz towards a more swinging style when he complained about the shortcomings of the Moten band's repertoire. Moten responded to this criticism by instructing the band's pianist, Count Basie, and guitarist, Eddie Durham, to come up with fresh ideas for the band and these included some riffs that became the basis for 'Moten's Swing'[8] (Driggs & Haddix 2005: 117).

Unlike the earlier stomps, which were so often blues-based, 'Moten's Swing' is based on the AABA refrain of 'You, You're Driving Me Crazy', Walter Donaldson's popular hit song of 1930. This lively song is given a jazz makeover by Moten's band in a string of solo choruses for Basie's piano, that are interspersed with ensemble passages that make good use of riff-based writing. The piece culminates, in the typical way of hot jazz, in a highly energetic final 'shout' chorus.

The recording of the piece by the Clouds of Joy features an arrangement by Mary Lou Williams that starts in a similar manner to that of Moten's version, with an introduction and solo chorus (0'00"–0'44") for piano, but the differently styling of the arrangement becomes immediately apparent in the smoother lines of the saxophone ensemble harmonies that are heard backing Williams's playing. As in the Moten's recording, Kirk's brass come to the fore to dialogue with the saxophones in the B section of the first chorus (0'22"–0'32"), before the saxes resume their smooth accompaniment figures to close the chorus in the final A section (0'32"–0'44").

In fact, the backings to most of the solos in 'Moten Swing' are all much more arranged in this smoother manner than in Moten's version and Kirk's ensemble sounds altogether tighter and better rehearsed throughout. The Clouds of Joy are somewhat slower paced that Moten's band and so their record contains one fewer chorus than on Moten's

---

8 The authorship of 'Moten's Swing' is unclear. The piece is attributed to Bennie Moten and his brother, Buster, on the record, but Basie always maintained that he and Durham were responsible for the tune. Driggs and Haddix also credit them but frame this in the context of the Moten band's working practices (Driggs & Haddix 2005: 117). As Moten's band, like Holder's, tended to work out arrangements collectively, based on riffs they would devise in rehearsal, it is most appropriate that the piece's authorship should remain inconclusive.

record. However, Kirk's band is notably cleaner and lighter in its execution of the final 'shout' chorus (2'15"–2'58"), with the closing coda tag (2'58"–3'03") showing an impressive control of dynamics that is entirely absent in Moten's recording. While Moten's version may be a harder-driven piece of hot swing that conveys a greater sense of galvanizing energy and swinging abandon, the Clouds of Joy's version of it, if marginally less energetic, is much more elegant and refined in its arrangement and performance. If their recording is a tribute to Moten, then, it is most surely a fond one presented in their more elegant dance-band style of swing as much as it, once again, deploys something of the style of Moten's music to represent a decidedly hot-black jazz identity for Decca's record producers.

While both 'Walkin' and Swingin" and 'Moten Swing' represent a distinctly refined-but-bouncy style of swing, neither of those tracks was the biggest seller amongst the band's 1936 hot-styled swing records. That came in the form of 'Christopher Columbus' (60874-A), a rather different style of riff-based piece that Kirk's band recorded for Decca on 7 March 1936. When that record was released (Decca 729), somewhere around 15,000 copies were sold, which, according to Kirk, constituted a big hit in the race market for the Clouds of Joy (Kirk 1977: 8). The arrangement was most likely not by Mary Lou Williams. It has been attributed to Kirk's trumpeter and sometime arranger Earl Thompson, but for reasons that will become clear, if Thompson did help produce materials for the band's recording, they were likely based on a stock arrangement that was supplied by the publisher of the sheet music of the piece.[9]

Ross Russell lists Kirk's recording of 'Christopher Columbus' amongst the records that are emblematic of the Kansas City style of riff-based jazz (Russell [1971] 1983: 51). However, listening to the recording in the context of the band's other tracks from the late 1930s reveals it to be atypical of their usual style of swing: the starker juxtaposition of contrasting riffs, which occurs right from the start of 'Christopher Columbus', is a rarity amongst the 1936–1941 instrumentals that were recorded by Kirk's band. In fact, the unusual character of the piece for the Clouds of Joy can be attributed to the fact that it originated with Fletcher Henderson's band in

9 Thompson is credited with the arrangement in Bernard Niquet's liner notes (in French) to a 1975 LP entitled *Andy Kirk and his Clouds of Joy 2: 1936–1938—The Lady Who Swings the Band* (MCA 1343), Volume 70 in MCA's Jazz Heritage series of reissues.

New York City. Henderson did not have to emphasize melodic and smooth, unobtrusive music in the way that regional bands like Kirk's did, because a different culture of more energetic swing dancing, exemplified by the Lindy Hop, had emerged in New York's ballrooms. The greater abandon of such dancing was suited to a galvanizing riff-based piece like 'Christopher Columbus'.

The authorship of 'Christopher Columbus' is confused, but it seems that Horace Henderson (Fletcher's brother) developed this highly influential piece based on a bassline riff that Fletcher Henderson's star saxophonist, Leon 'Chu' Berry, was keen on playing.[10] That riff may well have come from another source and there is some evidence to suggest that it started life as a melodic motif taken from a bawdy song which was adopted by one of Jimmie Lunceford's band. Other riffs in the piece have been claimed by others in the Henderson band.[11] The fact remains, however, that this is wholly a riff-based piece that was developed within Henderson's circle rather than the regional dance-band culture in which Kirk operated. We also know that Kirk did not propose the piece, but the suggestion to record it came from the producer, Jack Kapp, who indicated it was an essential track for Kirk's band to record for Decca's race records market (Kirk 1989: 84). Kapp evidently saw the market potential of the voguish black modernity in this riff-based composition.

Kapp's brother-in-law was the sheet music publisher Joe Davis, who owned a company that specialized in publishing black popular music of the period. Kirk had met Davis in New York in the 1930s because the publisher had an office in the Roseland building where Kirk's band worked (Kirk 1989: 85). The office was frequented by Fats Waller, whom Kirk had met in Kansas City, and Alex Hill, one of Holder's former band members with whom Kirk had remained friends. In his autobiography, Kirk makes it clear that he only recorded 'Christopher Columbus' because Davis, who published it both as a song sheet and as a stock arrangement, asked Kapp to get Kirk to record

10 Horace Henderson's arrangement, if it was his alone, was published (not in his name) by Joe Davis and was covered by several bands aside from Kirk's during 1936. It was perhaps most influential when it formed a part of Jimmy Mundy's arrangement of 'Sing, Sing, Sing' for Benny Goodman.

11 The Henderson band's 1936 recording actually followed in the wake of a recording made on 5 February by Chu Berry with a small group drawn from Henderson's band that was led by the trumpeter Roy Eldridge. That recording was the basis for Eldridge's later claim that he was responsible for the counterpointing brass riffs in the piece.

it (Kirk 1989: 85).[12] As we will see in the next chapter, Kirk only did so in order to get Kapp to record a romantic ballad and a study of the published song-sheet shows why Kirk may have been hesitant in agreeing to record this uncharacteristic piece.

The song-sheet of 'Christopher Columbus', which is subtitled 'A Rhythm Cocktail', shows the way that such hot swing was racialized as African-American modernism by publishers. For Davis's publication, Andy Razaf fitted lyrics to the riffs of 'Christopher Columbus', and they represent an amusing but telling scenario filled with stylistic-racial discourse. They tell us that, 'Mister Christopher Columbus, Sailed the sea without a compass' (Razaf & Berry 1936: 4).[13] Then they go on to explain that, when faced with the mutiny of his despairing crew, Columbus showed that hot (black) swing rhythm was all he needed for direction. His deployment of swing not only wins around his shipmates, who, we are told, partied to Columbus's music for the rest of the voyage, but it also led to Columbus and his crew making history by (presumably) discovering America. In short, the lyrics suggest that the special rhythmic-racial character of swing music founded and unites Americans and leads them within a notion of a shared modern-urban culture that is essentially black.

This voguish paean to the galvanizing and collectivizing effects of swing seems innocent enough but the song-sheet carries a cartoon on its front cover showing a saxophone-playing and top hat–wearing Columbus leading a band of his white shipmates (see Figure 2.2). They are also depicted in period costume while playing on a banjo, harmonica, clarinet, and sousaphone, respectively. This band has just restored order through their playing, as a sword has clearly been dropped to the deck of the ship by a dumbfounded 'black' mutineer: he is shown wide eyed and stunned at the sound of their playing, which is depicted in the notes projected from their instruments. That highly caricatured image trades in notions of musical-racial authenticity that are ascribed to the rhythmical style of swing in the song.

The 'black' mutineer is clearly a minstrel-like caricature: he has white limbs but highly exaggerated bulbous lips and a blacked-up face. Given

---

12 Davis credited Fletcher Henderson and Chu Berry on the published score and parts. Davis is said to have paid Henderson $100 and Berry $275 for the arrangement. According to Bruce Bastin, Davis's returns for 1937 show that in that year alone 'Christopher Columbus' received over 21,500 licensed performances (Bastin 2012: 89). That accounted for roughly 20% of Davis's entire income from royalties in that year.

13 Razaf obviously fitted lyrics to the riffs in the Berry/Henderson piece.

FIGURE 2.2   The cover image of the sheet music to 'Christopher Columbus'.

the enduring cultural currency of blackface representations of race in American popular culture, his wide-eyed astonishment suggests that the band of the Columbus of the song has trumped even the exaggerated blackness offered by minstrel stereotypes. The message thus seems to be that this music will get you swinging like only *real* hot-black American swing can. In other words, it suggests that the rhythm in Columbus's swing represents an even more powerful expression of authentic blackness than the exaggerated stereotypes of minstrelsy. The highly rhythmical riffs of the piece are thus not just emblematic of a modern style of jazz but of swing's rootedness in authentic hot-black expression.

The stylistic-racial authenticity that is implied in the song's lyrics and the cartoon surely explain why Kapp felt the song was essential material for Kirk's band to record for the race market. Nevertheless, the racism in such notions of authenticity, even though Razaf frames them within a race-pride agenda of black contributions to American culture, might also explain Kirk's hesitance to record the piece. From that perspective, it is telling that Fats Waller sent up the song's lyrics in his inimitable vocal style in his contemporary recording of 'Christopher Columbus' (Victor 25295). Nevertheless, by recording this sort of racialized swing piece for Kapp and Davies, the Clouds of Joy were, once again, effectively blacking up their music, but in the very latest style of hot-black jazz: riff based swing.

Fletcher Henderson recorded 'Christopher Columbus' with his band for Vocalion (3211) just three weeks after Kirk's band made their recording for Decca (729). Kirk had become friends with Henderson in the earlier 1930s, but it still gave Kirk great satisfaction that he got in before Henderson with 'Christopher Columbus' and sold more records of the song that ultimately became Henderson's theme tune (Kirk 1989: 67). Henderson's recording is bold, brash, driving, and brassy but, from the start, Kirk's version of the piece sounds more refined and cleaner in its execution. This certainly has something to do with the better audio quality of the Decca recording (or its transfer to CD), but it is even more down to the lighter touch and neater execution of Kirk's players and a greater concern for balance between ensemble sections within the band. That leads to a more transparent texture in which the different riffs are more clearly discernible when they are set against one another.

A distinctive four-bar bassline riff for the saxes, trombones, piano, and the bass is repeated (with slight variants at its close) to form the introduction of the piece (0'00"–0'11"). Unlike Henderson's trumpets, Kirk's are tightly muted when they set their quirky two-bar 'escape note' motifs against the bassline riff (see Figure 2.3) to open the first chorus (0'10"–0'53"). A steady, danceable tempo and a bouncy swinging quality are supplied beneath such counterpoint by well-articulated offbeat accents, provided by the brisk strums of Ted Brinson's guitar and by Ben Thigpen's neat drumming. The audibility of these swing-inducing off-beats throughout the piece only goes to show the remarkable clarity of texture that was achieved through careful attention to articulation

FIGURE 2.3   Counterpointed riffs that open the first chorus (bb.9–13) of 'Christopher Columbus'.

and the balancing of the different instrumental groupings in relation to one another within the ensemble texture. That care for aural clarity represents a key part of the refined elegance that was a hallmark of the swing of Andy Kirk and his Clouds of Joy and it extends way beyond 'Christopher Columbus' to all their swing recordings of the 1936–1941 period.

In the first two phrases following the opening chorus (0'53"–1'15"), Paul King's trumpet solo is heard unmuted, but it is noticeably easier going and less brash than the one performed by Roy Eldridge on Henderson's record and it is accompanied by lilting riffs from the saxophones that underline an unhurried but still swinging character. The trombone solo by Ted Donnelly in the B section (1'15"–1'26") of this second chorus sounds a little brasher for using the upper register of the instrument but, in terms of rhythmical-drive, it is similarly laid back, as is Williams's more percussive piano phrase (1'26"–1'36") which closes the chorus in lieu of a return of King's trumpet.

Dick Wilson takes over as soloist for the whole of the next chorus (1'36"–2'19"). He opens his tenor sax solo with a witty quote from Rossini's overture to *William Tell*, but then he winds his solo up into ever more agile but always light-and-liquid twists and turns.[14] Despite the obvious technical accomplishment in his solo, Wilson conveys an overall impression of a casual, unhurried, and understated approach. Wilson's amazing facility as a light-toned swing soloist is ever apparent but his style, like that of the band as a whole, is never too showy or obtrusive—it is witty, cultivated, limpid, but above all, understated and laid back. That non-showy character perhaps helps to explain why Wilson is not better known as a great jazz soloist.

After the two solo choruses, the final ensemble chorus of Christopher Columbus (2'19"–2'40"), which actually turns out to be just a half chorus (two A sections plus a closing tag), at last lets the unmuted trumpet section loose. The trumpets counterpoint the rest of the band, which recapitulates the riff-based theme of the opening. Although the trumpet riffs are highly syncopated, Kirk's players don't articulate them as 'stabs', with hard accents at the front of the notes, as Henderson's trumpets do, but they use less striking 'pushed' accents which place rhythmical

---

14 Wilson's quotation is quite possibly a reference to another 1936 Davis publication by Berry and Razaf that was based on Rossini's theme (Bastin 2012: 87). The tune would, however, have been familiar to thousands of Americans as the theme from *The Lone Ranger*, a radio serial that began on a Detroit-based station in 1933 and by 1936 was the cornerstone programme of the nationwide Mutual Broadcasting System (Dunning 1998: 404).

emphasis slightly after the start of the notes. This makes the trumpets sound less urgent and driving than those on Henderson's recording.

Kirk's trumpets only play one phrase of riffs in their top register (2'19"– 2'29") before descending to mid range for their second phrase (2'29"– 2'40"). That phrase recaps the trumpet riffs that formerly accompanied Wilson's solo, albeit now without mutes. The effect of this different articulation and material for Kirk's trumpets is to subdue their volume, and their diminuendo leads to the neatly executed saxophone-led tag (2'38"– 2'40"), which closes the track. Henderson's trumpets, on the other hand, sustain loud riffs and brash playing right to the very end of the piece.

In such contrasting features, Kirk's band shows that what it lacks of the swinging energy of Henderson's recording, it makes up for with much greater finesse and relative delicacy. Nevertheless, their music still swings in a subtly bouncy way. In other words, 'Christopher Columbus' might be figured as a typically hot-black piece of swing, but the Clouds of Joy present that mask of blackness with their usual veneer of dance-band sophistication. It was that veneer that was interpreted as sweeter or whiter-sounding than the norm for a black band, and as in their stomping jazz recordings of 1929–1931, their working identity as a white-society dance band cannot quite be contained in their masked performance of hot riff-based swing. If such swing represented black-jazz authenticity for critics, then there was something disconcertingly inauthentic about the comparatively elegant refinement.

REINVENTING STOMPS AS SWING: MARY LOU WILLIAMS'S REARRANGEMENTS

The reinvention of the band's stomping jazz as black-sounding swing for the race-records market is underlined by the fact that Williams set about producing new swing arrangements of five of her pieces that the band had recorded for Brunswick. The rerecording project began in the same March 1936 session in which the Clouds of Joy recorded 'Walkin' and Swingin'', with a reworking of 'Lotta Sax Appeal' (60854-A) as a swing-styled tour-de-force. The original 1929 record (Vocalion 1453) of Williams's sax feature had her then husband, John Williams, in the solo role, but for the 1936 record (Decca 1046) his baritone sax was replaced by Dick Wilson's tenor.

Gunther Schuller described John's 1929 playing of Mary Lou Williams's piece as utilizing a 'gruff tone and a rather stiff, old-fashioned slap-tongue style' but in 1936, Wilson's playing was altogether looser, easier-going, and more swinging (Schuller 1989: 351). Williams's rearrangement follows the same basic form as the 1929 version of 'Lotta Sax

Appeal', with pairs of 12-bar blues choruses that are devoted to Wilson's saxophone, and, later, to Ted Donnelly's trombone. As in 1929, however, these blues choruses eventually give way to eight-bar phrases that are formed into an AABA structure (from 1'36"). In the 1936 version, that shift from a blues-based structure towards 32-bar song form represents a transition from the old black-jazz traditions of the Southwest to up-to-date swing especially because of the way that ensemble riffs are incorporated into the arrangement from that point.

Within the two AABA choruses that close the track, saxophone riffs are punctuated by the brasses' interjections in the A sections, and the B sections introduce solos for John Harrington's clarinet and Paul King's trumpet, respectively. In the 1929 recording of the piece, the rhythm section tended to provide the only accompaniment to the soloists but in the 1936 version, ensemble backings are added by Williams and this gives the rearrangement a much fuller and smoother quality than in the original recording. Much like the horizontal flow, which characterized swing dancing and contrasted the more vertical movements of earlier jazz dance styles, the revised piece embodies a new sort of smooth and forward momentum that is as emblematic of the new style of swing as the riff-based AABA-structured music.

A couple of days later, on 4 March 1936, the Clouds of Joy also rerecorded Williams's 'Froggy Bottom' (60865-A) for a Decca record (729) in another new swing-styled arrangement. 'Corky Stomp' got the same treatment on 7 March (60887-A) and, as if to emphasize the replacement of the outmoded stomping jazz with the more current swing style, the word 'stomp' was dropped from the piece's title when the new track appeared on the Decca disc (772).[15] While there was some adjustment in titles and structures, all of these reworkings essentially add riff-based ensemble writing to the old arrangements to bring them in line with the swing style of jazz that prevailed at the time. In other words, the hot jazz of the early 1930s was replaced by riff-based swing as a marker of the music's contemporary blackness: the band now blacked up in swing to record, albeit their relatively sweet, smooth and refined kind.

The 1938 Decca recording of 'Messa Stomp' (64615-A) demonstrates that Williams tended to retain the structure of her original arrangements (including the instrumentation and order of solos) in her updates.[16] She

15 Despite this, Williams's new swinging version of 'Mess-a-Stomp' appeared in late 1938 with the more similar title of 'Messa Stomp' (64615-A).
16 Rye lists the title as 'Mess-a Stomp' in his discography (Rye cited in Kirk 1989: 132) but the Decca disc has the title 'Messa Stomp' clearly printed on its label.

otherwise adjusted details of instrumentation, rhythm, and phrasing, and added riffs within those structures in order to convert the old stomping-jazz character into a swing-styled one. The Decca recording of 'Messa Stomp' starts without an introduction. Instead, after just an alerting tutti staccato chord, it opens with a pair of lilting blues choruses (0'00"–0'18" and 0'18"–0'36"). Those, as in the original recording, feature a clarinet solo (Harrington).[17] As in the 1929 recording, a guitar interlude of four bars (0'35"–0'41") then leads to two eight-bar phrases; the first (0'41"–0'52") featuring the saxophone ensemble and the second (0'52"–1'03") a solo trumpet (probably Clarence Trice). The latter is backed by ongoing saxophone ensemble material that features busier riffs than in the original arrangement. As in 1929, a pair of 12-bar blues choruses (1'03"–1'21" and 1'21"–1'38") for Williams's piano follow this section. Unlike in 1929, the piano is backed by the drums (Thigpen) and bass (Collins).

After Williams's solo, the repeated broken-chord and 'stomping' trumpet-ensemble phrase of the original arrangement is included (1'38"–1'55" and 1'55"–2'11") but it is transformed into a much more swinging and less stomping passage. These two 12-bar phrases, as I suggested in chapter 1, are central to the character of Williams's original arrangement, and so a comparison of them with their rendition in the 1938 recording illuminates the sort of stylistic changes that Williams made within the extant structure of her earlier music.

In the 1938 revision, the first of the two 'stomping' phrases starts out with much the same sequence of harmonized broken-chord riffs for muted trumpets (1'38"–1'48") as in the 1929 version, but the subsequent on-the-beat 'stomps' in the original record are replaced by more syncopated writing by Williams. This more syncopated passage starts on an offbeat accent and it is marked 'swing' in Williams's manuscript. On the 1938 recording, it has a decidedly swinging feel as it is stylishly phrased by the cup-muted brass (1'48"–1'55"). A saxophone ensemble statement takes over from the brass and leads to a reprise of the 'stomping' phrase but it proves to be a syncopated variation of it (1'55"–2'17"). The broken-chord trumpet riffs are now transformed to make a yet more agile, varied, and swinging phrase. The original 'stomping' bars, at the close of this second phrase, are pushed even further towards a

17 The manuscript scores in the Mary Lou Williams Collection of the Institute of Jazz Studies at Rutgers University indicate that Williams wrote an eight-bar introduction that is not heard on the recording. No doubt this element (and others) was cut in the studio to fit the music to the time constraint of one side of a 10-inch record.

syncopated swing feel by the addition of a saxophone line that provides a counterpoint to the crescendo of the syncopated brass chords.

The 1938 arrangement then dispenses with the guitar solo on the original record and instead a unison passage for the reeds leads to a brassy cadence and then not just one (as in 1929) but three blues-based 'shout' choruses follow. The first of these choruses (2'17"–2'34") features a harmonized tutti statement with minimal ensemble interplay but the second one (2'34"–2'50") features eight bars of swift exchanges between brass 'stabs' and saxophone riffs, which lead to a short solo break for Wilson. The final chorus (2'50"–3'09") is ever more dialogic and leads to nimbler ensemble exchanges that serve to bring the piece to its close. Taken together, the last three choruses represent some of the hottest swing-styled music that the Clouds of Joy ever recorded and they show how far their hot style was transformed from their earlier stomping jazz in Williams's highly effective rearrangements.

A few months later, on 6 December 1938, the Clouds of Joy recorded Williams's revision of her 1930 piece, 'Mary's Idea'. In many respects, this particular rearrangement marked the most radical of Williams's transformations of her earlier music for the Clouds of Joy. The success of the band's 1936 recording of 'Christopher Columbus' surely accounts for the new opening to the rearrangement because Williams handles her materials in a similar vein to the Henderson piece. As in 'Christopher Columbus', a distinctive two-bar bass-line riff, which is initially set for unison saxophones, piano, and bass, is simply repeated to form a four-bar introductory section (0'00"–0'06"). This riff then forms counterpoint to the more angular, rhythmically contrasting, and crisply articulated brass riffs that characterize the melody of the A sections in the first AABA chorus (0'06"–0'51").

Theodore Buehrer has pointed out how Williams bases the brasses' melody on the trumpet solo featured in the opening chorus of the 1930 recording (Buehrer 2013: xl), but the additional syncopation that Williams introduces in its 1938 transformation to become an ensemble line is reminiscent of the swinging rhythmic character and greater sense of line that she brought in to 'Messa Stomp'. Furthermore, the unison bass-line riff, which provided the accompaniment to the trumpets in 1938, is also much more syncopated and yet more smoothly articulated than the stomping on-the-beat figure that Williams set against the solo trumpet in 1930 (see Figure 2.4).

In 1930 the B section of the first chorus of 'Mary's Idea' was devoted to the saxophone ensemble, but on the 1938 record (0'29"–0'40"), it is split between the saxophones and a trombone solo. The second AABA

FIGURE 2.4 The 1930 trumpet solo in 'Messa Stomp' with its 'stomping' accompaniment, compared with Williams's harmonized, syncopated, and riff-based version of 1938.

chorus (0'51"–1'37") is also divided between a trumpet and a piano solo (it was a baritone sax solo in 1930), and it is followed by two eight-bar phrases (1'37"–1'58") that feature solo clarinet. The second phrase of this half chorus is curtailed by an interrupting unison statement for the saxophones that is immediately taken up by the brass. This four-bar interlude (1'58"–2'02") serves as a lead-in to the final shout chorus. As Buehrer has noted, the slower tempo of the 1938 recording (ca. 168 bpm rather than ca. 208) meant that one fewer AABA chorus could be accommodated on the 10-inch side than in 1930. This most likely explains why the solos are pushed together or else curtailed (e.g., the clarinet shared a whole solo chorus with alto sax in 1930) (Buehrer 2013: xl).[18]

The final AABA 'shout' chorus (2'02"–3'00") is characterized by meter-defying riff interplay that, in the first two A sections, features accented bass-register notes in the saxes, piano, and bass that emphasize the weakest and most metrically unsettling (fourth) beat of the bar. Ted

18 The green-covered music manuscript book in the Mary Lou Williams Collection at Rutgers University suggests that Williams may well have conceived of her rearrangements in longer versions than are heard in the recordings. This notion is reinforced by the longer tracks that are heard on the Trianon broadcasts in 1937 (see chapter 3).

Donnelly's trombone solo opens the final B section (2'28"–2'40"), but the trombonist gives way to plunger-muted brass ensemble motifs, played over a walking bass, that lead to a recapitulation of the counterpointed riffs from the piece's opening in the final A section (2'40"–2'54"). A short coda tag (2'54"–3'00"), based on the same material, is added on to the end of that section to close the piece.

In sum, Mary Lou Williams's rearrangements represent her experience of both the riff-styled hot swing, which was the preserve of Eastern black bands like Henderson's, and the smoother style of regional dance-band music that was more melodic, refined, and much less raucous. I have established that her swing pieces represent black-sounding hot jazz of the mid-1930s, but in their style, they also show a mix of the band's experience of Kansas City jazz culture and the work of the Clouds of Joy as a sweeter-styled white-society dance band. Although 'Mary's Idea' might have been reconceived as an out-and-out hot-swing number, which, like 'Christopher Columbus', featured counterpointed riffs right from the start, the majority of such hot-swing recordings made by the Clouds of Joy tend to combine syncopated and polyrhythmic ensemble writing with smoother melodic lines in precisely the way that Williams did in her reworking of 'Mess-a-Stomp'.

As comparisons with the styles of music of the bands of Henderson and Moten have shown, Kirk's band brings a greater lightness of timbre and clarity of textures together with a less urgent drive and rowdy sonorousness to this sort of hot-swing music than is usual for black bands of the period. That approach can be accounted for by looking at the band's relationship to the particular sort of swing dancers that they played for at the Pla-Mor Ballroom in Kansas City and in the other Southwestern dance halls to which they most often toured.

BEATING OUT A SWING IDENTITY: MUSICAL STYLE FASHIONED FOR AND BY SOCIAL DANCING

Andy Kirk always maintained that despite the hot jazz that is heard in their recordings of Williams's pieces and 'Christopher Columbus', the Clouds of Joy were first and foremost a dance band (Kirk 1989: 62). In underlining this notion several times in his autobiography, Kirk suggests that the smoothly swinging, always crisp but light and laid back style of his band's music was rooted in their particular culture of live musical performance, which was primarily styled to suit regional dancing audiences. However, what is it about their live work with dancers that made the Clouds of Joy swing in their notably subtle-but-bouncy way?

Is it reasonable to consider dancing as a formative force for swing music, and, if so, how does this formative relationship between dancers and musicians work?

A general problem in addressing such questions is that almost all studies of swing music, if they attempt to define the famously illusive swinging quality of the music at all, offer rather nebulous definitions based predominantly on easily discernible rhythmical features. They do not tend to reference the movements and bodies of dancing audiences at all, even if they do sometimes point towards musicians' embodiment of swing. However, given that Kirk talks of his band's distinctive 'little bounce-beat style', we might start by exploring rhythmical considerations that articulate the live practices of social dancing with the swing style of jazz (Kirk 1989: 67).

In 1954 the French musician and critic André Hodeir offered one of the most detailed considerations of the 'essence of swing' in his book *Jazz: Its Evolution and Essence* ([1954] 1955).[19] Hodeir states that 'swing is an essentially rhythmic phenomenon', and in a footnote, he adds, 'The rhythmic phenomenon is not simply a question of *time values;* the succession of *attacks* and *intensities* is also an important part' (Hodeir [1954] 1955: 196, italics in original). Hodeir points out that an appropriate tempo and a stable (or very slightly accelerating) beat is a prerequisite for swing to occur, but the rhythm section must always give the impression of forward movement even within the confines of maintaining a steady beat. He writes:

> Swing is possible, in classical jazz, only when the beat, though it seems perfectly regular, gives the impression of moving inexorably ahead (like a train that keeps moving at the same speed but is still being *drawn ahead* by its locomotive). (Hodeir [1954] 1955: 198)

Although Hodeir considers accentuation within the bar to be of lesser importance than the underpinning beat, because of its great variance within jazz practice, he notes that, in general, 'the grave accent, falling on the uneven-numbered beat (or strong beat), contrasts with the acute accent, which comes on the even-numbered beat (the weak beat)' (Hodeir

---

19 Hodeir's rather generalized study of swing focuses on its instantiations in the smaller-band jazz of the post-bop era in which he was writing. Nevertheless, in the course of his chapter, it becomes clear that his analysis of swing is rooted in more 'classical' forms of jazz that presumably encompass 1930s swing as much as the hot jazz of the 1920s.

[1954] 1955: 199). The common use of instruments that tend to sustain notes, like bass drum and open high hat, on the strong beats means that Hodeir agrees with Bernard Heuvelman's earlier assertion that those beats tend to be accented 'by length (horizontally)'. By contrast, the use of the choked high hat and/or snare stroke on the weak beats shows that they are emphasized 'by force (vertically)' (Heuvelman, as cited in Hodeir [1954] 1955: 199). In this we can see that Hodeir is referencing lateral and vertical movements.

Above this rhythmic foundation, the next condition for swing to occur, for Hodeir, concerns the rhythmic articulation of the melodic phrase, which he feels always needs some syncopation but not too much of it. Hodeir writes about this in clearly racial terms as follows:

> It seems that the American Negro has found in an alternation of syncopations and notes played on the beat the best expression of his rhythmical genius. By turns the melodic phrase seems to depend rhythmically on what is being played underneath and to be completely independent of it, and this unending alternation gives rise to a kind of expectation which is one of jazz's subtlest effects. (Hodeir [1954] 1955: 200)

The rhythmic and, for Hodeir, essentially hot-black character of a melodic phrase in swing depends on the division of the beat into smaller rhythmical units—usually triplet-quavers. At faster tempi, swing tends to lose its ternary division of the beat (its triplet 'feel') as it approaches a binary division and Hodeir argues that this effects 'the internal equilibrium of the phrase' (Hodeir [1954] 1955: 202). Thus, the soloist must adopt phrasing practices relative to the tempo of the arrangement or phrase therein, but in doing so, must also always aim to retain a vitalizing 'expressive contrast' with the underlying rhythmic foundation (the groove or beat) if swing is to be felt (Hodeir [1954] 1955: 204). In effect, Hodeir illuminates the polyrhythmic character of swing, which is not only about the relationship between soloist and rhythm section but also about the contrasting rhythmic character of juxtaposed ensemble sections (reeds, brass, rhythm section).

For Hodeir, soloists as much as ensembles cannot place notes just anywhere in the bar but must generally follow rhythmic-pitch conventions so as not to sound 'corny'. He explains that in ensemble passages, there is a greater risk of swing-undermining errors occurring because individualism in articulation, which is prized in solos, must submit to following that of the lead player of the section. That leading player may, of course, have a poor rhythmical sense, and, in Hodeir's view, swing-undermining errors in rhythmic phrasing and articulation are common enough for him to suggest 'big bands are much rarely more satisfying than small ones in swing' (Hodeir [1954] 1955: 206).

Finally, Hodeir turns from measurable technical considerations to more bodily-rooted and felt ones. In that shift his analysis becomes notably vaguer:

> Relaxation plays an essential role in the production of swing. It gives to the rhythm section's pulsation the bounce that characterizes swing; it is what makes it possible for soloists to get everything in the right place without seeming to try, which is the ideal way. Many musicians, both accompanists and soloists, have a perfectly correct idea of tempo and phrase structure and just where the notes should go, but still cannot get across the swing because their bodies betray them. (Hodeir [1954] 1955: 206–207)

In a clear tension with such apparently vital relaxation is another precondition that Hodeir calls the 'vital drive' of swing. This movement-imparting 'rhythmic fluidity' stems from what he calls 'a combination of undefined forces', but when it is absent, the musicians appear to him dry, overly intellectual, and non-emotive, as if 'carrying out a plan rather than playing jazz' (Hodeir [1954] 1955: 207). Hodeir's notion of combined but opposing forces is important here, because it implies that his vagueness about the causes of such a drive have to do with them stemming from a compounding of the competing rhythmical elements within an ensemble arrangement and their complex interaction relative to the rhythmic expectations that are set up by an arrangement.

On 26 July 1937, the Clouds of Joy recorded 'A Mellow Bit of Rhythm' for Decca (62446-A), which represents a sort of manifesto for the mellow, or, in Hodeir's terms, 'relaxed' character that must be exhibited by musicians if their jazz is to swing. The piece is co-credited to Mary Lou Williams and Herman Walder. Walder was a Kansas-City-based saxophonist, who recorded with George E. Lee's band in 1929 (Brunswick 4684). He was also the younger brother of Woodie Walder, the tenor player in Bennie Moten's band. So, once again, the piece marks a connection with the black jazz tradition of Kansas City, which made it appropriate fare for Decca producers to record for the race records market

♩=c.156 (swing quavers)
Trumpets
Trombones

FIGURE 2.5 The meter-defying brass riff featured at the opening of 'A Mellow Bit of Rhythm'.

(Kirk 1989: 50–51).[20] The riff-based piece was later revised by Mary Lou Williams for the bands of Benny Goodman and others.

As in 'Christoper Columbus' and 'Messa Stomp', the eight-bar introduction section (0'00"–0'12") immediately presents a repeated two-bar riff. Williams sets it low in the range of the brass and ties notes across both the middle of the bar and the bar line. This syncopation undermines the expected accentuation of the strong (first and third) beats of the bar and puts emphasis on the movement-motivating weak off-beats. It thereby imparts a feeling of rhythmic drive—the piece immediately seems to chug along like in Hodeir's train metaphor. The articulation of the brasses' riff also enhances the forward-leading rhythmic quality of Hodeir's swing 'locomotive' (see Figure 2.5). The saxophones underline the syncopation in their ascending accompaniment line in the first four bars before coming to the fore to maintain the rhythmic momentum in an ensemble dialogue with the trumpets.

The first 32-bar AABA chorus (0'12"–1'01") follows this introduction, and its A sections feature the saxophone section in a laid-back, riff-based ensemble melody, which, to my ears, has a sultry or moaning quality. The snare (hit with a brush), together with guitar strums, prominently accent the second and fourth beats to maintain the movement-motivating ('vertical') off-beats of the swing beneath the saxes' 'moans'. The playing of the saxophones is rife with stylish portamento and the on-the-beat emphasis in their two-bar riffs is soon undermined by the greater syncopation of the B section (0'37"–0'49"). This highly syncopated phrase

20 It is worth noting here that George E. Lee's band was considered by Kirk to be the only other one of similar style to the Clouds of Joy in Kansas City. Like the Clouds of Joy, they stressed a sweeter style of jazz and offered a similar mix of ballads and showmanship alongside music for dancing (see Kirk 1989: 79–80). Thus, Herman Walder was well acquainted with the smooth and bouncy style of music exhibited by the Clouds of Joy.

is heralded, in the closing bar of the second A section, by a sudden off-beat tutti chord that sets the tone for the syncopation thereafter. What follows in the B section of the chorus is another quasi-improvised but harmonized ensemble line (see Figure 2.6), which is scored for all the horns (brass and saxophones). It features ever more urgent offbeat accentuation (after the third beat) in its phrasing before the 'moaning' sax riff returns with the reprise of the A phrase.

The second chorus (1'13"–2'01"), which features solos from Wilson's tenor sax in the A sections and King's trumpet in the B section, is prefaced by an eight-bar interlude (1'01"–1'13"). That section features a pair of jaunty clarinets in a syncopated shuffle-styled riff that features prominent dotted rhythms. This quirky duet is heard above a variation on the saxophones' ascending accompaniment line from the piece's opening, which is now orchestrated for the (muted) brass. Although it features ties across the middle of the bar, there are no longer ties across the bar-line. A similar figure, but now in a form that is completely void of syncopating ties, next becomes the accompaniment riff for Wilson's solo (see Figure 2.7). The brass, however, play their part in maintaining the offbeat swing here by accenting the 'weak' second beat of the bar in the first couple of their counterpointing two-bar riffs. What we get here, though, is a gradual relaxation of hot syncopation.

Wilson opens his solo with a series of laid-back trills, which span the interval of a minor third, before he relaxes into a lilting swing in a line

FIGURE 2.6 The quasi-improvised ensemble passage from the B section of the first chorus of 'A Mellow Bit of Rhythm'.

♩=c.156 (swing quavers)

Saxes' riff at the opening

Saxes' (and muted brass) riff under clarinet duet

Saxes' riff in the second chorus of the tenor-sax solo

FIGURE 2.7   Similar sax riffs from different points in 'A Mellow Bit of Rhythm' showing the gradual relaxation of syncopation as the piece progresses.

that descends through the range of his tenor, coming to rest on a low B-flat as the clarinets interject their earlier riff. His second (A) phrase (1'25"–1'37") is much more syncopated and the effect of Wilson's emphasis of the half beats is to produce the curiously contradictory sense of a sort of lazy precision. That gives way to some agile but seemingly easygoing arpeggio figures that again bring the phrase to rest on a low-ish note (E-flat).

King's solo in the B-section (1'37"–1'49") is effective enough but a bit more pedestrian, and it is concluded by an interrupting trill from the brass section, which was prefigured by similar but less urgent motif heard in Wilson's solo. Wilson re-enters to take the last A section (1'49"–2'01") with a characteristically swinging figure that rests for a moment on a dissonant slide. As if responding to this aural mellowness, Wilson follows it with repeated notes (E-flats) that serve to restore the rhythmic momentum and allow the solo to close with a swinging swagger.

The third chorus does not cover the whole AABA structure, possibly because it features a solo for John Harrington on clarinet and shows him to be a rather faltering soloist in comparison with Wilson. In the first A section (2'01"–2'13"), he drops out of the phrase rather early (in the fifth bar) and an ensemble passage of four bars is tagged onto the end of his second A section (2'13"–2'29") to save him finishing the phrase. This tag extends the second A phrase to 10 bars, restores the swinging momentum, and forms a bridge to the final 'shout' chorus (2'29"–3'18").[21]

21 Mary Lou Williams's autograph score (edited in Buehrer 2013: 83–109) shows that the B section and the concluding A section of the third chorus were cut from the arrangement for the 1937 recording.

The closing chorus presents an entertaining interplay of ensemble riffs that move from those that juxtapose syncopated writing (in the first and second bars) with on-the-beat material (in the third bar) to those that feature call-and-response dialogue between reeds and brass. They disappear when the 'moaning' A section returns in the final phrase of the chorus to close the piece much as it began. A two-bar tag serves to cap off the last phrase with a syncopated tutti statement that leads to a final cymbal splash from Thigpen.

The overall impression left by 'A Mellow Bit of Rhythm' is of a decidedly unhurried but highly swinging and danceable piece. It seems that the more the players are laid back or 'mellow' in approaching the syncopated 'drive' of the riff-based music, the more they engender a subtle but bouncy momentum in their swing. This mellow bounciness stands in contrast to the approach shown in other recordings of the piece. Those made by the bands of Earl Hines (Jazz Archives JA2) and Les Brown (Decca 3155), for instance, don't sit back nearly as much. Instead, they push the tempo to somewhere around 200 bpm. The faster tempo of the Hines's band (featuring slapped bass) means that they offer a much more clipped articulation of the riffs and Les Brown's soloists seem in even more of a hurry, and thereby neither band swings in anything like the easygoing, bouncy vein heard on Kirk's recording.

The Clouds of Joy, with their smooth and comparatively un-hurried style of swing, can thus be conceived as a highly 'relaxed' band in Hodeir's terms. This implies that the band members generally exert extraordinary 'neuromuscular release' so as to embody the swing—they, as it were, lose themselves in the swinging groove and become one with it through their mellowness exerted in the face of the tension caused by the onward-driving imperative of the swing beat. In a 1989 interview with Stanley Dance, Mary Lou Williams underlined the importance of such rhythmical relaxation when she reflected on a tendency of younger jazz musicians to play ahead of the beat. She stated, 'They're pushing *over* the beat—zuzz, zuzz, zuzz. That isn't jazz. That's corny. The delayed thing, the relaxation, is it' (Williams cited in Dance 1989: 9). That sort of relaxed approach of the Clouds of Joy can only really be accounted for by considering the band's live work as a band that most often played for social dancers in regional ballrooms.

Hodeir argued, in undoubtedly racist terms, that such relaxation is an innate characteristic of the African American but he also concedes that it can be learned (Hodeir [1954] 1955: 207). Given that swing is first and foremost a dance music, it seems reasonable to argue that the 'mellow' or 'relaxed' swinging bounce of the Clouds of Joy resulted from, or at least was refined by, their particular function as a white-society dance band working in the context of social-dance culture of the Southwestern Territories. Few jazz scholars, however, have gone much beyond Hodeir's rather vague and contradictory notions of 'relaxation' and 'drive' in approaching swing from the perspective of embodiment, and fewer still have considered the relationship between the movements of dancers' bodies and the character of the music itself.

An important step in that direction was made following Hodeir's work. In 1966 the American ethnomusicologist Charles Keil drew on Hodeir's analysis and especially his notion of 'vital drive', to argue for a new analytical conception for approaching musical genres like jazz. Keil proposed his approach to contrast the musicologist Leonard Meyer's attempt to define 'masterpieces' of music based on observations of musical features found within the canon of European art music. Meyer's methodology prioritized what Keil (somewhat confusingly) called, 'embodied meaning'—meaning arising from within the syntax of musical works. By contrast, Keil suggested that musical forms like jazz are better understood in terms of what is felt as a result of the processes deployed in performance. He thus suggests the qualities of such music should be conceived more in terms of what he calls 'engendered feeling' (Keil 1966: 338).

Keil presents a table which sets characteristics of music that involves 'embodied meaning' (classical music) against those features of music like swing that involve 'engendered feeling'. Fourth on Keil's list of characteristics is the 'mode of response'. Keil indicates that music which involves 'embodied meaning' tends to evoke 'mental' responses, but music that engages with 'engendered feeling' is more about 'motor' responses (Keil 1966: 338). In using such terms, Keil references the way that jazz makes one want to move the body (e.g., tap one's toes to the beat), whereas Meyer's venerated 'classics' generally seem to appeal more to the mind. In his explanation of his table, Keil relates what he calls 'the metaphysical spectre of mind-body dualism' is implied in this juxtaposition, but he feels it is important not to be too quick, like he felt Meyer was, to resolve this dichotomy, 'along Christian Science mind-over-matter lines' (Keil 1966: 339).

Keil points out that 'choreographic references' appear throughout his list of characteristics on the 'engendered feeling' side of his table. Although such references undermine his earlier claim that music may be meaningful in and of itself, Keil suggests that choreographic understandings might be fundamentally important to music that involves 'engendered feeling'. He states: 'Far from being a mere flirtation, there often seems to be an out-and-out romance going on between music of the "engendered feeling" type and dance' (Keil 1966: 339). Keil's view is that much process-orientated music, like jazz, is effectively inseparable from dance, and just because it evolved into a listeners' music, increasingly experienced by an immobile audience in concert-like conditions, did not mean that it somehow became no longer choreographic in its meaning. Thus, Keil questions, as follows:

> Can we not infer a great deal from choreographic responses or 'symbolic action', from the 'conversation' between dancers and musicians (the stimuli and responses go in two directions, I suspect), not to mention the relationship between man and instrument? If music 'is so closely associated with bodily effort', why not build a bodily aesthetic adequate to the task? (Keil 1966: 340)

As Keil admits, however, the 'mind-body duality is something of a false chicken-and-egg sort of issue' (Keil 1966: 339). So, whilst he acknowledges that there is a need for 'a bodily aesthetic' understanding within an alternative analytical discourse for music like jazz, because such musical forms are rooted in dance, his subsequent analysis does not really address that task. Instead he simply develops Hodeir's notion of 'vital drive' to propose that swing stems from a complex of multilayered rhythmical interactions within the rhythm section of a band and from interplay between soloists and ensemble.[22]

In extending the sorts of observations made by Hodeir and Keil, Paul F. Berliner (1994), J. A. Prögler (1995), and Ingrid Monson (1996) have all pointed towards ever subtler rhythmical interactions that are observable within the playing of and against a rhythm section in jazz. They survey the vital 'participatory discrepancies' (to use Keil's term) that arise to illuminate what gives swing its swing. All these studies agree that standard analytical frameworks need to be extended beyond mere syntactical analyses of musical details to get closer to understanding where the illusive phenomenon of swing is manifested in the music. None of them, however, really take up Keil's challenge to develop a bodily-choreographic model as part of the analytical methodology, except in considering the movements of musicians when they are engaged in the act of performing.

---

22 Towards the end of his article Keil touches on the mind-body duality briefly in his consideration of the value of relational linguistics in his 'processual analysis' of music (Keil 1966: 345). However, he quickly moves away from bodily matters to abstract musical 'gestures' within the progress of a phrase.

In his 1997 article 'Swing and the Lindy Hop: Dance, Venue, Media, and Tradition', Howard Spring investigates what he calls 'the dynamic relationship between musicians and dancers' in the early swing era (Spring 1997: 183). Spring's focus is on the Lindy Hop, an apparently ubiquitous social-dance style of the 1930s that developed at New York's Savoy Ballroom at the end of the 1920s. It mixed energetic close-partner dancing, built freely upon a set pattern of fairly easy basic steps, with 'breakaways' that gave room for improvised individual moves. In the way that it was practiced at the Savoy in New York, Lindy Hop was a highly vigorous dance that utilized the whole body much more than earlier social-dance styles had done and, for Spring, that meant it required suitably energetic music in the form of hard-driving (hot) swing.

It is tempting to articulate the Lindy Hop directly with what Kirk described as the 'little bounce beat' of the Clouds of Joy because, as Spring notes, in the Lindy Hop, 'the bouncing of the dancers is more conspicuous' than in earlier dance styles (Spring 1997: 186). In referencing some early Lindy Hop dancing in the 1929 film *After Seven,* Spring further explains:

The dancers bounce to four beats during most of their routines, even when their feet are not moving in a four-beat rhythm; their movement in four, either by step or bounce (or both), provides a constant four-four rhythm. Inasmuch as hot musicians made much of their living playing for dancers, it is not surprising that they would respond to the new dance style by increasing the use of four-four rhythms in music that they played. (Spring 1997: 189)

Spring also explains changes in the instrumentation found within the standard rhythm section of bands in terms of the way the guitar and string bass were acoustically better suited to the energetic four-to-the-bar movements of the Lindy Hop because of the more appropriate articulation they offered in comparison to the banjo and brass bass of earlier jazz.[23] The more 'assertive' drumming of the likes of Chick Webb, for Spring, also gives hot swing the vital energy required for Lindy Hop (Spring 1997: 199). Such features are, of course, notable in the changes made to Kirk's band earlier in the 1930s.

Spring next points to the increased utilization of riffs as the basis for swing arrangements of the early 1930s as evidence of musical changes that were made in response to the new momentum requirements of

23 The argument that is more often made is that the shift from acoustic to electric recording around 1926 influenced the change in rhythm-section instrumentation.

Lindy Hop. Spring draws on Eddie Barefield's experience of working out riffs with his colleagues in Bennie Moten's saxophone section to explain that 'the idea was to use riffs to build "momentum"' as an arrangement progressed (Spring 1997: 198). Such a riff-based building of momentum is, of course, evident in the Decca recordings of the Clouds of Joy, but as we have established, the riff-based swing of Kirk's band deviated from the practices employed by Moten and Henderson, and that was precisely because they worked in a different context.

Although Kirk's band did play at the Savoy Ballroom in the early 1930s and no doubt absorbed there some of that four-to-the-bar bounce of swing, the band's musical style was by no means typical of the energetic hot swing music offered for Lindy Hoppers at the Savoy. As Kirk noted in 1977, 'The New York bands were playing a lot of 2/4 drive, and we called ours bounce, and it was a little different' (Kirk 1977: 7). In an earlier interview he goes further in explaining that difference:

> We'd play everything with a little bounce, always swinging, while the other bands were always shouting, with high brass, etc. Our stuff was muted much of the time, but always rhythmic. (Kirk 1959: 17)

This more muted approach to swing hardly sounds like one conducive to the high-energy levels required for the Lindy Hop, and as the analysis of 'A Mellow Bit of Rhythm' showed, an essential characteristic of Kirk's band was the relaxed or 'mellow' quality of their swing. This means that the swing music of the Clouds of Joy tends to feel much less brash and rhythmically driven than the music played by other bands that performed at the Savoy. The comparison made with Fletcher Henderson's band further suggests that the emphasis on a clearer, cleaner texture engendered by rehearsing for a more elegant articulation of the ensemble passages also differentiated the Clouds of Joy from the rougher-edged and more rowdy Lindy Hop aesthetic that was common in New York. So, from where did their comparatively refined swinging style come from?

In his biography Kirk states that he 'was "brought up" in the dance music field', but, it seems, he experienced mostly the more classy, white dances during his upbringing in Denver (Kirk 1989: 62). As we learned in the introduction to this book, Kirk's first proper job as a bandsman was with George Morrison, who ran a number of groups in Denver. In 1977, Kirk remembered Morrison during the course of an interview:

> There were a lot of fiddle players around, but George Morrison was a violinist. He was a trained musician, and, of course, his bag was

society music. That was how he made his living—off the society people in Denver. They would go to New York, and they would see the shows, and they would come back, and they'd want to hear the music that was playing in the theatres. I recall one time 'Alice Blue Gown' was a hit. And 'Irene'. We played that in 1920. (Kirk 1977: 6)

Here Kirk stresses the comparatively sophisticated nature of both Morrison as a musician and the classier sort of dances for white audiences for which he supplied music. 'Alice Blue Gown' is a waltz, and in its implied contrast with hot-black jazz, it connotes a comparative musical elegance and sophistication. In fact, the waltz forms a sort of musical emblem of race pride for Kirk, because in his biography he references playing waltzes almost every time that he mentions playing for dancing. Kirk also makes it clear that waltzes became a fundamental part of the Clouds of Joy's repertoire after he heard Jack Teagarden's group play the tune 'Let Me Call You Sweetheart'. Kirk remembered, 'it came out the jazziest, swingin'est waltz I ever heard' (Kirk 1989: 57).

Although Morrison had a large dance band that was the focus of his activity, when necessary he hired out smaller bands for society dances around Denver. On one occasion, Kirk took charge of a four-man group that shared the billing with the pianist Ferdinand 'Jelly Roll' Morton. Kirk recalled,

Morton said, 'Man, you all play too fast'. We were doing what they call the Peabody. Everybody was racehorsing, you know? Get hot. They called it gettin' hot when you play fast. But I learned a few tricks from Jelly. (Kirk 1977: 6)

The Peabody, a lively partner-dance with a distinctive hold that was a forerunner of the quickstep and thereby the Lindy Hop, might have suggested a hot (fast and driving) tempo but Morton encouraged Kirk to 'lay back' into an easier, more relaxed groove. It seems that this lesson stayed with Kirk into the swing era because this is precisely the approach of his band when it came to providing swing music like 'A Mellow Bit of Rhythm' for dancing. By the time Kirk was with Holder's band and rehearsing the group for smoothness of melodic line, as was required for waltzes, the foundations of the smooth and subtle style of the music that he would develop with the Clouds of Joy were already set.

The Clouds of Joy did not record any waltzes, but Kirk is clear that they remained a staple part of the band's live repertoire. He states, 'All the time we were making race records we were playing our pop tunes, romantic ballads and waltzes for the dancing public. Most of our work in ballrooms was for Whites and these were the things they liked to dance to' (Kirk 1989: 73). On that point, Kirk also recalled the following:

> We had two forms of waltz, the 3/4 and the 6/8. That type of waltz, real pretty, where you could hold the girl close to you and talk at the same time. And everybody did about the same thing. It wasn't everybody doing their own things. This was the beauty of standing on the bandstand, or being elevated on the bandstand and watching the people. We could tell whether they were enjoying it by the tempo, how they were expressing themselves. Some would do a little twirl. They were called ballroom dancers. They went every Saturday night to the dance, so they learned little extra steps, and the others would be watching. (Kirk 1977: 8)

Although it was undoubtedly highly influential, the centrality of the energetic Lindy Hop to the development of swing as a popular jazz style has quite likely been overstated. Even Spring, in discussing the Savoy Ballroom, concedes that 'though it was the home for famous hot dance styles such as the Lindy Hop, it was also the scene of a wide range of popular dance and music—including "sweet" and "symphonic" jazz, waltzes, and tangos' (Spring 1997: 189). Such a range of music required, of course, a much greater range of styles from both the musicians and the dancers than just the energetic hot swing that was required for Lindy Hop. It was such hot swing, however, that was most often recorded by black bands and venerated by critics. There were, of course, bands that specialized in such energetic hot swing, like Chick Webb's, but Kirk's band was clearly not one of them, even if such uptempo music formed a part of their style and repertoire. They otherwise embraced waltzes, ballads, and melody-driven sweet instrumentals precisely because that was the sort of music to which their audiences liked to dance and from which they derived their living.

Kirk's observation that he could sense the appropriateness of his band's music for dancing from the bandstand concurs with testimony from other musicians that recalled their work in dance halls. Spring quotes Count Basie's trombonist Dicky Wells (brother of Kirk's trombonist, Henry) as recalling the following:

> In a dancehall, you're not as self-conscious, and you do a whole lot of things on the horn you wouldn't do at a concert—a whole lot of relaxed

things. For the dancer, you know what will please him. It has got to be something that will fit around him and with his step. When you see a dancer take his girl, and then drop her hands and walk off, something isn't right. Most likely the rhythm's wrong. But when you get that beat he's right there saying: 'play that again!' (Wells, as cited in Spring 1997: 191)

Despite his heavy emphasis on the way that a specific style (Lindy Hop) shaped swing music, Spring does suggest that 'the relationship between dancers and the musicians was not one-way. It was more akin to a reinforcing feedback loop' (Spring 1997: 200). A sort of communal 'drumming up' of swing rhythm, between the musicians and their dancers' feet in the dance hall, is emblematic of the production of this feedback loop. As Eddie Barefield noted:

When you went to a dance you could hear the feet on the dance floor. Everybody was beating in time, it was one of those things, you could hear the patting of the feet right along with the music. And this made a lot of the momentum of the swing more predominant. (Barefield, as cited in Spring 1997: 192)

In his study of drumming, John Mowitt explores the intersections of psychoanalytical, sociological, and musicological divisions that cut across what he calls the 'percussive field' (Mowitt 2002: 3). His self-proclaimed aim is 'to come to terms with the sense made in and of senseless beating', so his thinking is particularly applicable in the context of the apparently unfathomable beat of swing, especially if it involves the seemingly meaningless beating of dancers' feet (Mowitt 2002: 2). Mowitt's notion is that drumming, precisely because the drum is an instrument that is normally both sounded and received through forms of skin contact, offers a particularly potent area for conceiving of the interrelations between music, the body, and individual subjectivity:

Percussive sense-making is caught up in the way that skin contact produces a subject who at once makes sense of various patterns of contact and who is itself the locus of sense for such contacts . . . as with drumming itself . . . the subject forms in and through the limits of embodiment . . . drumming touches on and plays with these limits and, in doing so, makes sense. (Mowitt 2002: 7)

Although Mowitt's study has a focus on drumming in rock 'n' roll music, his approach is readily transferable to swing, because that is another form of popular music rooted in dance and 'engendered feeling', in which, as Hodeir and Keil explained, sensing the beat or groove is fundamental to its meaning. The four-to-the-bar swing groove of bands like the Clouds of Joy can thus be read as the equivalent of the so-called 'backbeat' in rock 'n' roll, with its movement-motivating syncopation deriving from a similar rhythmical emphasis of the second and fourth beats of the bar. The effect of accenting these weak beats is, for Mowitt at least, ultimately a form of profoundly important syncopation, as to continually keep the music from the predictable and safe emphasis of the strong beats speaks of and to the body and ultimately to and of individual subjectivity.

In his provocative analysis of Chuck Berry's 'Rock 'n' Roll Music', Mowitt states that the backbeat's importance is that it 'tells the body where to be in such a way that one never feels out of step or off-beat' (Mowitt 2002: 30). Mowitt goes on:

> Because it is hard to imagine that one might truly be shaken by his or her inability to dance in step, it is important to recognize that the backbeat's beacon might also be the source of comfort for the performers—that is those for whom losing the beat might have more immediately humiliating consequences. (Mowitt 2002: 30)

Thus, the rhythmical 'beacon' of the backbeat (or swing beat in jazz) serves to test the musical subject's position (whether the subject is conceived as a social dancer or a musician), and in doing so it motivates the subject to locate and anchor their identity relative to that beat—to choose to belong to the beat or not. This choosing is, however, no simple finality but—like subjectivity formation itself—is rather an ongoing, continually deferred encounter with the choice to identify that is perfectly embodied in the syncopated deferral of the strong beats of the bar in the backbeat.

The notion of interpellation, as conceived by the French-Marxist philosopher Louis Althusser has an important influence on Mowitt's understanding of subjectivity and drumming. In his now famous metaphor, Althusser explained the mechanism by which the subject is 'interpellated' or called into conception in terms of a policeman—the embodiment of ideology—'hailing' an individual and thus causing them to turn to acknowledge the fact that they are indeed being addressed.

However, Mowitt counters a tendency to read Althusser's account as a purely psychovisual encounter by emphasizing the oral-aural dynamic in it and the resultant embodiment in the crucial turning of the undifferentiated subject to acknowledge its differentiated (individual) subjectivity. Mowitt writes:

> The sonoric event of interpellation-qua-event is embodied in shock or . . . in the beat of the hail or knock. The interpellative call strikes and moves the body hailing it 'into position'. Thus, in addition to music's interpellative dimension, there is the matter of music's irreducibly percussive character. Which means . . . that beyond the beat effected by the rhythmic organization of any given piece of music, there is the duration and extension of the piece, the time and space of the performance, that breaks in on the subject in formation. The piece strikes us, catches our ear, regardless of whether it is scored for percussion instruments. We are, one might say, subject to its blows. (Mowitt 2002: 58)

Mowitt's emphasis is very much on the way that the beating of the music, produced by the musicians' repeated rhythmic 'calls', continually moves bodies to become conscious subjects of the music. In the dance hall, however, as Barefield attested, the dancers are as much beating back with their bodies and especially their feet in what might be termed an act of counter-interpellation. Their 'senseless beating' was clearly sensible to dance band musicians like Kirk's 'and it caused them to' turn, in the musical sense of adjusting their swing beat, as they sensed and embodied the dancers' counter-beat to the rhythmic groove in their playing. In doing so, they ultimately adjust their swing character relative to it. Thus, a communal dancers-band swing feel is identified through a drumming-up of a feedback loop. As Kirk played predominantly for regional white-society dancers, is it thus no wonder that his band's swing music came to embody a peculiarly sweet (white) quality in its elegant smooth and mellow style, as they were so often subjected to the interpellating return beat of the feet of relatively restrained close-partner dancing.

So, it seems that swing bands, like Kirk's, which predominantly played for social dancing, both motivated *and* responded to the rhythmical movements of their dancing audiences. When Kirk's band returned to recording in 1936, however, their distinctive style of bouncy swing music was itself striking, in Mowitt's sense, despite the fact that they initially blacked up that style in hotter swing to appeal to Decca and their race records market. Their melodious, mellow and elegant style of swing music shocked stylistic expectations of hot-black authenticity that underpinned prevailing critical judgements of jazz, and never more so than when they started to record numerous sweet-sounding ballads. Those songs and their relationship to critical notions of musical-racial authenticity are considered in the next chapter, which explores the vocal records made by the band in 1936 and thereafter. Before we get to that consideration, however, there is one further aspect of the hot swing music that was recorded by Kirk's band in the 1936–1941 period that deserves our attention.

PAINTING SIGNIFYIN(G) PORTRAITS WITH HOT-AND-SWEET SWING

Many of the hot-swing numbers recorded by the Clouds of Joy between March 1936 and July 1941 directly reference dance movements or else the distinctive rhythmic qualities of swing in the voguish language of their titles. The likes of 'Steppin' Pretty' (60867-A), 'Wednesday Night Hop' (61598-A), 'Keep It in the Groove' (61951-A), and 'Jump, Jack, Jump' (64696-A) are four tracks that most obviously do so. Aside from such movement-referencing swing pieces there are some upbeat vocal recordings of the period that stand apart from the band's sweet commercial ballads as more theatrical novelty or entertainment numbers in the line of 'Casey Jones Special'. These are the songs that are most often sung by the band's drummer-vocalist, Ben Thigpen, or else feature all of the band members in a vocal ensemble that sounds somewhere between a unison sung chorus and a chant. They also have quite a different stylistic function from the ballads, and, not least, in the playful expression of the experiences of the band as a community of black musicians. In this, they present an important measure of humour that underlines much of the band's stylistic mask-play.

They include such tracks as 'Git', (60861-A-C) an amusing dialogue between the band and their drummer, in which Thigpen repeatedly refuses to sing the chorus (until the last one) and thus prompts solos from the other players. 'Toadie Toddle' (64642-A) is a similarly entertaining Mary Lou Williams number, full of tongue-twisting lyrics penned by Sharon Pease. Increasingly, these swing novelties cross over with another subgenre within the band's hot-swing recordings that depict individuals that were in or were associated with the band. Such 'portraits' include 'The Lady Who Swings the Band' (61464-A), 'Big Jim Blues' (66880-A), and 'Big Time Crip' (69519-A), which portray Mary Lou Williams,

Harry 'Big Jim' Lawson, and a one-legged Harlem tap-dancer, Henry Heard, respectively.[24] However, the most interesting portrait piece, for its musical-racial discourse, is one that doesn't depict a performer at all but makes critical use of the band's distinctive style of swing music.

In late 1936, shortly after their first ballad recording came to light, Louis Armstrong's notorious manager, Joe Glaser, took on the full-time management of the Clouds of Joy. 'Little Joe from Chicago' (63259-A) is a portrait of Glaser penned by Mary Lou Williams and Henry Wells that the band recorded for a Decca disc (1710) on 8 February 1938. According to the lyrics of the song Glaser 'wears a big blue diamond ring' and 'never wants for anything' but 'handles plenty o' money' and 'dresses up like a king'. The song goes on to suggest that he 'never spent a day in school', but 'how he handles money, makes you know he's nobody's fool'. This wording in the context of the swing styling of the arrangement makes this highly entertaining boogie-woogie piece double-voiced: it can be taken as a swing anthem, celebrating the cunning of the band's manager, as much as a critique of Glaser's profiteering from his charges—something Williams felt strongly.[25] Such a double meaning extends as much from its stylistic admixture of hot boogie-woogie and elegant swing and it thereby represents the subversive quality of the Signifyin(g) stylistic mask-play.

The song opens with a 12-bar blues that is founded on a typical boogie-woogie type of bass line. This is immediately apparent in the two-bar piano introduction (0'00"–0'03") in which the swung quavers, in the left hand octaves of Williams's playing, immediately convey a jaunty bounce. Set over this bass line in the first 12-bar blues chorus (0'03"–0'23") is a quirky duet for clarinets accompanied by rather brash, offbeat and low-tessitura chords for the brass. In the second blues chorus (0'23"–0'44") these syncopated interjections are hat- or plunger-muted and played

---

24 'The Lady Who Swings the Band', recorded on 9 December 1936, was written by Decca's resident songwriting team of Cahn and Chaplin, who were responsible for reworking 'Until the Real Thing Comes Along' (see chapter 3). Williams's 'Big Jim Blues', recorded on 15 November 1939, uses an 18-bar-long variant of the blues structure. 'Big Time Crip' was co-written by Mary Lou Williams and Kirk's trombonist Henry Wells. It was recorded on 17 January 1941, in the last session before both Williams and Wells left the band (Wells was to return in 1946). It is similar in its boogie-woogie styling to 'Little Joe from Chicago'.

25 Williams described the band's management in ironic terms as a 'Golden System' and explains how they hired new 'stars' (Smith and Richmond) to oust both her and Terrell when the pair proved persistent in asking for more money. She cited 'barnstorming and the "New System" of management' as amongst the reasons that she decided to leave Kirk's band (Williams [1954] 1997: 109–110).

with more growl and with some ominous-sounding crescendos. This gives the impression of a 'lowdown' boogie-woogie that underpins the otherwise rather 'clean' ensemble timbres and textures that were always the hallmark of the elegant and subtle swing of the Clouds of Joy. The tension between lowdown hot (black) character and the band's elegant sweet (white) dance-band style is essentially what constitutes the stylistic mask-play in the number.

The vocals that feature in the third and fourth blues choruses (0'44"–1'04" and 1'04"–1'25") are more chanted than sung by the chorus of players above Williams's piano figurations and that gives them a black-vernacular modernity. The boogie-woogie quavers then disappear in a four-bar bridge (1'25"–1'32") to a new section of music, an interlude that contrasts the 12-bar blues form used in the rest of the song with two eight-bar phrases. The first eight-bar phrase (1'32"–1'45") features a solo for Wilson's tenor, which leads to a two-bar trumpet break for Clarence Trice. The full brass section then features in the second eight-bar phrase (1'45"–1'59") in a repeated and emphatically swinging riff. However, the return of the boogie-woogie bass line signals the immediate revival of the lowdown blues changes (1'59"–2'20"), and what a powerhouse of a swinging blues chorus it is—the high point of the arrangement and, perhaps, of the whole blues-based output of the Clouds of Joy. The remaining blues chorus (2'20"–2'41") and its additional four-bar coda (2'41"–2'48") effectively form a gradual relaxation after that climax. The quirky clarinet duet returns in final section and that gives the piece a satisfying formal symmetry.

There is no doubt that this piece was intended as a fun 'novelty' number. However, the way the boogie-woogie style is rendered in the piece allows for a powerful and even ominous bluesy quality as much as the bouncy momentum of good-time commercial swing music. This gives the piece its peculiar double-voiced character that acts as Signifyin(g) commentary on Glaser: is this a celebration or a critique of their manager? Within that dichotomy, the brief solos for Wilson and Trice seem to exist in an entirely different context of eight-bar phrases, as if their jazz artistry is indifferent to the blues-based dance-music populism that got Glaser his money. The brassy riffs of the second eight-bar phrase ultimately energize the return of the boogie-woogie style and thereby suggest that a vital discourse involving the meeting of black-jazz artistry with more commercial dance music are at play in the stylistic critical admixture of the piece. This is a complex Signifyin(g) on styles and positions in which the musicians seem to be able to slip as easily between celebration and critique as between upbeat dance-band music and the lowdown blues.

FIGURE 2.8 The opening saxophone and brass figures in 'The Count' showing the striking hot-syncopation that overpowers sweetness in the piece.

By contrast with 'Little Joe', 'The Count' (68317-A) is a relatively straightforward 'hot' portrait of Count Basie that was arranged by Mary Lou Williams.[26] It is a fun, swinging, and brassy arrangement of a piece that was originally composed by Thomas Gordon and recorded by Bennie Moten for Victor in 1930 (Victor 23391). It is the last in the line of Moten-inspired arrangements that were made by Williams. It marks her swan song as a hot-swing arranger with the Clouds of Joy, as it was recorded in November 1940, just a year or so before her departure from the band. It shows how she Signified on the marriage of the hot-black jazz traditions of Kansas City with the sweeter swing music that befitted the band's work of playing for white social dancers.

Williams sets the piece in a brisk four-to-the-bar tempo (ca. 188 bpm), which Russell described as being typical of 'one of those bounce tempi that set feet dancing all over Eastern America when the Clouds of Joy appeared in ballrooms' (Russell [1971] 1983: 170). However, Williams's arrangement opens with a rhythmically disconcerting eight-bar introduction (0'00"–0'10"), featuring what Mowitt might term a 'striking' series of snatched syncopated chords for the brass interwoven with a saxophone line, to which dancing would be tricky (see Figure 2.8). A danceable tempo is established with the first AABA chorus (0'10"–0'50") but that features the muted trombone of Ted Donnelly, who clearly emulated the

26 We know this because manuscripts in Williams's hand are in the Mary Lou Williams Collection at Rutgers University.

original hot-sounding 'gutbucket' extemporizations of Moten's trombonist. Saxophone-ensemble riffs accompany Donnelly in neatly executed phrases before the brass lead the whole band in the contrasting B section (0'30"–0'40"). The brass return at the end of the final A section to herald the second AABA chorus (0'50"–1'31").

After four bars of brassy ensemble writing, Williams takes over on the piano and plays a highly swinging solo. In the second A section (1'02"–1'11"), she is backed by long-held chords in the saxophones before the hot-swinging brass, once again, interrupt this sweeter-styled atmosphere to frame the clarinet solo of the B section (1'11"–1'22"). Harrington's clarinet is accompanied by brief dialogue between trumpet and trombone motifs before the full ensemble closes the phrase with an arresting and reiterated dominant-ninth chord (F^9). That leads to an ascending scale, rendered in accented swung quavers, which reaches a climactic tonic chord (Bb^6) that opens the closing A section (see Figure 2.9). This chord immediately drops down through two octaves of reiterations ahead of a return of Williams's piano solo, which is ultimately interrupted by another brassy cadence.

A sudden change of timbre is offered in the next section (1'31"–1'52"), a sixteen-bar interlude which is effectively an extended bluesy solo break for Clarence Trice's trumpet. During this interlude the whole band falls silent save for Trice himself, Floyd Smith, who provides some chimes-like chords on his guitar, and Ben Thigpen, who simply marks time on his bass drum and snare. Trice maintains the swing momentum of the piece, partly by adopting a full tone at the start of each eight-bar phrase before letting the volume drop as he progresses through each one. The relatively sparse texture is shattered, once again, by the return of the brass-led ascending-scale figure that, at its climax (without the octave drops this time), marks the start of the third AABA chorus (1'52"–2'35").

FIGURE 2.9 The accented passage for brass and saxophones in 'The Count' that interrupts the clarinet solo in the B section of the second chorus.

This third chorus features a tenor solo for Wilson in its first three sections (AAB). He has to work hard at times so as not be to be drowned out by the plunger-muted brass riffs that accompany his solo, but his characteristic swinging agility and sense of line is very apparent in his wonderfully characterful playing. The final A section of Wilson's chorus is given over to a homophonic passage for saxophones, harmonizing with the trombones' melody in another one of Williams's characteristic passages of inventive orchestration.

The piece ends with a half chorus (2'35"–2'55"), comprised of just two A sections, and a concluding coda (2'55"–3'07"). The first of the resulting A sections is effectively a dialogue between brass and saxophone sections that soon fuse before Donnelly's muted trombone melody returns in the second A section. A walking bass line is introduced to increase momentum for the eight-bar coda, bringing the piece to an upbeat, highly swinging, and brassy close.[27]

In sum, 'The Count' is one of Williams's most characterful, varied, inventive, and hot-swinging arrangements. It features characteristics of the subtle, smooth, and bouncy swing, which had become the hallmark of the Clouds of Joy, but that is made to surrender, time and again, to the hot-swing styling in the piece. From its 'striking' opening, through the 'gutbucket' trombone solo, the surprising changes in timbres, and the brassy disruptions of every sweet-styled atmosphere, it is as though hot-styled syncopated writing bludgeons the band's sweet musical commerciality to death. Through such stylistic Signifyin(g), Williams shows that she will no longer mediate hot-black Southwestern jazz through smooth-styled melodic music of the usual type of the Clouds of Joy. From that perspective, it was no wonder that she left the band just a year or so after recording this arrangement, citing boredom with its musical style as one of her prime reasons for going.

In these portrait pieces, then, we can see how the bouncy or hybrid style of the elegant but hot swing of the Clouds of Joy was harnessed to Signify on the band's situation and individuals in its orbit. Whether the tone of that Signifyin(g) is subtly celebratory and subversive, as in the depiction of Glaser, or else critical of the ever more sweet and white-sounding

---

27 The manuscript score in the Mary Lou Williams Collection at Rutgers University suggests Williams actually wrote a full AABA chorus but made a cut after the first A section and inserted a reprise of the first (trombone-solo) A section from the opening chorus ahead of her original coda. This gives the arrangement a formal symmetry and shortened the arrangement by 16 bars which, no doubt, allowed it to fit on a three-minute side of a 10-inch record.

commercial style of Kirk's band, as in the depiction of Basie, it shows how the hotter instrumentals provide comment without recourse to the sort of direct expression of words that might get black musicians in to trouble. The next chapter considers how the band courted such racialized trouble with vocals that offered more direct expression but were no less subversive in the way their played with notions of racial authenticity.

CHAPTER 3

'UNTIL THE REAL THING COMES ALONG'
POP SONGS AND AUTHENTICITY, 1936–1949

THIS CHAPTER EXPLORES the development of Kirk's band from their recording of 'Until the Real Thing Comes Along', a 'special ballad' that Kirk convinced Decca to record in 1936, to the disbanding of the Clouds of Joy in 1949. So it begins by covering a similar period to the previous chapter, but it extends analysis to the recordings of the later 1940s because it has a rather different focus: it is primarily concerned with the band's commercial success with vocal records that increasingly dominated the Decca releases during the 1940s.

The vocal recordings are the most critically controversial and maligned part of the band's output and yet they represent the most popular and widely consumed records that the band made. To critics, like Gunther Schuller, the turn towards commercial vocals in the sweet style of jazz, which was usually the territory of white bands, was a betrayal of the supposed authenticity of hot-black jazz. So, the first part of this chapter covers the most illuminating aspect of the recordings made by Andy Kirk and his Clouds of Joy, because the sweet vocals speak (or sing) loudest of the position and actions of a black band operating within a highly racialized musical culture and society. By considering the vocals relative to the band's increasingly more modest hot-jazz (swing) output, this chapter challenges any notion that Kirk's band sold out on their black-jazz credentials with their turn to popular vocal recordings and swing music after 1936. Instead, it suggests how they found new ways to Signify on their situation within the racist culture in which they operated.

Pha Terrell's singing of ballads drew on the 'crooning' style, which had been popularized by white singers during the 1920s, but his crooning was especially distinctive for his use of falsetto. We will see that critics read this feature not just as racially inauthentic but also as decidedly effeminate and queer-sounding. Some renamed Pha Terrell as 'Fay Terrible', and the likes of Schuller struggled to cope with the popular appeal of such falsetto singing within abiding notions of jazz as a heteronormative, if not macho, black creative culture. So, the first question for the chapter is, what might Terrell's appalling (for critics) yet appealing (for audiences) ballad recordings mean within debates of racial identity and authenticity that surrounded the band's music?

Terrell's sweet ballads came to dominate the recordings of the Clouds of Joy in the later 1930s and early 1940s. Critics, like Albert McCarthy, suspected that the commercial imperatives of the record business meant that the hot jazz of Kirk's band became confined to its live performances because of the popularity of the ballads (McCarthy 1971: 23). So, to what extent does the apparent imbalance of sweet to hot jazz on the Decca records of the late 1930s represent the live practices of Kirk's band? This question is addressed in the second section of this chapter, which considers the set of recordings that resulted from broadcasts that the Clouds of Joy made from Cleveland's Trianon Ballroom in the spring of 1937.

This enterprise requires a little reverse engineering because the LP of the Trianon recordings represents a reordered and selective collection of music that was drawn together from four separate broadcasts. Once the tracks are reorganized into the original sets, what do they show of the impact of the success of 'Until the Real Thing Comes Along', the general balance of musical styles within the live work of the Clouds of Joy, and the way that the band's live practices compared with their Decca recordings? Furthermore, what do the Trianon recordings suggest of the band's reaction to their sweet ballad recordings with respect to their supposed musical-racial character?

Terrell left the Clouds of Joy in mid 1940, and the third part of this chapter begins by documenting how the void that was left by his departure was initially filled by other singers that emulated his 'crooning' style. However, the larger-than-life singer June Richmond, who joined the band in 1939, increasingly came to the fore after Terrell left. In her highly characterful and theatrical performances, she offered a contrasting direction for the vocal recordings of the Clouds of Joy. She moved them away from the seemingly white-sounding and strait-laced ballads, back towards a more bluesy, co-medic, and stereotyped musical portrayal of black authenticity on records.

This shift back towards a more stereotypical black style helped to position Kirk's much-enlarged band at the forefront of the early R & B market. On Richmond's departure, they had some success in backing black male vocal quartets in making records in the doo-wop genre. What did this continued domination of pop vocal recordings within the band's output mean for the ever-smaller quantity of jazz that the band recorded for Decca, and what does that say of their musical-racial identity on records?

The last section of this chapter considers the recordings that resulted from wartime broadcasts made for Coca-Cola and the Armed Forces Radio Service (AFRS), together with the band's role in the 1948 movie *Killer Diller*. By exploring the brassy swing numbers that featured in those recordings and the film, the chapter challenges the abiding crit-ical notion that the 1940s represented a period of profound commer-cialism and artistic decline for Kirk's band, which ultimately led to its demise.

How can we account for the comparatively hard-driven swing and modernistic jazz that appears in the broadcast recordings and what do the theatrics seen in the film say of the band's positioning of their musical and racial identity at the end of the 1940s? Why are the band's commercial recordings so different from the broadcasts and the film, and why did Kirk wind up his band as a full-time concern in 1949? These are questions that occupy the end of this chapter and point towards Kirk's actions in the 1950s, which are the subject of the next one.

'UNTIL THE REAL THING COMES ALONG': SWEET BALLADS, FALSETTO, AND JAZZ AUTHENTICITY

Kirk relates in his autobiography that he wanted to get the Clouds of Joy back into the recording studio in 1936 because he was increasingly aware that their extant recordings did not represent the true breadth of their repertoire or the full extent of their popular appeal (Kirk 1989: 73). They were presented on their records as a band that appeared only to play music of a hot-black type that was limited to the relatively low-value race market, when their actual repertoire and style was more wide-ranging, classy, and commercial than that. Kirk wanted to make records that better represented their appeal to audiences beyond the limited African American market, which played only a relatively small part in their live work as a dance band. He felt that representing the full range and cross-racial appeal of their music was not only truer to their identity as an enterprising black dance band, but it was also a statement of racial pride that could challenge the racist culture of recording and open up the wider market for their records. As Kirk put it, 'I [had] decided it was time to try to crack the race barrier in recordings' (Kirk 1989: 84).

In an interview with Frank Driggs, Kirk recalled how he struck a deal with the Decca executive Jack Kapp that ultimately led to his band's escape from recording solely the type of music that record producers wanted for race records:

> We were getting set to record when he [Kapp] got something he wanted to record right away. That was *Christopher Columbus*. I told him okay we'd make it, but that I wanted him to listen to something special we had. He said to make his tune first and then we'd talk about it. (Kirk 1959: 15)

Undaunted, Kirk put the idea of recording a sweet-styled ballad to Kapp and he recalled the producer's reaction in terms of the way he associated musical style with racial authenticity and appropriateness:

> 'Andy, what's the matter with you?' Kapp said. 'You've got something good going for you. Why do you want to do what the white boys are doing?' Right then I saw his commercial motives, saw why he had originally wanted to record us in Kansas City. It was for the race market only. He told us that for that session *Christopher Columbus* was a must. (Kirk 1989: 84)

After the Clouds of Joy recorded 'Christopher Columbus', Kapp was full of praise for the band and Kirk seized his opportunity to remind Kapp of their agreement and to convince him to record their 'special' ballad. He recalled their exchange as follows:

'Great, fine', Kapp said, after hearing the playback. He gave me a pat on the back, one to Mary Lou, and all the rest of the band. 'You did a wonderful job'. He started for the door. 'Wait', I said, 'you said you'd listen to our other things'. 'Oh—OK', he said, 'go ahead'. We played our special ballad. He said it was OK, but I could see it didn't really strike him. He had the race thing on his mind. But as a compromise he finally said, 'All right, we'll record it'. (Kirk 1989: 85)

Although Kapp ultimately agreed to record the 'special ballad', 'Until the Real Thing Comes Along', he was worried enough about the uncharacteristic material to insist that changes were made to the song before rerecording it for release. The extent of these changes is made clear by comparing the two different recordings of the ballad that were made by the Clouds of Joy during the spring of 1936: the first one was made four days after the recording of 'Christopher Columbus', on 11 March (60887-A), and the second on 2 April (60973-A). The earlier recording was rejected by Kapp but sometime after the second version was issued by Decca (802), it was released by the British arm of Columbia records (DB5004).[1] These two recordings are especially different in their lyrics. In a song that is all about authenticity, Terrell's vocal treatment of the different lyrics is fascinating, especially when considered relative to the published sheet music and intersecting notions of racial integrity and musical style that were bound up with recording such commercial material.

The song was published by Chappell in 1936 and the sheet music credits five authors: Mann Holiner, Alberta Nichols, Sammy Cahn, Saul Chaplin, and L. E. Freeman. Two of these (Holiner and Nichols) were the song's original writers, and the others were most likely credited for their roles in revising the piece. In reality, only one of these revisers, the lyricist Sammy Cahn, was heavily involved in reworking the song, because the changes do not extend much beyond adjustments of the lyrics. Although it is possible that Kirk's tenor saxophonist, Lawrence 'Slim' Freeman, played a part in arranging the song for the band (he is also

---

1 The discographies of Kirk's recorded output disagree over who sang on the 11 March session. Charles Garrod (1991: 3) and Howard Rye both list Pha Terrell as the vocalist (Rye, as cited in Kirk 1989: 127), but in the liner notes to the Classics CD, *Andy Kirk and His Twelve Clouds of Joy 1936–1937*, Ben Thigpen is listed as the singer. To my ears both vocals are sung by Pha Terrell. Even though Thigpen sang the other vocal recorded in the session, 'I'se a Muggin'', he generally did not sing 'swing' ballads but tended to stick to hot numbers and novelty songs.

credited with 'Sweet and Hot'), Kirk maintained that he had as much to do with it as a 'bucket' (Kirk, as cited in Driggs & Haddix 2005: 141).

The published vocal score represents the song in a form that was typical for ballads of the period: after a four-bar introduction for the piano alone, it features a fairly perfunctory verse section of 12 bars that is followed by a repeated 32-bar refrain (marked 'Slowly with expression'). The refrain utilizes the standard AABA structure of Tin Pan Alley ballads and is made up of four eight-bar phrases. In the usual manner of such songs, the key is shifted (to G major) for the B section to temporarily 'release' listeners from the E-flat major of the A sections. As is typical of most band arrangements of the period, only the refrain part of the published song is featured on the two recordings made by the Clouds of Joy, and short passages of additional instrumental music were added to frame it.

Each recording offers a different introduction. The one made in March 1936 opens with a brassy fanfare-like phrase (0'00"–0'06") which is not in the published vocal score but was no doubt supplied by the arranger. The fanfare phrase was dropped for the version recorded in April 1936, when it was replaced by a sweeter, more ponderous, and less striking piano phrase (0'00"–0'08"), which was most likely improvised by Williams. Thereafter, though, both recordings are identical in their musical form and its scheme runs as follows:

The first AABA chorus (0'06"–1'23" / 0'08"–1'27") is sung by Terrell and then it is repeated by the band, after a short interlude that is led by the trumpets. The four-bar interlude (1'23"–1'33" / 1'27"–1'37") is, again, not in the published song sheet but was provided by whoever made the band arrangement. In the second rendition of the chorus (1'33"–2'54" / 1'37"–2'59"), the saxophone section features the song's melody in the first two A sections. The saxophones are set in close harmony and perform in a decidedly sweet style. Terrell resumes his singing from the B section of the second chorus and continues to the end of the song. The song is capped off with a fanfare-like tag (2'51"–2'54" / 2'55"–2'59") which echoes the original introduction and, once again, that is not featured in the published music of the song but was most likely the work of the arranger.

According to Kirk, the ballad was originally entitled 'A Slave Song' (Kirk 1989: 85), and it contained a decidedly black sensibility in its lyrical content because of its original 'Southern' context in the Broadway show that featured it. The white songwriters, Holiner and Nichols, wrote it for one of Lew Leslie's reviews called *Rhapsody in Black: A Symphony of Blue Notes and Black Rhythm* (1931). It starred Ethel Waters and Valaida Snow, and it was noted for being relatively progressive for its depiction of blackness (Mordden 2005: 90). Kirk recalled that a performer named Harriet Calloway (no relation to Blanche and Cab) brought the song to Kansas City from Chicago when Leslie's review toured to the city after the Broadway run.[2] The Three Chocolate Drops, a trio that Kirk describes as 'three kids with ukuleles' (Kirk 1989: 85), heard the song when Leslie's show played at Kansas City's Schubert Theater in January 1933 (Driggs & Haddix 2005: 141). They reinterpreted it, and it was in that mediated form that the song became popular around Kansas City's nightclubs and thereby made it in to the repertoire of the Clouds of Joy.

Save for the short additional passages that frame the two choruses in the band arrangement, the later (April 1936) recording of 'Until the Real Thing Comes Along' is nearly identical in form and content to the published song sheet. This indicates that it represents the final version of the song, after revisions had been made to it by Cahn and Chalin. The earlier (March 1936) recording contains different lyrics and is thus representative of the form of the song before it was revised (the Chocolate Drops's version of Holiner and Nichols's 'Slave Song'). A comparison of the different lyrics in the two recordings indicates that the adjustments that were made at Kapp's behest were an attempt to tone down some of the more overt black representation and suggestive expression (see Table 3.1).

The March 1936 recording of the original song was double-voiced in that it was concerned with bodily, psychological and behavioural stereotypes associated with black slavery as much as romance and sex. The black body in hard labour, suggestively moaning and groaning, and the ever-present threat of death are central metaphors in the lyrics in the March version. The contrasting B section implies emancipation and the legacy of the black diaspora in its references to travel and separation. In short, the band's first recording of 'Until the Real Thing Comes Along' was full of highly suggestive and stereotyped African American imagery. This is a song that very much represents the legacies of stereotyping that came with and from blackface minstrel traditions.

By contrast, the band's April 1936 recording contains lyrics that are similar to those in the published sheet music but they are not absolutely

---

2 Calloway first appeared in the second incarnation of Leslie's revue called *Blackbirds of 1929*, which did not feature the song. It did, however, appear in Leslie's later *Rhapsody in Black* of 1931, performed by Valaida Snow with the orchestra (Peterson 1993: 291). It seems likely that Calloway performed the song when that show toured.

TABLE 3.1 A comparison of the lyrics in the 1936 recordings and published sheet music of 'Until the Real Thing Comes Along'.

Recording of 11 March 1936 (Decca, New York)	*Recording of 2 April 1936 (Decca, New York)*	*1936 published sheet music (Chappell, New York)*
(Brass fanfare introduction)	*(Piano 'laid-back', arpeggio-filled introduction)*	*(4-bar introduction and 12-bar verse)*
I would work for you, slave for you,	I would work for you, I'd slave for you,	I'd work for you, I'd slave for you,
Work my body to a grave for you,	I'd be a beggar or a knave for you;	I'd be a beggar or a knave for you;
If that ain't love, it's got to do,	If that ain't love, it will have to do,	If that isn't love, it will have to do,
Until the real thing comes along.	Until the real thing comes along.	Until the real thing comes along.
I would moan for you, groan for you,	I'd gladly move the Earth for you,	I'd gladly move the Earth for you,
Work my fingers to the bones for you,	To prove my love, dear, and its worth for you,	To prove my love, dear, and its worth for you,
If that ain't love, it's got to do,	If that ain't love, it'll have to do,	If that isn't love, it'll have to do,
Until the real thing comes along.	Until the real thing comes along.	Until the real thing comes along.
Maybe someday, I'll go far away,	With all the words, dear, at my command,	With all the words, dear, at my command,
I should leave, you know I won't stay;	I just can't make you understand,	I just can't make you understand,
I need you now more than ever, somehow,	I'll always love you, darling, come what may,	I'll always love you, darling, come what may,
If you should leave, you know we'd both grieve.	My heart is yours, what more can I say?	My heart is yours, what more can I say?

(continued)

TABLE 3.1 Continued.

Recording of 11 March 1936 (Decca, New York)	*Recording of 2 April 1936 (Decca, New York)*	*1936 published sheet music (Chappell, New York)*
I would rob, steal, beg, borrow, and I'd lie for you, Lay my body down and die for you, If that ain't love, it's got to do, Until the real thing comes along.	I'd beg for you, I'd lie for you, I'd draw the stars down from the sky for you, If that ain't love, it'll have to do, Until the real thing comes along.	I'd sigh for you, I'd cry for you, I'd tear the stars down from the sky for you, If that isn't love, it'll have to do, Until the real thing comes along.
(Saxes take harmonized refrain melody for first two A sections)	*(Saxes take harmonized refrain melody for first two A sections)*	*(Straight repetition of refrain—repeat marks)*
Maybe someday, I'll go far away, I should leave, you know I won't stay, I need you now more than ever, somehow, If you should leave, you know we'd both grieve.	With all the words, dear, at my command, I just can't make you understand, I'll always love you, darling, come what may, My heart is yours, what more can I say?	
I would rob, steal, beg, borrow, and I'd lie for you, Lay my body down and die for you, If that ain't love, it's got to do, Until the real thing comes along.	I would rob, steal, beg, borrow, and I'd lie for you, I'd draw the stars down from the sky for you, If that ain't love, it'll have to do, Until the real thing comes along.	

identical with them. The suggestive bodily aspects have been expunged in favour of a more poetic, wholly romantic and race-neutral tone. All the African American vernacular and suggestive expressions have been replaced with a much safer and less racialized sensibility. In this sense, then, the song has been whitened and morally sanitized, as its apparent blackness and sexually suggestive connotations have been removed for the band's Decca release. However, Terrell's performance of this ballad suggests that despite these revisions, the April 1936 recording represented no straightforward abandonment of black identity in favour of a whitened commercial one at the behest of white record producers. Instead, his singing represented another opportunity for Signifyin(g) mask-play around the restyling of the song that spoke of race, even if the lyrics no longer did.

In both of the band's recordings of the song, Terrell sings the refrain in a fairly straight (in both senses) manner in his light baritone, which has qualities of the crooning of Nat 'King' Cole. However, the retention of the vernacular 'ain't' in the lyrics of the April 1936 version suggests that the more polite and white standard form of 'isn't', which is in the published song, was a step too far for Terrell's African American sensibilities. Furthermore, when the final A-section comes around (2'35"–2'58"), Terrell uses the increasing momentum of the original line 'I would rob, steal, beg, borrow' to push into falsetto for the words 'lie to you', and he thereby marks out the word 'lie' as the high point of the phrase with his fluted top B-flat. This voguish vocal quality is a highly distinctive feature of Terrell's Signifyin(g) performance of the sanitized song.

If there is anything false about falsetto, then it sounds all the more so when it is aimed at a word such as 'lie'. Importantly, this particular line is not in the published iteration of the ballad, but it is a vestige of the lyrics of the original 'Slave Song' (or, at least, the Chocolate Drops's remediated version of them) as can be heard in the March 1936 recording. The original line is surely retained by Terrell in the band's April recording for its better rhythmic drive. However, his 'lie' is nevertheless telling, because, as if to underline the vocalized deceit in this whitened version of the song, Terrell uses falsetto again, just moments later, for his final rendition of the titular line (2'50"–2'58"). Its reference to waiting for the authentic experience of true love to arrive, once again ends on his 'lying' top B-flat. This falsetto emphasis suggests that the 'real thing' of the song, whether it be love, musical style, or racial identity, is always anything but that—it is a falsehood, an affectation, a construction with no sure foundation—and one could be left waiting for ever for it to come along.

The Decca release of 'Until the Real Thing Comes Along' proved to be an unprecedented success for the band and the record label. It marked more than a fivefold increase in record sales on 'Christopher Columbus', which was itself considered to have been a hit by Kirk and Kapp, albeit within the limited scope of the race-records market.[3] The folks at Decca were, of course, surprised and delighted by the success of the band's first ballad, and Kapp sought to record much more of such material with the Clouds of Joy thereafter. This meant that 'Until the Real Thing Comes Along' was followed by many similar sweet-styled ballads that were increasingly recorded at the expense of hot-swinging instrumentals.

That move away from hot jazz towards a more commercial style of popular vocal music ultimately tarnished the reputation of the Clouds of Joy with jazz critics who had long argued that the hot style was the only true jazz, especially for a black band. Gunther Schuller, for example, bemoaned in his 1989 assessment of the band that, 'by 1937 and there-after, as a result of an immensely popular recording by the band's singer, Pha Terrell, its [hot] *jazz* playing days, while not exactly numbered, were certainly threatened' (Schuller 1989: 353). It is interesting that Schuller does not mention the problematic recording by name but he goes on to contextualize the style of Terrell's singing with reference to established values of sophistication, taste and authenticity in jazz that stand in con-trast to such musical commercialism:

Virtually every band [of the period] had—or tried to have—a pop-ular singer who could cater to less sophisticated musical tastes and bring in dollars at the box office, which in turn would permit the continuance of instrumentals and a true jazz repertory. (Schuller 1989: 353)

Schuller's main objection was to the style of singing known as 'crooning' that emerged with the development of vocal amplification during the 1920s. It was popularized by the likes of Harold 'Scrappy' Lambert and Hubert 'Rudy' Vallée, and by the 1930s it had become a mainstay of the vocals that were offered by swing bands. It exploited the way a micro-phone could amplify softer, more intimate, and conversational vocal

---

3 Various figures are quoted by Kirk with regard to the jump in sales brought about by their move to ballads. In his autobiography, Kirk claims sales increased from 10,000 to 100,000 (Kirk 1989: 87).

expression. This contrasted with the more robust and demonstrative style of blues 'shouting' or Broadway 'belting' that had developed in the days when singers had to fill large theatres with their voices without the aid of amplification.

Crooning brought with it a different approach to using the voice, such as utilizing the lighter-sounding 'head' voice rather than the louder 'chest' voice of the lower vocal register. It also involved some specific stylistic traits, such as a concern for a really smooth melodic line, an evenness of tone, and approaching notes with a slide rather than attacking them right on pitch (Goldstein 2001). However, the understated and anodyne qualities of crooning were its most defining characteristic, and for jazz critics like Schuller, they meant it contrasted the ideals of performance and immediacy of expression in hot-jazz singing. To the likes of Schuller, the comparatively hushed and effeminate expression of crooning represented a debasement of the muscular and masculine style of 'true' jazz in the pursuit of mere commercialism: it represented an emasculated and sold-out form of real jazz artistry.

Schuller cites the vocal recordings made by the bands of Ellington and Basie as 'more successful in resisting these inroads of the marketplace' on account of them 'having better and more jazz orientated singers'. However, he lumps the Clouds of Joy together with a whole lot of other bands of the period that featured popular crooners, and he clearly blames what he calls 'the mystery of the male crooners' mesmerizing successes' for turning the band's '7:5 jazz-to-pop ratio around to 4:15' (Schuller 1989: 353, n.1). This sort of criticism is revealing of the complex mix of markers of jazz artistry, commercial populism, and racial authenticity that are bound up with such prevailing discussions of style in jazz. In this context, Terrell's use of falsetto within his 'crooning' is especially interesting for the way it adds overt notions of effeminacy and implied homosexuality into that mix.

After the song's release, Terrell's falsetto was often read by audiences and critics as an indication that the singer was gay. On one particular occasion, a thickset audience member threatened Terrell, and Kirk reflected in highly derogatory language that 'you could see he didn't like his looks or the way he sang in falsetto—sounded to him like a fag, I guess' (Kirk 1989: 102). Kirk also described how members of his bands would tease Terrell and would assume he was 'soft' because of his high voice (Kirk 1959: 16). In a bid to put the record straight, Kirk emphasized how the diminutive singer, whom we are told was a former nightclub bouncer and very much a ladies' man, would quickly use his fists to settle any doubt about his sexuality (Kirk 1989: 102). This was also the recollection of the saxophonist, Buddy Tate, who stated:

> [Pha Terrell] never hit anyone in the world [but] he'd knock out, I mean down-out. Little skinny cat, man. You know, people used to jive with him and they say, must be a faggot, high voice, and the name, Pha. They soon found out, if they tackled him. (Tate, as cited in Pearson 1988: 61)

In subsequent criticism, and notably in Schuller's writing about the Clouds of Joy, the apparent queerness of Terrell's falsetto becomes symbolic of the perceived derivative commerciality and racial inauthenticity of the sweet ballads relative to the hot-jazz artistry that is heard in the band's earlier recordings. In other words, critics articulated connotations of falsity, emasculation, and homosexuality, which were evoked for them by Terrell's falsetto, with the sweet-white style of his crooned ballads. They thereby denigrated the black band's move away from their 'rightful' territory of hot jazz to a more commercial and seemingly derivative style of sweet vocal music on records. Terrell's falsetto is therefore used to queer the sweet-styled music that was increasingly recorded by Kirk's band on the basis of its racial-stylistic inauthenticity and overt commercialism.

In this vein, Schuller felt that the overwhelming popularity of such 'effeminately voiced crooners' demonstrated the 'appalling taste' in the consumption of popular music of the period (Schuller 1989: 323, n.1). Schuller considered that 'the generally "macho" outlook of the average American male consumer' could not possibly account for the huge sales of such material, and yet he remained mystified because 'women were surely not the main buyers of records—especially in the lean depression years'. What his gendered reading misses is the attraction of falsetto as a popular vocal style both within and beyond connotations of gender and sexuality. It was, in fact, a style that evoked for audiences the unworldly qualities of true love, and it could also be harnessed for subversive maskplay in a way that had long enjoyed a currency in African American forms of black representation within American popular culture.[4] In that

---

4 In this context, it is interesting to think of the song as an extension of the cross-dressing and gender-bending roles commonly found in the blackface minstrel shows of the previous generation of African American performers.

FIGURE 3.1   A publicity photograph of Pha Terrell sent to the journalist and record producer Dave Dexter in the later 1930s.

respect, one of Terrell's publicity photographs captured precisely that ethereal, unworldly quality (see Figure 3.1)

There were, of course, other black singers of the period who displayed a similar style of crooning to Terrell. These included Orlando Roberson (a singer with Claude Hopkin's band), Dan Grissom (who sang with Jimmy Lunceford's orchestra), and Hayes Pillar (of the Jeter-Pillars Orchestra and formerly a singer with Alphonso Trent's band). All of these singers utilized the same sort of light baritone as Terrell, and they articulated the musical line in much the same emotionally indulgent way and were often equally criticized for it.[5] The smooth vocal articulation as much as the lightness of tone in their singing allowed all these singers to slip into falsetto quite effortlessly within a vocal phrase, when or if they saw fit to do so. It is in that aspect that Terrell stands apart from those others because his move to falsetto brings with it a marked change of vocal timbre: it is more noticeable or telling in its difference from the rest of his vocal character and he played on that in his vocal performance.

Interestingly, all of these singers were from the Southwestern region, where falsetto was often employed within blues singing. In the 1950s and 1960s, the likes of Willis James (1955), R. A. Waterman (1952), and Harold Courlander (1963) identified the feature of the 'falsetto cry', 'snap', or 'break' in blues singing and sought to trace its origins back to the field cries of plantation slaves and West African vocal traditions. However, the falsetto cry has a vocal character that is similar to yodelling, and this has led others to suggest that it may have come from the Amish community who brought yodelling with them from Switzerland (Ravens 2014: 202). What is clear, however, is that falsetto 'breaks' became a part of the distinctive character of Southwestern blues vocals. According to Russell, they involved 'a sudden change in pitch combined with changes in dynamic and perhaps in timbre' (Russell [1971] 1983: 252, n.1). Terrell's use of falsetto may well have roots in such blues traditions, but it is not quite so striking or abrupt a change of vocal quality as that typical in the 'falsetto cry' in the blues, and it is thus most likely a mediated form that as much grew out of black minstrel usage of falsetto.

In his book about falsetto singing, Ravens writes:

From the 1860s onwards the Georgia Minstrels—a genuine negro group which spawned many imitators—toured America and played to vast audiences—their act incorporated the falsetto singing (partly as female impersonators) of T. Drewette. This tradition of falsetto as part of the minstrel act was to continue into the twentieth century.

(Ravens 2014: 191)

---

5 Friedwald wrote: 'These men [Terrell and Grissom] dealt with the blues and jazz influences by replacing it with a sort of open-toothed sibilance drawn from the genuine but nonetheless obnoxious black tradition of falsetto singing that found a better place in the perversely misnamed "soul" movement of the sixties and seventies. Still, while jazz collectors (usually white) nicknamed these two Dan "gruesome" and Pha (pronounced, appropriately, "Fay") "Terrible", they had their admirers . . .' (Friedwald 1990: 121).

Ravens goes on to identify three 'routes' that falsetto singing took from black minstrelsy into recordings. The first is exemplified in the yodelling qualities of the records made by blues singers like Jimmie Rodgers, who, Ravens reminds us, had been associated with black minstrels early in his career. The second was in the singing of the early barbershop groups, like the Mills Brothers, the Ink Spots, and the Revellers. The third 'led to the Soul Stirrers and the ecstatic falsetto of Robert Harris', who 'introduced the false soprano which was to become fundamental to gospel' (Ravens 2014: 202). In this way, Ravens suggests that such singers and groups perpetuated a tradition of falsetto singing which, although it had roots in the female impersonations of minstrelsy, was increasingly symbolic of a decidedly black-male vocal style for recording.

The idea of a black tradition of falsetto singing extending from black-face minstrelsy has important implications for understanding its function for a black singer in the 1930s. Will Friedwald has suggested that the sort of vocal pretention represented by Terrell's falsetto also formed a part of a wider tradition of vocal styling that black singers had to adopt within the racist discourse that surrounded vocal performance. He explains:

> [For a black ballad singer, the] quality of your singing impressed people less than the nerve it took to dare to suggest that blacks were capable of feeling the same things white folks were and, consequently, able to sing the same songs. Louis Armstrong, Bill Robinson, Stepin Fetchit, and Ethel Waters had made a start by proving that black entertainers, if they didn't stray too far from white preconceptions of how blacks were supposed to act, could be accepted by whites and even become wealthy and famous. No one minded if Little Jimmy Rushing sang a blues with Basie, if Pha Terrell went through his campy parody of crooning, if Cab Calloway hi-de-ho'd, or if Ivie Anderson expounded on how all God's chillun had rhythm, but no black man dared attempt a 'straight' love song.
>
> (Friedwald 1990: 255)

Friedwald goes on to cite 'Flamingo', a ballad recorded in 1940 by Herb Jeffries (a notably pale-skinned black singer with Ellington's orchestra) as the first hit record that was sung 'straight' by a black singer. So, within Friedwald's pre-1940 context, falsetto represented a necessary vocal mask that was distancing, because it suggested that this was not a real (white) man singing about real emotions. In that context, the effeminate and homosexual connotations of falsetto only helped to distance the black singer from the serious romantic content of the song, as much as it represented a tradition of black-vocal identity coupled with a voguish 'crooning' modernity that the microphone had brought to it. From that perspective, Terrell's falsetto in 'Until the Real Thing Comes Along', is all the more powerful for its double-voiced Signifyin(g) on authenticity both in terms of true love *and* racial-vocal expression.

Such stylistic mask-play is always open to different interpretations and it can be read as much for its Signfyin(g) on racial commercial concerns that were bound up with the styles of music recorded by the Clouds of Joy, as for its apparent expression of emasculation and homosexuality. Critics like Schuller, in their fixation on the inauthentic, emasculating and homosexual connotations of Terrell's falsetto, overlooked the racial identity politics that such an apparent camping-up or queering of musical styles represented. As much as the Clouds of Joy 'sold out' on their black integrity with such supposedly queer-sounding sweet ballads, Terrell's singing in the context of the band's apparent whiting up of their musical style with 'Until the Real Thing Comes Along' shows how Kirk's band continued to subvert the racist discourses and structures that were associated with black-musical identity and recording. Thus, Terrell's sweet-falsetto crooning not only served as a protective measure and a voguish marker of cross-racial commerciality for the band, but it also pointed to the falsity of articulating musical styles with racial and/or sexual absolutes.

'LIVE' FROM THE TRIANON BALLROOM: PLAYING WITH STYLISTIC-RACIAL EXPECTATIONS

Most of the critical writing on the Clouds of Joy reports how the sweet ballads came to dominate the hot jazz in their recordings of the later 1930s, but Albert McCarthy suggested that this imbalance may not have been a true reflection of the live practices of the band (McCarthy 1971: 23). Given the place of the band and its records within critical debates of musical-racial authenticity, this is an important suggestion to explore. However, the trouble is that the band's live practices are not very easy to assess because relatively few live performances were recorded and released. But, there is a set of recordings from 1937 that will serve to explore McCarthy's suggestion while showing something of the way that the band responded to the nationwide fame they found with 'Until the Real Thing Comes Along'.

In early 1937, riding high on the back of their hit ballad, the Clouds of Joy were booked by their new manager, Joe Glaser, to play for dancers at the Trianon Ballroom in Cleveland, Ohio. This ballroom was formerly known as the Crystal Slipper and could accommodate 4,000 dancers (Strasmyer 2015). However, the main attraction for Kirk and his band was that it had a 'wire' that linked the microphones in the ballroom directly to the NBC radio network and thereby gave the Clouds of Joy far-reaching exposure. As Kirk explained, it was not easy for a black band to access such broadcasting venues:

> We couldn't play white hotels then. The hotel jobs were good because they had radio wires, and usually a band stayed in a hotel spot for a long time—years sometimes. But those spots were controlled by white agents and so white bands got them. (Kirk 1989: 94)

So it was something of a coup when the Clouds of Joy broadcast live from the Trianon Ballroom on the Friday and Saturday nights of two consecutive weeks: 29 and 30 January and 5 and 6 February 1937. The broadcasts were recorded directly from the ballroom's radio feed on to acetate discs. Some decades later, selections from these discs were edited for a commercial release, an LP on the Jazz Society label (AA503).[6] While the selections from the broadcasts were no doubt chosen by the record's producers to display the jazzier aspect of the band's style rather than its commercial side, one can still get a sense from them of the typical sort of set that the band offered in its live appearances and thereby explore the balance and breadth of the styles of music that they played in person. We can also measure how the band adapted its music for recording by comparing the Decca releases with their live equivalents.

As the lists of broadcast numbers show (see Table 3.2), the Jazz Society LP offers the whole of the set of numbers that was broadcast on Saturday 6 February 1937, and all bar one of the pieces ('In the Chapel in the Moonlight') that the band broadcast on Saturday 30 January 1937.

These sets of six pieces each were prefaced by a short rendition of the band's new opening theme, 'Until the Real Thing Comes Along', and they were followed by its closing theme, 'Clouds' (which they went on to record in 1938). Each of the sets featured just one sweet ballad ('Trust in Me' and 'What Will I Tell My Heart', respectively) and one hot-styled vocal ('All the Jive Is Gone' and 'Froggy Bottom', respectively). They were

---

6 The Jazz Society LP (AA503) is still widely available through suppliers of secondhand records and online auctions, but it has been reissued by Hallmark as an album of mp3 files entitled *Sepia Jazz* that is available for download.

TABLE 3.2 The pieces recorded during four 1937 broadcasts from the Trianon Ballroom in Cleveland, Ohio.

29 January 1937	30 January 1937	5 February 1937	6 February 1937
Opening Theme ('Until the Real Thing Comes Along')	Opening Theme ('Until the Real Thing Comes Along')	Opening Theme ('Until the Real Thing Comes Along')	Opening Theme ('Until the Real Thing Comes Along')*
'You Turned the Tables on Me'	'You're Slightly Terrific'*	'Honeysuckle Rose'	'Swingtime in the Rockies'*
'Never Slept a Wink Last Night'*	'Yours Truly'*	'There's Frost on the Moon'	'Froggy Bottom'*
'Goodnight My Love'	'Trust in Me'*	Medley ('Boo Hoo'; 'One, Two, Button Your Shoe'; 'Trouble Don't Like Music'; 'Once in a Minute')*	'What Will I Tell My Heart'*
'You Do the Darndest Things'	'All the Jive is Gone'*	'Walkin' and Swingin''	'Moten Swing'*
'Spring Holiday'	'Dear Old Southland'*	'Dedicated to You'	'There, I Love You Coast to Coast'*
'When I'm With You'	'In the Chapel in the Moonlight'	'Oh Say Can You Swing'	'Organ Grinder's Swing'*
'Make Believe Ballroom'*	Closing Theme ('Clouds')	'King Porter Stomp'	Closing Theme ('Clouds')*
'Sepia Jazz'*		'Liza'	
'[I Went to a] Gypsy'		Closing Theme ('Clouds')	
Closing Theme ('Clouds')			

* Indicates reissued on Jazz Society LP (AA503) and *Sepia Jazz* downloadable album.

otherwise entirely made up of instrumentals. Two of the instrumentals in each set were arrangements of popular tunes drawn from the repertory of Broadway, Hollywood, or Tin Pan Alley pop songs, and the remaining two were characteristic hot-swing numbers. So, in sum, in contrast to the band's post-1936 commercial recordings, which greatly emphasized ballads, there is roughly an equal split in the Trianon repertoire between vocals (of contrasting styles), popular tunes for dancing and swing numbers that show off hot-styled jazz.

Alongside these two sets of music, the LP also contains three numbers from the Friday 29 January broadcast. These are all titles that do not appear elsewhere in the discography of the Clouds of Joy, probably because they represent stock arrangements of popular tunes: 'I Never Slept a Wink' is a song by Andy Razaf and Nat Simon (like 'Christopher Columbus', it was published by Joe Davis) that is reinvented as a fairly unremarkable solo vehicle for Mary Lou Williams; 'Make Believe Ballroom', which Charlie Barnet recorded the previous year as a radio theme (alongside his version of 'Until the Real Thing Comes Along'), is rendered as a mid-tempo dancing number; and 'Sepia Jazz' is an uncharacteristically hurried hot-swing number (ca. 290 bpm) that, unlike the comparatively understated swing on the Decca records, shows that Kirk's band was capable in its live music of the more energetic style of swing that was ideally suited to Lindy Hop dancing.

A medley of popular tunes is the only number on the Jazz Society LP that was included from the Friday 5 February broadcast, and it is the only such medley that the band recorded in the later 1930s. In fact, it is such pop tunes, whether styled as a medley or as music for dancing or improvising, that dominates the Trianon Ballroom recordings. Nevertheless, unlike in the ballad records, there is still plenty of evidence of jazz within that output. A comparison of the Trianon version of 'Moten Swing' with the one recorded for Decca illustrates the restrictions that studio-based recording imposed on the Clouds of Joy, as well as the influence that the band's commercially successful recordings had on their subsequent live performances.

The Trianon version of 'Moten Swing' uses the same arrangement as was featured on the Decca recording of 2 March 1936, but the live track is considerably longer as it encompasses seven AABA choruses rather than just the four that are heard on the Decca record. The first chorus (0'00"–0'43") on the Trianon recording is notable for the way Mary Lou Williams's piano solo is more dissonant and harmonically experimental in the closing A section (0'32"–0'43"). The second chorus (0'43"–1'25"), which is not heard on the Decca recording, features the saxophone ensemble trading motifs with the brass in the A sections before a baritone-sax solo (John Williams) is heard in the B section (1'03"–1'14").

The third chorus (1'25"–2'07"), like the second one on the Decca recording, features Harrington's clarinet with a trombone (probably Ted Donnelly) taking over in the B section (1'45"–1'56"). The fourth chorus (2'07"–2'48") is given over entirely to Dick Wilson's tenor saxophone, as Paul King's trumpet (which featured in the B section of the third chorus in the 1936 recording) is given its own 32-bars in the fifth chorus (2'48"–3'29"). The same 'sotto voce' ensemble chorus (3'29"–4'09") as was heard on the Decca disc closes the Trianon version of 'Moten Swing', except that it is repeated in its entirety and at a louder volume (4'09'–4'50'), before we get the same dynamic-controlled coda (4'50'–4'56') that is tagged on to its end.

This scheme shows the sorts of compromises that the Clouds of Joy had to make in shortening such five-minute pieces to fit the three minutes or so of a side of a 10-inch 78 rpm disc. In general, it suggests that in the recording studio, ensemble choruses could be cut whereas solo choruses were more often telescoped together in order to feature the same number of soloists but without having to give each one a full chorus of their own. There was, of course, more room in live performance situations for a greater number of longer solos and the Trianon sets show that such live solos were sometimes more experimental, as in Williams's solo, but they can also appear to be derivative.

Jan Evensmo noted in his study of Wilson's playing that his solo in 'Moten Swing' is, in its first part, very similar to the version heard in the 1936 Decca recording. This is unusual of Wilson, because elsewhere in the Trianon recordings he shows his readiness to completely reconceive his solos. Evensmo notes, for instance, that his solo on 'Walkin' and Swingin'' (not on the Jazz Society release) differed markedly from either of the Decca takes of the track. This leads Evensmo to question, 'Lack of capability to improvise we know it is not. Maybe it is just a coincidence?' (Evensmo ca.1977: DW5)

Wilson's apparent derivativeness may not be a coincidence but simply attributable to a typical 'lick' he deployed in his soloing. As so often happens when a band becomes well known for popular recordings, it is also sign that the recorded identity of the Clouds of Joy was increasingly becoming a part of their live aesthetic. In his autobiography, Kirk explains how audiences at the live gigs increasingly requested to hear the band's music in the form that it was performed on their records. Furthermore, he reported that their audiences so expected the same solos that they could be bitterly disappointed when a recording master wore out and Decca was forced to issue a second pressing using an alternative take, which featured different solos (Kirk 1989: 72). So, as the band's recordings became better known, there was increased demand for them to be authentic to their recorded character and faithfully reproduce their recorded music when they played live, solos and all.

Kirk reports that when his band played for a cruise down the Mississippi, shortly after the release of 'Until the Real Thing Comes Along', they were met at the quay by a huge crowd (Kirk 1989: 86). As soon as they started playing the ballad they realized that it had become a hit because the audience on the boat immediate stopped dancing, crowded around the bandstand, and demanded a further six renditions. By adopting a shortened version of the song as their opening theme, as is heard on the Trianon recordings, the band could succinctly present the record for which they were best known and thereby signal musical familiarity for their audience before going on to play the rest of the music in their set. In a similar vein, when figures like Wilson reference a solo they had recorded they are as much 'calling' on an audience's recognition of their recorded musical identity: it is an interpellative 'strike', in Mowitts terms, that asserts their recorded character.

So, it seems that by 1937, the music heard on their commercial recordings was increasingly merging with and recolouring their live music. As Philip Auslander points out, this is typical of a more general dynamic of the effect of mediatization on liveness:

> The incursion of the mediatized into the live has followed a particular historical pattern. Initially, the mediatized form is modeled [sic] on the live form, but it eventually usurps the live form's position in the cultural economy. The live form then starts to replicate the mediatized form.[. . .] To the extent that live performances now emulate mediatized representations, they have become second-hand recreations of themselves as refracted through mediatisation. (Auslander 2008: 183)

In that respect, the blurring of the line between the live and recorded music of the Clouds of Joy afforded Kirk's band yet another level of Signfyin(g) mask-play. It meant that they could easily slip between expected and unanticipated styles with reference to their mediated musical-racial identity. In this way, they could both please and confound audiences' expectations of a black band and call upon them to identify with their particular brand of sweet-hot swing in their dancing or listening. In Mowitt's terms (see chapter 2), the popularity of their records meant that their hybrid musical style 'struck' their audience even before the band appeared in person. In live appearances, the expected musical-racial identity of the Clouds of Joy was reified through the familiar 'call' of their sweet-styled opening theme, but the range and character of their jazz thereafter would confound any expectations of racial authenticity: they could not be pigeonholed wholly as a sweet-commercial dance band or as a hot jazz one. In this sense, the playing with or between live and recorded musical identities was as much a subversive act that spoke of their racialized position as a black band operating within a racist culture.

As Andy Kirk recalled, the effect of 'live' radio broadcasts, as much as records, was that the Clouds of Joy reached audiences (especially in the South) that might otherwise have rejected them because, as he puts it, 'Since they came to know us only by radio, they didn't know whether we were white or black' (Kirk 1989: 82–83). This confounding of racial expectations through musical style was clearly striking, in Mowitt's sense of the word, and it was harnessed by Kirk to appeal across the racial line. It seems then that Kirk and his band hit upon a formula that worked by shocking audiences' racist-stylistic expectations through their hybrid jazz style. It made ever-increasing numbers of both white *and* black people into subjects of their music, moved to identify with their sweet *and* hot style of swing. In this way, the band envisioned a culture and society beyond their racist contemporary one that limited the freedoms and incomes of African American musicians, as much as the wider black populace, within specific categories of style and race.

BALLADS AND CONCERTOS: SWEET-WHITE COMMERCIALISM AND HOT-BLACK EXHIBITIONISM

The unprecedented sales of 'Until the Real Thing Comes Along' meant that sweet-styled ballads increasingly outnumbered the hot-jazz sides that were recorded by the Clouds of Joy during the later 1930s and early 1940s. These ballads most often featured Pha Terrell and they were sometimes contrasted by more upbeat, bluesy or novelty vocal recordings. These contrasting vocals featured Harry Mills (of the Mills Brothers quartet), Ben Thigpen (the band's drummer), or O'Neill Spencer (of John Kirkby's sextet), until June Richmond came on the scene in 1939. Henry Wells, a trombonist with the Clouds of Joy, recorded a couple of songs with the band in 1937 and 1938, and when Terrell left the Clouds of Joy, in the summer of 1940, Wells assumed full responsibility for performing the ballads.[7] Wells's continuation of Terrell's crooning vocal style meant that sweet-styled ballads predominated the Decca records for a five-year period between 1936 and 1941.[8]

Whether they were sung by Terrell or Wells, the ballads are generally in one of two forms that represent relatively common approaches to arranging such songs. The first form presents a complete chorus (generally in a 32-bar AABA form) for the band that prefigures a vocal one that follows it. The 'prefiguring' chorus introduces the whole of the song's melody, and although it sometimes features a little ornamentation (portamento, pitch bends, mordents, and so on) and background piano figurations, the tune is never obscured and those features do not constitute improvisation in the sense of a jazz solo. In the second form of ballad, the vocal chorus opens the arrangement, usually after a fairly cursory introduction from the band. This is then succeeded by an instrumental 'echo' of the vocal chorus from the band. This 'echo' chorus more often features improvisation because the melody is already familiar, as it has been heard in the vocal refrain, and because the vocalist most often re-enters towards the end of the chorus to restore familiarity by rounding off the song with the final phrase of the familiar melody.[9]

A survey of the 60 or so sweet-styled ballads that were recorded after 'Until the Real Thing Comes Along', suggests that these two forms are fairly equally deployed. Despite the room available for solos in the 'echo' chorus form, these vocals are hardly exemplars of jazz exhibitionism of the sort that is found in the swing instrumentals of the period (examined in

---

7 At that point, Wells had just returned from an unsuccessful period away from the band during which he'd tried to set up as a bandleader in his own right. He'd then worked as a sideman for Gene Krupa and Teddy Hill before returning to Kirk (Chilton 1985: 352).

8 The song '(Ev'rything Happened) When I Saw You' (68319-A) was the first of a small batch of ballads recorded by Wells between November 1940 and January 1941. A notable feature of the song is that, at the end of the number, Wells breaks into falsetto, in just the same way that Terrell had done in numerous earlier ballad recordings. In his next recording session, however, Wells opted not to use falsetto at the end of his two songs: 'If I Feel This Way Tomorrow' (68363-A) and 'Or Have I?' (68364-A) The first of these two songs still sounds as though it lies a little too high in Wells's voice for his comfort. This suggests that Wells was still recording Terrell's material, but thereafter exploited his own, rather different, vocal qualities rather than imitating Terrell's crooning.

9 Most of the ballads, precisely because of their slow tempi, usually contain just two AABA choruses plus an introduction and interlude (secondary introduction) of some sort. In this sense, they represent a simple form that was similar to that used by the Clouds of Joy for jitney dances in the late 1920s (see chapter 1).

chapter 2). Two of Pha Terrell's ballads that were recorded in 1937 will serve to illustrate the typical structures of these vocals and the limited scope that was available within them for hot-jazz features like improvisation.

'In My Wildest Dreams', recorded on 26 July 1937 (62447-A), is a ballad cast in the first of the forms that was just described. It opens with a short, riff-styled introduction (0'00"–0'09") that takes the form of short exchanges between brass and saxophone motifs. The instrumental AABA chorus (0'09"–1'29") is then opened by a muted and vibrato-laden trumpet melody that is backed by very quiet saxophone harmonies. As is common in such ballad arrangements, the soloist never quite plays a complete phrase of the melody in the A sections, but each melodic line is, instead, ended for him by the band—here the saxophones suddenly come to the fore to do this. The B section (0'47"–1'06") is given over to Dick Wilson's wonderfully languorous tenor saxophone, with soft brass and the other saxes shadowing him. Wilson's rich-toned and laid-back solo barely departs from the song's melody, save at the end, and it is thus more noticeable for its mellow style of performance than its musical inventiveness.

There is a quality of excess about the sweet-styled playing of the melody by both the trumpet (probably Paul King) and saxophone (Wilson) in this opening chorus. In Wilson's solo especially, the style is so sweet sounding in its vibrato and rhythmic lethargy that it could even be read as ironic in its overindulgent sweetness. Ironic exaggeration was, of course, a part of the long-standing performance conventions of blackface minstrelsy where, in the acts of black minstrels like Bert Williams, it could form a subtly double-voiced mode of Signifyin(g) critique in which serious racial points were made beneath its obvious comedy. From such a perspective, we might read such sweet-melodic solos as offering powerfully ironic comment on the apparently white-sounding commercialism of the ballad style of the band. In that respect, as a stylistically rooted commentary, such solos are actually all the more powerful for not departing far from the vocal melody: they speak more loudly about the artifice of white-commercial sweetness by Signifyin(g) upon it *only* by exaggerating such stylistic markers as vibrato, portamento, and rhythmic license.

In contrast to his melody playing, Wilson makes a more characteristically agile, liquid, and jazzy interjection in the return of the A section (1'06"–1'29"), which follows his rendition of the song's melody. This is otherwise an ensemble phrase that is capped off by a short clarinet figure which leads into a cadence and extends the section by two bars. Pha Terrell's vocal chorus (1'29"–2'50") then arrives, accompanied by Mary

Lou Williams's hushed piano figurations and some long-breathed ensemble harmonies from the saxophones. Between Terrell's phrases, the brass fill in with material that is sometimes muted and at other times not. Wilson's tenor very briefly appears for a final flourish in the two-bar tag that closes the song (2'44"–2'50"). This ending is otherwise rather uncharacteristic of the ballads for not featuring Terrell's trademark break into falsetto at its close.

A typical ballad of the contrasting form is 'What's Mine Is Yours' (62453-B), recorded the day after 'In My Wildest Dreams', on 27 July 1937. It opens with a four-bar introduction (0'00"–0'11") for the full band before Pha Terrell enters with his AABA-structured vocal chorus (0'11"–1'35"). After Terrell's characteristic but straightforward vocal chorus, there is a four-bar interlude (1'35"–1'46") that serves to shift the key and as a fresh introduction for the following 'echo' chorus (1'46"–3'12") for the band. In this chorus, the trombones lead the saxophones in the melody in the first A section (1'46"–2'06"), before the trumpets join in and the phrase culminates in a two-bar clarinet break for John Harrington. Wilson, again, takes a solo for the first four bars of the second A section (2'06"–2'27") and the full band rounds off Wilson's short solo by returning to the melody of the song. The B section (2'27"–2'49") features a short piano solo for Williams, which, like in Wilson's solo phrase, is initially quite pedestrian before it becomes increasingly filled with nimbler improvisation. The full ensemble, once again, rounds off Williams's solo phrase before Terrell re-enters to sing the final A section (2'49"–3'12"). He closes this final phrase of the song by breaking into his idiosyncratic falsetto (3'05"–3'12") for the titular lyric.

If such short instrumental solos mark a small measure of hot-jazz blackness within what was perceived as the wholly sweet-white style of the ballads, then the handling of the standard AABA form in the band arrangement does so even more. The call-and-response character of ensemble and solo interactions (e.g., the band finishing soloists' phrases) and the nature of the accompaniment riffs and short interjections from the band (e.g., syncopated stabs and solo breaks) all point towards an underlying hot-swing sensibility that colours the song, albeit subtly, beneath any apparent whiteness in the way the vocal is crooned by Terrell. If this reading is reasonable, in their desire to contain the black band within racist notions of the expected style of black jazz, critics were, perhaps, too quick to write off the sweet ballads for their seemingly inauthentic, derivative, and jazz-threatening whiteness when there are still stereotypically black-sounding characteristics that undermine that essentialist understanding.

Even behind the mask of sweetness in the ballads, then, there is some room for the musicians to express themselves and thereby challenge the apparent whiteness of the popular-song style. However, such room is strictly limited and one can readily imagine the frustrations of great soloists like Wilson and Williams at having to make do with such meagre expressive opportunities in the face of recording so many sweet-styled ballads. In fact, Williams cited being bored in her playing with the band in that period as a major factor in her decision to leave the Clouds of Joy.[10] Within that context, the comparatively fewer instrumentals recordings represented precious opportunities for the soloist band members to express everything else beyond the melodiousness and saccharine romantic emotions of the ballads.

Probably because of the need to satisfy the band's leading soloists in the face of so many solo-limiting ballads, a significant development in 1938 was the introduction of what might be termed 'concerto' numbers. These were numbers that featured just a single soloist throughout the number rather than, as in 'Lotta Sax Appeal' (60854-A), other soloists sharing in the limelight. The first of such 'concerto' numbers was 'Twinklin'' (63256-A), a piano feature by and for Mary Lou Williams, which the band recorded on 8 February 1938. It was followed up in March 1939 by another Williams vehicle, co-composed with Andy Kirk, entitled 'Close to Five' (65190-A). This was recorded in the same Decca session as 'Floyd's Guitar Blues' (65191-A), which exploited the novelty of Floyd Smith's electric slide-guitar playing. These pieces paved the way for such later vehicles as Ken Kersey's 'Boogie Woogie Cocktail' (71050-A) and Howard McGhee's 'McGhee Special' (71053-A).

These 'concertos' have already received quite a lot of critical attention, precisely because they represent substantial vehicles for the leading soloists in Kirk's band and thus better display the band's 'true' (hot-black) jazz for critics. Gunther Schuller in his assessment is critical of 'Floyd's Guitar Blues' for what he sees as its exploiting of voguish novelty over real jazz. He writes,

> *Floyd's Guitar Blues* was a strong seller, as much for its novelty of featuring the then very new 'electric' guitar as for its intrinsic musical

---

10 Williams recalled, 'At this time I was feeling dragged so far as Kirk's outfit went. I could not play or write my best for thinking about my share of the loot, and my sacrifices before we made a hit. All my piano solos I turned over to [our guitarist] Floyd [Smith]. I had gotten sick of playing the same ones long ago. Our repertoire consisted of recorded hits, and the solos had to be exactly like those on the records' (Williams, as cited in Gottlieb 1997: 109).

values. For Smith's opus is rather shallow musically, content to explore the newly-won *technical* capacities of the instrument: its ability to sustain notes in lengthy durations, thereby also enabling the greater use of glissandos—whose wailing and moaning effect Smith overdoes considerably—and, above all, it dramatically increased dynamic levels. With a sometimes unpleasingly piercing sound, Smith's guitar sounds like a full band, one reason the brass and reeds may have been relegated to the introduction and coda of the piece. (Schuller 1989: 356–358)

On the other hand, Schuller was full of praise for 'Boogie-Woogie Cocktail', which he described as 'quite perfect' (Schuller 1989: 360). He wrote in highly gendered terms:

Whereas Mary Lou Williams had taken the boogie-woogie, with its murky and somber primitive visions, and given it a more cheerful lacy legato touch, Kersey took the same idiom, tightened its variation structure, energized its rhythms, stylized it and turned it into both a pianistic tour de force and an excellent dance number. It was boogie-woogie cleaned up a bit, efficient, and quite perfect—a miniature boogie-woogie concerto. (Schuller 1989: 360)

Schuller has even more praise for 'McGhee Special' to which he devotes several pages of analysis (Schuller 1989: 360–367). That piece comes from a period in the early 1940s, which saw the wartime drafting of several members of Kirk's band to serve in the armed forces. This meant that a younger generation of musicians entered the Clouds of Joy and brought with them some of the new modernistic approach to jazz that would later become known as bebop. The trumpeter Howard McGhee was one of these figures, and Schuller describes him as 'a leading transitional figure in the incoming bop movement' and his composition as 'harmonically/melodically advanced beyond the norm of the day' (Schuller 1989: 360–361).

As a classically trained musician with European modernist inclinations, it is not surprising that Schuller's criticism prizes technical innovation. He thus particularly admires the originality of the chord changes in 'McGhee Special' and the way the piece, as an original composition, contrasted the tendency of bebop players to rely on 'standards' (established songs) as a basis for improvisation. Schuller is especially taken with McGhee's employment of 'a secondary tonic on the flattened third degree (A-flat) of the key (F major)' in the bridge section (Schuller 1989: 361). For Schuller, this key relationship presages the more chromatic harmonic structures that were to come in bebop. It is such features that mark 'McGhee Special' out for Schuller as a pre-bop masterpiece.

'McGhee Special' is, as Schuller analyses, a marvellously effective vehicle for McGhee's trumpet playing. Despite the modernistic harmonic adventurousness in the piece, a lot of the excitement of the music actually comes from the way that McGhee simply shifts the key up by a semitone or half step for each of his last two trumpet phrases (at 2'22" and 2'31", respectively). If McGhee was a musical innovator, he was as much one that understood how to be theatrical and dramatic within a jazz idiom.

It is, of course, not just the shifts in key that give the piece a sense of drama but also the bright tone, rhythmical drive, and well-calculated momentum of McGhee's soloing. At first McGhee tends to play in what might be termed 'dynamic waves', which involve reaching a peak in pitch and volume towards the start of a phrase that energizes the rest of it. Such peaks of energy become more pronounced and frequent as the arrangement progresses and the ascending half-step shifts in key only add to the increasingly climactic sense of McGhee's high-wire trumpet act as the arrangement comes to a close.

So, by the early 1940s we begin to see the ballads, with their apparent sweet-white style, interspersed with 'concerto' numbers, like 'McGhee Special', which represent exemplars of black-jazz exhibitionism within the recordings of Kirk's band. The contrast between the two, however, is not quite so cut-and-dried as it may seem: in the sweet ballads, there is often at least a small measure of hot jazz character, and in the hot-jazz 'concertos', there is often a populist theatricality over and above any musical modernism. As much as critics, like Schuller, want to disavow the sweet ballads and venerate hot-jazz vehicles like 'McGhee Special', the recordings of the Clouds of Joy show in their music and performance that they resist such categorizations and assessments in the way they manipulate and Signify on jazz styles.

BACK TO BLACK: JUNE RICHMOND, GOSPEL QUARTETS, AND RHYTHM NUMBERS

It was not just in the instrumental numbers that 'theatrical' innovations took place during the 1940s. When Henry Wells left the band in 1941, sweet ballads of the type that had been recorded in such quantity by Kirk's band were suddenly no longer the mainstay of its output. The reason for this was not only changing tastes and expectations of recorded music but also a change of emphasis that had come with the addition of June Richmond to the Clouds of Joy in 1939. The songs she recorded with the band were much more stereotypically black sounding on account of their decidedly rhythmical or else bluesy character. Furthermore, Richmond's appearance was highly stereotypical of a classic type of black female jazz singer: she was comedic, large, and playful, or else powerful, poignant, and pensive.

Richmond can be understood to have ushered in another new stylistic phase in the recordings of Andy Kirk and his Clouds of Joy. If the first of these phases was the 'stomping-jazz' one of 1929–1931, and the second the 'sweet-ballad' phase of 1936–1941, then the third and final phase, which extends until 1949, might perhaps be called the 'proto-rhythm 'n' blues' phase. Likewise, if the first phase is characterized by a certain amount of stylistic 'blacking up' in hot jazz for recording and the second by a sort of 'whiting up' of that style with the sweet ballads, then the third phase might be conceived as a return to a stereotypical black aesthetic that embraced a new racialized dance-music sensibility mixed together with the character of the blues. That sort of aesthetic is embodied in Richmond's recorded performances.

Richmond made her first recording with the Clouds of Joy on 23 March 1939. She came to Kirk's band on the back of a short spell working with Cab Calloway, during which she recorded a couple of sides for Victor: 'Deep in a Dream' (Vocalion 4511) and 'Angels With Dirty Faces' (Vocalion 4498). She had made far more records in her previous job, singing with Jimmy Dorsey's band. Her appearance in early 1938 with Dorsey's orchestra marked her out as one of the first black singers to front a white band. According to Dave Oliphant, Richmond arrived to sing for Dorsey at about the same time that Artie Shaw contracted Billie Holiday (Oliphant 2002: 120). However, these two black singers could not have been more different interpreters of popular songs, even if they did share a certain affinity with the pathos of the blues.

Holiday was a much slighter figure whose voice was lighter in tone but still highly expressive. As James Lincoln Collier summarized, '[it] carried a wounded poignancy which was part of her attraction' (Collier 1994: 533). Richmond, on the other hand, was a decidedly rotund figure with a big, sonorous vocal presence, and she could bring a comedic theatricality to even the most serious of songs. In that regard, Howard Rye assessed Richmond as, 'a powerful and effective blues shouter', but suggested that 'her approach to popular songs often relied on the techniques of cabaret singing rather than of jazz' (Rye 2015). The comic theatre of what Rye calls her ' "cabaret" style' helps explain why she was considered a suitable pairing for the highly theatrical antics of Cab Calloway in the period before she worked for Kirk.

In his fascinating book exploring cover versions of Jerome Kern's ubiquitous 'black' song 'Ol' Man River', Todd Decker includes a review of a 1946 performance by Richmond that illuminates her comedic approach to popular-song interpretation. The review describes her as a tastefully dressed 'hefty comic' and praises her for 'bringing some good yocks as well as showing nifty pipes' to her performance, which the reviewer observed, 'depends heavily on little bits of business, especially facial expressions, to get across' (cited in Decker 2015: 104). Decker stresses the way that this review at once expresses Richmond's artistry as a singer and the comedy that extended from her stature and facial expressions. Thus, through the agency of her big-black feminine physicality and comedic mask, she was able to transform even the most serious material into fun entertainment and comedic comment.

Richmond reflected such transformative intentions in the new lyrics that she put to the verse section of 'Ol' Man River' when she recorded it for the *Jubilee* show with the Count Basie Orchestra for the Armed Forces Radio Service in June 1945:

Everyone likes to sing 'Ol' Man River'
But I would like to get in the groove.
Everyone wants to be so dramatic
But here's how I'd like to sing that song for you.

Decker describes the remainder of Richmond's performance on the *Jubilee* recording as follows:

Having set the terms, she launches into a very fast chorus: 162 bpm. The next chorus shifts tempo several times: cooling down to make room for some scat vocalizing; going into a deliberate pace for the big finish, which is drawn out—'routined' in the show biz sense—for maximum impact. Indeed, Richmond ends with a long high G-sharp. The audience of GI's loves it. (Decker 2015: 104)

The sort of bodily rooted and comedic-theatrical performance that Decker references is evident in a more muted form in a series of three short films that Richmond made with Roy Milton and his band in 1944. These films each feature a track that Richmond had previously recorded with the Clouds of Joy, so they are the nearest that we can get to witnessing the way in which she performed with Kirk's band. Although accompanied by a smaller band, Richmond's vocals and the structures of the songs on the films are very close to the versions that were recorded by the Kirk's band in 1941 and 1942. So, observing her physical actions on the films is especially instructive for understanding her particular mode of highly theatrical performance in her fronting of the Clouds of Joy.

In 'Forty-Seventh Street Jive' (RCM 2015a [1944]), Richmond stands as an imposing figure before the band. She coyly engages in nonsense-dialogue with the bass player, while swinging her shoulders along with the boogie-woogie styled groove of the introduction. The first vocal chorus is accompanied by the odd knowing glance and tilt of the head from June, and then she breaks into a 'step-and-clap' sort of a dance as the band takes the next chorus. A few more lines of soulful singing follow. Richmond then breaks into scat and offers small circular motions with her open right hand as she shifts her weight from one foot to the other in a swaying sort of dance to the beat of the music. She stops this, tenses her shoulders, and fixes us with her gaze as she indulges in the most intense parts of her scatting, as if to invite us in on her evident enjoyment of extemporizing. She continues to shift between her feet until near the end of the song, when her stasis underlines her 'big finish'. These small but significant movements enliven her full-voiced performance no end and highlight that a physicalized blackness (the stylized small movements of a large black body) underpins her vocal performance.

In 'Hey Lawdy Mama' (RCM 2015b [1944]), the song that secured the No. 4 spot for Kirk and his band in *Billboard*'s Harlem Hit Parade chart in April 1943, Richmond sings the song with ever-increasing amounts of theatrical physicality. In particular, she responds to Milton's drum solo by dipping to one side with each of his repeated snare strokes and then she purses her lips in evident self-satisfaction. In the scat-singing part of the following chorus, she again purses her lips, this time as if blowing us a kiss, but otherwise opens her eyes wide and playfully wiggles her head, and then, as if she cannot hold it back any more, she bursts into full-blown dance after her exclamation of, 'Papa, meet me in the bottom!' Her surprisingly graceful and unexpected energy in this dance conveys a sense of embodied fun that comes from sending up the hotness (blackness) of the music. Milton's pianist, Camille Howard, is evidently greatly amused by Richmond's antics at this point.

By contrast in 'Ride On, Ride On' (RCM 2015c [1944]), a famous Billie Holiday number, Richmond is filmed seated at a table. She sings this slow-tempo, intense, and powerfully bluesy song without any hint of playful theatricality. Instead, she uses a full-bodied tone, faces straight to camera, and there is a particular seriousness and poignancy in her gaze that is not evident in the other films. This is highly appropriate to the subject matter of the song, which, through the agency of the figure of a disembodied voice (referenced in the lyrics), is essentially a plea to 'ride on' with persistence and solidarity to a better place, 'Where the livin' is fine'. The racial politics of this metaphor are clearly not a laughing matter and the song shows that Richmond knew when to send up a number and when it would prove a step too far to do so. In other words, she was politically astute enough to know when to emphasize an apparently sincere or authentic blackness and when to undermine expectations of a 'race' number by sending it up.

In Richmond's performance, then, we can identify three styles: the comedic sending up of material in a theatrical manner that was somewhat similar to Cab Calloway's minstrel-like mask-play, a sense of bodily-rooted fun stemming from dance-orientated showmanship and the deeply felt and poignantly meaningful expression of a bluesy authenticity that was more common in the singing of the likes of Billie Holiday. These three styles effectively map onto the musical styles that were offered by the Clouds of Joy, such that Richmond maintained their dance-orientated swing and novelty-entertainment aesthetics whilst also bringing a distinctly authentic blackness back to their vocals—she effectively transformed the ballads into the blues. At first, Richmond was recorded alongside Terrell, but with his departure and the subsequent loss of Wells to military service, the apparent whiteness signified by the ballads was entirely replaced by Richmond's swinging black-song sensibility. Furthermore, there is a sense in which her form of bodily rooted humour, literally emphasizing her mask, marked a return to a minstrel-like black style of representation for the Clouds of Joy.

The apparent blackness that Richmond brought back to the band on their records put them firmly back in the specialist race-records market in the early forties, even if it wasn't called that by then. This is underlined by the band's recording of 'Take It and Git' (71240-A), made on 29 July 1942. On 24 October 1942, that became the first No. 1 in the Harlem Hit Parade, the first of *Billboard*'s race record listings, which eventually became their famed R & B chart (Whitburn 2006: 322).[11] If, as a result of their

---

11 The Harlem Hit Parade was compiled from sales reports obtained from six record stores (five in Harlem), and its hits were aired on New York's WHOM radio station every Thursday night (Ennis 2006: 192).

ballad recordings, the Clouds of Joy were not instantly recognizable as a black band on their earlier Decca records, they certainly were after they had this chart success with Richmond. In other words, Richmond's songs redefined them as popular black musicians within the race market. This did not mean, though, that there was not room within that categorization for some subversive, if minstrel-like, renegotiation of the band's musical-racial identity through Signifyin(g) mask-play.

The 1942 recording of 'Take It and Git' (71240-A) opens with Kirk's vernacular call of, 'Boys, take it and git!'. This is immediately followed by a three-bar response from the band that forms the introduction to the number (0'00"–0'06"). The first 12-bar chorus (0'06"–0'24") simply alternates the bandsmen chanting of 'Take It and Git' with two-bar statements from the band. Floyd Smith next responds to their call with 'Solid, man, I got it!' and goes into his electric guitar solo (0'24"–0'41"). The pattern after that is to pair a chorus of the chanting with a responding solo one that is prefigured by solo breaks within the chanting chorus. Thus, pianist Ken Kersey is heard to riff between the chanted statements in the third chorus (0'41"–0'59") before his shout of, 'Okay, I got it!' signals his proper solo chorus that follows it (0'59"–1'17").

Similarly, the trombone of Ted Donnelly is heard between the chants on the fifth chorus (1'17"–1'34") before his, 'Boy, I got it!' signals his following solo chorus (1'34"–1'53"). Kersey returns for the next pair of choruses (1'53"–2'29") before Kirk's shout, 'Take it and git now!', signals for a final pair of swinging choruses for the full band (2'29"–3'03"). This is led by the saxophones (topped by a clarinet) and leads to brass riffs, which are interspersed with sax ensemble motifs. Kirk's voice eventually returns with 'Boys, you got it and gone!' and this is the cue for a big finish of a coda (3'03"–3'13"), which, in a rather witty dynamic and textural contrast, closes with an unanticipated solo chord from Kersey's piano.

The black-vernacular call-and-response nature of the number is great fun and the interplay of voices, solos, and ensemble gives it a sense that we are listening to a community of vibrant individuals at play and we want in on their fun. This, in an instrumental form, is similar to the impression left by the fun vocal numbers performed by Richmond and, indeed, the reverse side of 'Take It and Git' on the original record (Decca 4366) featured her in 'Hip Hip Hooray' (71241-A), a piece of swing-styled flag-waving wartime propaganda, complete with bugle-call motifs, references to 'star-spangled skies', and calls to 'let freedom reign'. If ever there was a hot-swing record that was intended to convey a sense of an all-united American community, then this one was surely it. Thus, the number is typical of a broader black political strategy: to confound racism by appealing to the need for a cross-racial communal war effort.

The wartime was a difficult period for recording artists because of a dispute between the American Federation of Musicians and record companies. The dispute was over the fairness of royalties, and it meant that the Federation's head, James Petrillo, imposed a ban on recording. This lead to deadlock, and the effect of the recording ban was that there were precious few Decca recording sessions for the Clouds of Joy between July 1942 and November 1945. The session held in New York City on 3 December 1943 yielded just two sides that featured typical Richmond numbers, 'Fare Thee Honey Fare Thee Well' (71536) and 'Baby Don't You Tell Me No Lie' (71537).[12] When the band next appeared in Decca's studios on 27 November 1945 they had lost Richmond, who had decided to go it alone as a solo act in Hollywood and subsequently ended up in Europe. Nevertheless, Kirk's band kept up a decidedly black-popular aesthetic by recording with the male gospel quartet, the Jubalaires.

During the immediate postwar period, black vocal-harmony groups like the Jubalaires increasingly performed and recorded arrangements of show tunes and romantic ballads alongside a repertoire of gospel hymns and work songs. However, Stuart L. Goosman has suggested that this should not be taken as any indication that they were simply assimilating into the white 'mainstream' of popular culture in performing such material (Goosman 2005: 84). Instead, influential and long-standing African American traditions of choral-harmony music making, together with analysis of the practices and understandings of postwar black vocal-harmony performers, suggest that they, as much as the Clouds of Joy, always maintained a vital black difference in their treatment of such white-mainstream materials. Furthermore, this difference shows that they were actively developing the notion of black aesthetics relative to that of the mainstream of popular culture.

The essential black difference in the aesthetic of black gospel quartets was and is still often overlooked because of tendencies to stereotype black performers within essentialist notions of musical genre and authenticity. Thus, black race-record (or R & B) performers were typically

---

12 It seems the instrumentals 'Shorty Boo' (71535) and 'Hippy-Dippy' (72646) may also have come from this period, but they were released only some years later in Japan on an LP (MCA 3151). This overseas release was, perhaps, an indication that the recordings were not issued in the US because of the recording ban: 'pop' vocals most often escaped censure by the Federation (union) but such jazz instrumentals would not have done so.

not expected to sound too much like mainstream 'pop' acts by white producers and audiences for fear of them seeming to cross a racial line that such 'race' genres were intended to hold. When performers did appear to cross that line, as when the Clouds of Joy recorded their sweet ballads with Pha Terrell, or when black vocal quartets recorded pop numbers in a seemingly white 'crooning' style, there was, as Goosman puts it, 'a palpable tension between stereotyped expectations and black performers who moved beyond that in performance' (Goosman 2005: 84).

Such a tension meant that black musicians, and especially vocalists, were positioned in a performed and critical negotiation between expectations of black authenticity and white aesthetic values that governed the mainstream of popular music taste. Goosman argues:

> Vocal groups maintained cultural continuity with pre-existing musical forms while balancing them with emerging post-war sensibilities. A social aspect to this was that in the neighborhood, harmony singing was more than just something to do, it was also a manner of doing something that reflected deep black American values. Group harmony was structure (underlying principles or organization) and style (manner of expression), both musically and socially. (Goosman 2005: 85)

Goosman further argues that because of the apparent isomorphism between musical practices and society, the way vocal harmony groups handle the AABA song form is not simply a matter of musical style but also a form of social discourse. Thus vocal quartets like the Jubalaires tend to embed such discernible black practices as call-and-response patterns within the standard AABA pop song but not, Goosman believes, such that 'one takes precedence over the other'. Instead, 'they are enmeshed, cooperative modes' (Goosman 1997: 85–86). Furthermore, the division of the melody into solos with ensemble backing (termed 'basing' or 'backgrounding' by black harmony singers) and more equally balanced close-harmony singing ('blending' but with the individual voices still distinguishable) points towards performance that is as much about social tensions established between individuality and community as about musical ones of authenticity and mainstream aesthetics.

Goosman explains how this works in terms of 'basing' as follows:

> Basing grounds a song, establishes a two-part organization, and maintains antiphonal and polyphonic relationships. This arrangement

during performance establishes a codependency between lead and background voices and between individual and group. Within the structure of a 32-bar AABA song form, performers articulate a vernacular sensibility through basing (which is essentially an openended, circular structure). Any contradictions (doubleness) inherent in using basing, for example in a mainstream-type Tin Pan Alley song form, are resolved in the performance itself (as would be *crooning* the blues). Any contradictions between imposed categories (what double consciousness really is supposed to be), such as 'pop' and 'rhythm and blues', are resolved in performance. (Goosman 1997: 87)

The way voices blend in the close-harmony singing of black vocal groups comes into this. 'Blend' meant (and means) something rather different in African American harmony singing than it does in European-derived choral practices. In black American harmony singing culture, the aim is not to erase all individuality in the pursuit of a seamless whole 'community' of sound but to acknowledge that individual differences are inherent in any such community. Goosman proposes the term 'heterogeneous blend' as more appropriate one for this decidedly African American understanding precisely because individual and community identities are implied in the sonic blend of black harmony singing. From that perspective, the effect of such singing is to instantaneously conjure a sonic notion of a society that is invigorated by its internal differences. Black harmony singing groups thus tend to 'feel' a good blend, rather than to simply listen for it, and that involves perceiving the invigorating energy that stems from the coming together of the differences within the group.

The heterogeneity in and of blend is a decidedly black American conception, and as Goosman puts it, 'Placed in the context of postwar black communities and the history of black harmony groups, blend as a social and musical process, as a sonic model for behaviour, makes it a [black] vernacular sensibility' (Goosman 1997: 90). When put together with the social implications of the technique of 'basing', singing a distinctive ostinato pattern behind a lead vocal, this means the following:

Basing and blending go beyond musical attributes. Both exemplify a social ideal that merges subjectivities and creates the kind of *communitas* or 'groove' that Steven Feld described as a 'feeling of participation' and a 'comfortable place to be'—a social groove both in and out of performance, a sonic locale. Singers could also use blend to reconcile difference and similarly in actual singing, in grouping, in repertoire, and in social identity. A true understanding of this requires that we acknowledge the acceptance of difference as its resolution. The communal cohesion embedded in group harmony was a process of social blending. Blending was an aesthetic notion agreed upon by singers, even if it embodied the contradiction implied in heterogeneous blend. (Goosman 1997: 90–91)

The Jubalaires carry connotations of the long-standing black gospel-harmony tradition in their name for it is a direct reference to the 'Jubilee' tradition of gospel-quartet singing. However, their name also carries connotations of secular ballads ('airs'), and a sort of Anglo-French sophistication and race pride is implied in its archaism. In that regard, the 'e' in their title was, no doubt, intended to show the distance of their urban-cabaret performance from that of poor, rural blacks of the South that are implicated in the notion of Jubilee-style harmony singing. Furthermore, it shows a link back to New Orleans and the vibrant culture that spawned jazz.

When the group was founded in the early 1930s in Jacksonville, Florida, they were called the Royal Harmony Singers (Nations 2004: 2). The change in name came about only following their move to New York and at the behest of their new manager, Paul Kapp (the brother of Jack Kapp), who also encouraged them to record more secular fare for Decca (Nations 2004: 4). Thus the Jubalaires, as much as the Clouds of Joy, were involved in complex racial-identity negotiations with leading white figures in the racist record industry. Like the Clouds of Joy, they were not entirely helpless in these negotiations but could manipulate their situation through their stylistic treatment of repertoire in performance and, especially, on records.

The first track that the Jubalaires recorded with the Clouds of Joy, on 27 November 1945, was a fairly typical example of music that was steeped in the Jubilee tradition of harmony singing because it was a pseudo-gospel number entitled 'Get Together With the Lord' (73161). The song was, in fact, written by the white songwriting team of Moe Jaffe and Bickley 'Bix' Reichner, and based on the chord changes of 'When the Saints Go Marching In'. So, for all its apparent black roots, it was actually nearer a jazzy pop song than a traditional gospel one.[13] Nevertheless,

---

13   Jaffe and Reichner may well have known the Jubalaires because the quartet had been resident in Philadelphia before moving to New York. They were employed to sing for sightseers visiting the naval dockyard. Moe Jaffe had a band made famous by broadcasts from the Benjamin Franklin Hotel in Philadelphia. Bickley 'Bix' Reichner was a crime reporter for the *Evening Bulletin* and wrote lyrics for Broadway in his spare time.

the treatment of the song by the Jubalaires is straight out of the Jubilee tradition, albeit in a mediated popular-music form, and it is complemented their by backing from the Clouds of Joy.

After an eight-bar introduction (0'00"–0'08") for the band, the first four 16-bar choruses are the sole preserve of the Jubalaires, save for a few short brassy interjections and instrumental fills. The choruses are each in an AABA form that is made up of 4-bar subphrases. The first chorus (0'08"–0'29") features the Jubalaires in close harmony, and this continues in the second chorus (0'29"–0'48"), but with added little breaks for the bass singer, George McFadden, and then a longer one for the baritone, Ted Brooks. The third chorus (0'48"–1'07") is entirely a baritone solo with percussive vocal backing, whereas the fourth chorus (1'07"–1'25") mirrors the second one. The band takes over for the fifth chorus (1'25"–1'45") before the solo chorus returns with its call-and-response character (1'45"–2'04"). The seventh (2'04"–2'23") and final choruses again mirror the second one with its brief solo breaks. The final chorus (2'23"–2'48") has additional backing from the band, initially just the saxophones but later the brass join in too, and it is extended by means of a coda (2'37"–2'48"). That coda allows for a big finish, with the band coming to the fore at last. In all of this, there is plenty of 'blending' and 'basing' that maintains the black-vernacular quality of the music in the face of its otherwise upbeat and mainstream popular style.

On the reverse of this pseudo-gospel track was quite a different number entitled 'I Know' (73162). This proved to be another hit for the Clouds of Joy, reaching No. 2 in *Billboard*'s race-music chart on 4 March 1946 (Whitburn 2006: 322). Like 'Get Together With the Lord', 'I Know' (73162) represents a decidedly black popular song in the standard AABA form but it is a much more secular and bluesy number. It was written by two of the Jubalaires, Theodore 'Ted' Brooks and John Jennings, and The number is essentially a solo for Orville Brooks, who had only just left the Golden Gate Quartet to become lead tenor in the Jubalaires (Nations 2004: 5). Behind Brooks's solo, the rest of the Jubalaires are restricted to 'basing' in hummed harmonies, except in the short passage of sung homophony that rounds off each phrase.

The band is even more limited in its contributions to 'I Know' than it was in 'Get Together With the Lord'. There is a short introduction (0'00"–0'16") and thereafter only the rhythm section is audible (notably Hank Jones's piano riffs) behind the vocal chorus (0'16"–1'58") until a reedy eight-bar saxophone solo (1'58"–2'21"), most probably featuring Jimmy Forrest, that is backed by hat- or plunger-muted brass follows a short brassy cadence. Jones's piano backing is replaced by Floyd Smith's guitar riffs with the return of the Jubalaires vocals (humming beneath Brooks) in the next phrase (2'21"–2'48"), which is simply a reprise of the B section. The final A section (2'48"–3'16") has a little more of a subtle accompaniment from the Clouds of Joy (faint saxophone lines), but the band only really comes to the fore for the final chord. In other words, individuality plays a much greater part in this mainstream pop song in terms of the vocal solo, but there is still a palpable sense of a supportive, black band/community behind this. However, this is not the sort of ebullient and entertaining community heard in 'Take It and Git', and this might well account for its lower chart position.

A couple of months after their first Jubalaires record, Kirk tried to reincarnate his success with June Richmond in records featuring vocalists Beverley White, Bea Booze, and Billy Daniels, which were released in Decca's 'Personality Series' of records, but none of these had the impact of 'Take It and Git' or 'Hey Lawdy Mama'. Another soulful number recorded with the Jubalaires, 'I Don't Know What I'd Do Without You' (73590), followed on the heels of 'I Know' and secured a No. 5 position in the Harlem Hit Parade chart of 9 November 1946. However, the band could not repeat such successes with their subsequent recordings with a different quartet, The Four Knights. Those records were made in December 1946, alongside some songs recorded with Joe Williams. That set of recordings ultimately spelled the end of a long period of releases on Decca records for Kirk and his band.

JIVE TALKING AND LOUD SWINGING BLACKNESS: AFRS BROADCAST RECORDINGS AND KILLER DILLER

One might think from the Decca records of the 1943–1949 period that the recordings of the Clouds of Joy were almost exclusively vocals in which the band had essentially an accompanying role that involved little jazz. For that reason, the later 1940s is most often represented by critics as a period of profound decline for the Clouds of Joy that led to its eventual disbanding. However, when one considers the recordings of broadcasts that Kirk's band made during the 1940s for the *Victory Parade of Spotlight Bands* and the Armed Forces Radio Service (AFRS), a very different picture emerges: we hear a powerful big band perform vibrant arrangements of hard swinging jazz that is sometimes highly modernistic in it style and which features some fine musicians in more extensive solo opportunities.

The Victory Parade of Spotlight Bands was a 25-minute radio show, sponsored by Coca-Cola, with a wartime morale-raising agenda. It was aired six nights a week across RCA's Blue Network, which later became the American Broadcasting Company (ABC). The programme was aimed at a civilian audience as well as at military personnel. Each show featured a different band (voted for by the civilian audience) and each was recorded before a live audience at a different military establishment (determined by a poll of servicemen). In March 1943, the AFRS began recording the shows and then editing them down to 15-minutes (expunging all advertising) for dubbing to 16-inch 'transcription' discs for distribution across their network of military bases in the United States and overseas. Andy Kirk and his Clouds of Joy made seven programmes for the *Spotlight Bands* series between February 1943 and February 1945 and some of the recordings that came from them have since been released.[14]

The *Spotlight Bands* show that was broadcast on 29 June 1943 from a naval base in Portsmouth, Virginia, featured Kirk's band in 'Wednesday Night Hop', which Decca had issued in 1937, and in 'Ridin' Along', 'Wake Up', and 'Back Home in Indiana', which the band never recorded commercially. These hot-swing tunes were heard alongside two vocals featuring June Richmond, 'We Mustn't Say Goodbye' and 'Liza', which were also not recorded commercially by Kirk's band. So this demonstrates that a different range and balance of music was performed by the Clouds of Joy for their wartime broadcasts that was not of the sort that they recorded for Decca. The reason for this difference had to do with the racial segregation that persisted within the US military that was somewhat hidden within the 'we're all in this together' tone of these wartime shows. Although the *Spotlight Bands* series aimed to portray a racially integrated reflection of the war effort, the truth was often very different on the ground where the broadcasts were made. Kirk reported the following regarding their Portsmouth, Virginia, broadcast:

> We did a segregated show because it was the thought of the officer-in-charge to have two shows, one for Blacks and one for Whites, so they wouldn't sit together. The black cook there said to me, 'Don't feel bad, Andy, but none of us will be there. The officer thinks this is a social gathering, he forgets we are at war.' (Kirk 1989: 108)

14 Some of the most readily available LP and CD releases of music from the *Spotlight Bands* broadcasts do not give enough discographical information to enable one to trace the recordings back to a specific broadcast. For example, Dave Dexter's otherwise excellent-quality LP, *The Uncollected Andy Kirk*, gives no discographical information beyond a general note about the origins of the tracks on the radio and a catch-all date of 1944.

Within this segregated world of the military, black bands like Kirk's were recruited to appeal to the African American troops, and thus their repertoire was tailored to a hot-swing aesthetic rather than the popular sweet vocals that was established on their Decca records. In this sense, Kirk's band was once again required to black up its musical style. However, the reported comments of the cook reflect the new confidence that the war had brought to African Americans, who increasingly felt their engagement in a conflict to end racial oppression in Europe must mean the end of segregation and racism at home. Kirk reports that after their Portsmouth show, the black servicemen in the audience 'let the officer-in-charge know what they thought of his [segregating] policies by cutting up the tires on his car' (Kirk 1989: 108). The confidence behind such direct action of this sort can be read in the style of Kirk's music, which is that much bolder and 'in your face' in its hot-swing style than it had been in the 1930s.

Even outside of military society, Kirk witnessed black and white people challenging segregation in public spaces, like in the dining cars on trains. Kirk reflected on that as follows:

> This kind of confrontation would never have happened before the war. It showed a changing attitude on the part of Blacks. In fact, you could see a different attitude developing in both Blacks and Whites. They were beginning to ask questions about the whole Jim Crow situation. We had incident after incident to point that up. (Kirk 1989: 107)

In addition to Coca-Cola's *Spotlight Bands* series, the AFRS produced a number of different radio shows of its own including *GI Jive, Yank Swing Session,* and *Downbeat,* which all featured music prerecorded by Kirk's band during the war. However, the AFRS series that most often featured the Clouds of Joy was *Jubilee!*, a show that was specifically aimed at showcasing black talent, even though white performers also featured later on in the series (Spragg 2015: 2). This was another morale-boosting show, but it was a weekly broadcast (on a Friday night) that was made exclusively for distribution across the AFRS military network. *Jubilee* featured upbeat popular music (usually provided by two ensembles—a big band and a smaller combo) together with comedy skits and voguish dialogue aimed at conveying a lighthearted and uplifting tone. Two 25-minute *Jubilee* programmes were usually recorded in a single studio session which usually lasted a little over an hour (Spragg 2015: 4). These sessions were then edited down and dubbed onto 'Vinylite' discs for distribution to military facilities at home and overseas, for broadcast over the radio or the public-address system on those bases.

Jubilee was a show conceived by Mann Holiner, the Broadway performer, producer, and composer who co-wrote the 'Slave Song' that ultimately became 'Until the Real Thing Comes Along'. The show was initially intended exclusively for an African American audience, but Holiner rejected the idea that it should only be aimed at black personnel and argued that any quality programme should be available for general consumption (Spragg 2015: 7). Holiner got his way because senior military officers were keen to avoid inflaming racial unrest within the ranks at a sensitive time. *Jubilee,* as much as the *Spotlight Bands* series, escaped the recording ban that was imposed by the musicians' union during the early 1940s because bands gave their services for the war effort (Spragg 2015: 7). So in the end, *Jubilee* represented a rare vehicle for bringing hot-swing music to a broad cross-racial audience, when there were few opportunities to record such music. However, there is no doubt that *Jubilee* had a distinctly hip-black character, and in its stereotyping of black performers and their music, the show represented a highly stylized space for black jazz within the AFRS output.

The hip blackness of *Jubilee* was reinforced by the comedic tongue-twisting rhetoric that was scripted for the show's host, the African American actor Ernest Whitman. These scripts positioned Whitman and his guests within prevailing stereotypes of slick, voguish, and comedic black entertainers, which extended from those of blackface minstrelsy. The entertainers were depicted as always-jolly figures of fashionable modernity and Ernie 'Bubbles' Whitman, as he was christened on the show, was himself the butt of many jokes on account of his size. However, Whitman often gave as good as he got as he went through the jive-talk dialogue on air and that shows how the performers in *Jubilee* wore the stereotype of contemporary hip blackness much as a subversive minstrel's mask. Behind the masked performance of jive-talking, there was a serious message about the representation of blackness within the war effort and a concomitant agenda of national-cultural pride and social advancement for African Americans.

In March 1944, Andy Kirk and his Clouds of Joy recorded the sixty-eighth edition of *Jubilee* at NBC's studios in Hollywood, California. It featured Kirk's band alongside the resident AFRS Trio, which, later in the show, backed Bob Crosby in two vocals. As well as playing the *Jubilee* theme (an extract from Basie's 'One O'Clock Jump'), Kirk's band featured June Richmond in 'Basin Street Blues', and it performed Mary

Lou Williams's 'Little Joe from Chicago' in a very similar manner to that heard on their Decca release. However, the other two numbers they performed, 'New Orleans Jump' and 'Flying Home', do not appear amongst the band's commercial releases. The former of these was based on a stock arrangement by Van Alexander that was published in 1942. The latter was a Fletcher Henderson arrangement, published in 1941, of a number in Benny Goodman's repertory. Kirk's band gives a pacey and increasingly riotous rendition of 'Flying Home', and although it is somewhat curtailed by a fade-out on the AFRS dubbing, one gets a very good impression from it of the capacity of Kirk's 1940s band for loud, hard-driven hot swing that we rarely hear on the Decca records.

One thing that one immediately notices on listening to the wartime broadcast recordings of Kirk's band is its much fuller and brassier sound. In 1936, the band consisted of five brass (three trumpets and two trombones), three reeds (the players doubling on different saxes and/or on clarinet), and four rhythm (piano, guitar, bass and drums).[15] In 1937 Kirk added a fourth saxophone to the reed section to avoid arrangers having to add brass to facilitate sax-section harmonies (as Mary Lou Williams did in her 1936 arrangements). The resulting lineup of 13 players remained intact until sometime in early 1943, when the band expanded more significantly.[16] By the time the Clouds of Joy recorded for Decca in December 1943, Kirk had dropped the guitar from the rhythm section (with the drafting of Floyd Smith), but he had expanded his brass section to eight (four trumpets and four trombones) and enlarged his reed section to six (two altos, three tenors, and a baritone, with most players doubling on other saxes and/or clarinet). So, the 1940s band was almost one and a half times the size of the 'Twelve Clouds of Joy' that had recorded in the 1930s and that brought with it a brassier, more assertive sound.

The unusual trio of tenor saxes within the reed section was a particular feature of Kirk's post-1942 band and one that was exploited in their music and their stage antics. This is demonstrated in 'Flying Home' on the March 1944 *Jubilee* recording. After a driving eight-bar introduction (o'oo"–o'o8"), which is enlivened by neat-but-vibrant shakes (mordents) from the trumpets, the band launches into the first AABA

15 The violinist and guitarist Claude Williams is listed in Rye's discography as being a part of Kirk's band from 2 March 1936, until February 1937 but Williams left the Clouds of Joy and joined Count Basie's orchestra during 1936.

16 Although there were 13 in the band plus Kirk out front, by billing Andy Kirk as the leader and Mary Lou Williams as a featured soloist, they could still be advertised as the 'Twelve Clouds of Joy' and most often were.

chorus (0'08"–0'42") in which the B section (0'25"–0'33") is given over to an alto-sax solo (probably Reuben Phillips). The first chorus is followed by a 16-bar interlude (0'42"–0'58"), made up of two eight-bar phrases. In its scoring for Harrington's clarinet accompanied by descending unison trombones and throbbing tom-toms, it references Mundy's 'Sing, Sing, Sing' and thereby gives a nod to the Goodman-band origins of the piece. The chorus after the interlude (0'58"–1'31") features the trio of tenor saxophones in ensemble phrases which alternate with solo breaks for each one in turn. Thereafter, each tenor is given a whole chorus to improvise and those solos are separated by four-bar interludes for the brass.

It is not easy to determine which player is which but the first tenor-sax solo chorus (1'35"–2'04") most probably features J. D. King and it is easily the weakest of them. The second solo chorus is the most sonorous (2'08"–2'37") and is most likely played by Ed Loving. The third chorus (2'40"–3'09") soloist sounds like Jimmy Forrest, who is distinctly rougher in tone but strong enough in his material. The final brass interlude (3'09"–3'13") leads to a wonderful 'shout' chorus (3'13"–3'46") featuring trombone glissandi and an interplay of riffs between the reeds and brasses. This chorus comes to a close as the recording starts to fade out, but beneath Whitman's voiceover, we can just hear that it leads to another one of very similar material but which is transposed up a half-step to lift the performance energy to the piece's conclusion. This is the exact same device as was used at the end of 'McGhee Special' to great dramatic effect.

'New Orleans Jump', which featured in the same *Jubilee* show, demonstrates how the modernistic character of bebop (the very latest style of jazz) came with the younger generation of players (Howard McGhee, Theodore 'Fats' Navarro, and the like) who entered the band with the drafting of other players during the early 1940s. The track is brilliantly executed from start to finish by the Clouds of Joy with tight ensemble playing, a bright-driving swing, and characterful forward-looking solos. A six-bar introduction (0'00"–0'06") opens the piece and it is followed by the first AABA chorus (0'06"–0'45"). This is led by the saxes and punctuated by neat stabs from the brass, who take over to lead in the B section (0'26"–0'36"). An eight-bar interlude (0'45"–0'55") follows the first chorus and a one-bar drum break for Ben Thigpen is tagged on to its end (0'55"–0'56"). The trumpets pick up from the drums to lead in to the second chorus (0'56"–1'34") with a unison line that is remarkably similar to the opening of Dizzy Gillespie's 'Be-Bop', a tune that was not recorded until the following year (see Figure 3.2). This section was not in the stock arrangement used for the recording but it was

♩=c.160 (swing quavers)

FIGURE 3.2 The unison trumpet theme in 'New Orleans Jump' displaying a bebop character that is prescient of Gillespie's later recording of 'Be-Bop'.

mostly likely added to it by Howard McGhee, who had learned arranging from Mary Lou Williams. The trumpet ensemble alternates with short (four-bar) solos (most likely McGhee) before the saxes take over in the B section (1'15"–1'24"). Then a higher-pitched trumpet solo (possibly Navarro) follows in the final A section (1'24"–1'34") to close the chorus.

A second eight-bar interlude (1'34"–1'43") follows the 'Be-Bop' chorus, which, again, features Thigpen's drums and leads to Johnny Young's pickup into his piano solo. Young opens what proves to be an extended final chorus with two A sections (1'43"–2'03") that show his solo style to be as modernistic as the bebop-derived trumpet material. An alto sax (probably Reuben Phillips) briefly takes over in the B section (2'03"–2'13") of the chorus before Young's piano is then replaced by the sax. This brings back the distinctive riff-built theme of the opening chorus for two final A sections (2'13"–2'30"), rather than just one, which are ultimately capped off with a brassy coda (2'30"–2'36"). The effect of this high-energy ending to a decidedly hot and modernistic swing track is to immediately induce cheering and applause from the military audience.

The character of the music in these *Jubilee* tracks is different from both that heard in the late 1930s Decca recordings and the commercial releases of the early 1940s. The comparatively subtle and bouncy style of the prewar records is replaced by a confident, driving, and brassy-sounding swing that is much less orientated towards pleasing a regional audience of social dancers, and which, in its leaning towards modernistic bebop, contrasts the pop vocals that the band put out on its commercial releases. The turnover of players in Kirk's band, which was only exacerbated by wartime conscription, brought a modernistic big-band character to the Clouds of Joy which is too often overlooked and undervalued. It positions the Clouds of Joy as a force akin to Earl Hines's band of the early 1940s, which, although it never recorded, is more often prized for its musical enterprise in the face of wartime commercial pressures.

The wartime influx of young players to the Clouds of Joy not only brought a contemporary musical style into Kirk's band but also some of the African American self-confidence that was engendered by the wartime atmosphere and this proved a challenge for Kirk, as he recalled:

> My original band rules—and they were not strict, but important—didn't work. My three basic rules were: no fighting, no drinking on the stand, be on time. [. . .] But, as I say, my original rules didn't work. We were changing men fast and they all came in with their own thinking. They'd be drinking and clowning and were not accustomed to the decorum and standards I thought were right. (Kirk 1989: 109)

The ill-discipline of the younger members of the band got too much for Kirk one night during the war, and after they had played their gig, he summoned them to a meeting to express his disgust at their behaviour. Kirk's tenor player, J. D. King, reminded the bandleader that they were only in the band because they had all escaped the draft on account of being rated as '4Fs' (Kirk 1989: 109). Although Kirk had to change his attitude, he remained unhappy about it, especially when heroin use came on the scene and began claiming the lives of young musicians like Fats Navarro and his own son, Andy Kirk Jr., a talented bebop saxophonist.

It was not just the younger players that proved a challenge for Kirk: after the war, the closure of ballrooms and dance halls increasingly effected the tours that sustained the Clouds of Joy with work. According to Kirk, new civil rights legislation had a further detrimental effect on the band's established circuit of tour venues. In Pennsylvania, for instance, ballrooms that had been regular fixtures on the band's tours suddenly refused to book the Clouds of Joy for fear of the black clientele that might come to hear them (Kirk 1989: 113). Some restaurants that the band often stopped at en route between gigs presented them with special menus that contained inflated prices, intended to deter black diners who could now legally access such establishments. Even in New York, Kirk was told by the manager of the Arcadia Ballroom that the ballroom's owners didn't want to attract a crowd from Harlem and so he would not be able to honour the contract that Joe Glaser had set for the band. Despite these new difficulties, which were presented by the legal erosion of segregation within the entertainment business, Kirk was still able to struggle on with tours for his band until 1949.

The movie industry was just as slow as the ballroom and restaurant business to embrace the new civil rights legislation. If the *Jubilee* shows represented a sort of rare but confined space for black swing music during the war, then the 1948 all-black film *Killer Diller* was no better as an example of racial integration, and in many ways it represents one of the last in the line of all-black comedies that was produced in the 1930s and 1940s. Nevertheless, it provides a rare opportunity to see, as well as hear, Kirk's band of the late 1940s perform repertoire that, like much of the *Jubilee* material, was not released on commercial records. This is instructive for what it says about the band's stage-performance conventions in the late 1940s and how they reflect the band's Signifyin(g) on the popular-music styles that they presented in broadcasts and recordings.

Killer Diller was a low-budget comedy directed by Josh Binney.[17] It had a narrative about staging a variety show in the face of backstage chaos caused by a stand-in magician. It featured a cast of well-known black actors, led by Thelma 'Butterfly' McQueen and Clinton 'Dusty' Fletcher, and the action was of the 'keystone cops' variety. However, the film's rather silly narrative is really just a frame for the stage show that is at the movie's heart. That show, performed before an all-black audience in the film, is comperèd by Kirk himself, and aside from the Clouds of Joy, it features the Nat 'King' Cole Trio, the Clark Brothers (tap dancers), the Four Congaroos (a Lindy Hop team drawn from dancers of New York's Savoy Ballroom[18]) and the Varietiettes dancing girls (from the Katherine Durham School of Dancing). Kirk's band prove to be the stars of the show though, as they offer a selection of numbers that show off the band both as capable accompanists and as an engaging stage act in their own right.

The stage show in the film kicks off with Kirk's band playing 'Gators Serenade', an upbeat and increasingly boisterous number featuring a duel of solos between the band's now two tenor saxophonists, Ray Abrams and Shirley 'Gator' Greene. Abrams and Greene were relatively

---

17 The 72-minute film has been released on a budget-priced DVD by Alpha Home Entertainment and is available to view complete on YouTube (see *Killer Diller* 2018).

18 The dancers were Frankie Manning, Anne Johnson, Russell Williams, and Willa Mae Ricker.

recent additions to the Clouds of Joy.[19] 'Gator' Greene came from Los Angeles, where the band had recorded its *Jubilee* broadcasts/discs, and he has been credited with writing the track. However, a *Billboard* review indicates that the piece was already in the band's repertoire by 1944, when the Clouds of Joy performed at the Orpheum Theatre in Los Angeles and before Greene joined the band, but the band never recorded the track except for the film soundtrack, so we lack definitive records about its authorship (Abbot 1944: 26).

'Gators Serenade' begins with a veritable explosion of sound from the band before the first 32-bar chorus is split into eight-bar (AABA) solo exchanges between Abrams and Greene. Then three solo choruses follow for Abrams before Greene takes over for a further three choruses. During Greene's choruses, Abrams repeatedly tries to cut in on the solo action, but Kirk repeatedly sends him away, deflated, to wait at the side of the stage until the final chorus, when he is finally permitted to duet with Greene. This stage business was something that the band had featured since the earlier forties, as Kirk described how J. D. King used to make to leave the bandstand when the other two tenor saxes (Jimmy Forrest and Ed Loving) would duel for a prolonged period on just such a number (Kirk 1989: 110). The routine is, in effect, a staged version of a Kansas City jam session or 'cutting contest', and its drama is supported by the way that the arrangement for the band gathers in volume and momentum as the track progresses.

After 'Gators Serenade', Beverley White is featured in two comedic songs with the band: 'I Don't Want to Get Married' and 'That Ain't Nobody's Biz'ness What I Do'. These demonstrate her capacity for theatricality that, in a somewhat more coquettish vein, mirrored that of June Richmond. White opens her first song by singing the line, 'Marriage was a beautiful thing', before she breaks out of her sung performance, puts her hands on her hips and confides in a spoken aside, 'Yes, back in grandma's day!' White returns to singing thereafter to explain that men have changed and that this has prompted her to stay single, because 'when you're single, you have so much *fun*'. Such emphasis, little gestures, and facial expressions enliven her performance and she always resorts to spoken patter for the suggestive punchlines in the B sections of her AABA choruses. At the close of the song, she adds a final 'wink' in a

19 Greene does not appear in the listings of Kirk's band in any of the standard discographies, but these listings are increasingly unreliable in the later 1940s. Joe Evans recalled that Greene was playing tenor with Kirk's band when he joined as the lead alto player in 1945 (Evans & Brooks 2008: 71).

spoken afterthought, 'Ask me, I know'. This underlines how her spoken asides, as much as White's physical and facial expressions, serve as a nudge and a wink within the racy context of the song.

White's second song is, if anything, even more racy with its suggestions of infidelity and 'cougar' inclinations, and the whole song, apart from the last line of the final chorus, is spoken rather than sung in the comedic manner of the joke lines in White's first number. The song is an updated version of "Tain't Nobody's Business If I Do', a classic blues song that was recorded in the 1920s by Bessie Smith (amongst others). The original song is usually credited to a songwriting duo that paired Smith's piano accompanist, Porter Grainger, with Mammie Smith's pianist, Everett Robbins, but by the late 1940s, their version had been given a makeover. White's rendition of the updated song mentions the jukebox and bobby socks, and the blues femininity in the song is transformed: Smith's representation of a woman that justifies unconventional behaviours relative to love within a relationship (albeit, a physically abusive one) becomes one that actively seeks fulfilment beyond her man by soliciting sex from younger men. While the racy character of White's songs undoubtedly position the black female singer as a stereotypical sex object, they also facilitate a performance of feminine power within the context of the postwar era: this is a woman who, as much as flaunting her sexual mores, celebrates not conforming to contemporary expectations of women (marriage and children).

After White's routine, the comedy duo of Patterson and Jackson performs some numbers with the band, which include a parody of the Ink Spots vocal quartet ('If I Didn't Care for You'), which sends up falsetto-styled crooning. Given the band's recording history with Pha Terrell, the Jubalaires and the Four Knights, this sequence is as much an updating of past engagements with popular black vocal styles, as White's represents a revision of blues femininity.

Terrell's ballads, as much as those of quartets like the Ink Spots, were voguish but apparently sincere expressions that utilized the sweet-ethereal quality of falsetto crooning to impart the transcendent or otherworldly experience of true love. This approach is sent up by Patterson and Jackson in 'If I Didn't Care for You' in their contrasting of that sort of singing with very much more worldly comments like, 'Ah, sweet essence of meatballs in spaghetti'. This comedic juxtaposition brings the ethereal crooning style down to earth with a comedic bump. One of the highest-pitched falsetto moments in the song (on the lyric 'love beyond compare') is met with a response that is drenched with innuendo, 'Ah, shoot the salami to me mammy!' which sends up the homosexual connotations of falsetto crooning. Such commentary comes in the second chorus of the song in the stylized dialogue between the performers (one imitating the gravelly quality of Louis Armstrong's vocals and the other Terrell-like crooning), and it follows the plea, 'Now, Honey-chow, you gotta change your style'. The song ends with a 'big finish' in falsetto of the exact sort that Terrell offered in the late 1930s, but it is made rather too big by Patterson and Jackson, as the singer's voice grates somewhat, but that Signifyin(g) caricature is, of course, the whole point of the skit.

Kirk's band is next heard accompanying the impressive tap dancing of the Clark Brothers, and then, after an interlude from the Nat 'King' Cole Trio (not their finest work), they provide backing for the rather frenetic and acrobatic Lindy Hop dancing of the Congaroos. They dance before a stereotypical palm tree setting.[20] However, it is in the following episode that the band really comes to the fore. First, they are heard accompanying the guitarist René Hall (who is also credited with 'musical arrangements' on the film) in a distinctive number that features an extensive and modernistic piano solo (possibly Hank Jones) as much as the distinctive guitar riffs. This is followed by a feature for a bassist (most likely Al Hall), in which the bass starts off by backing saxophone riffs before taking a rare solo. A solo chorus follows for muted trumpet before an extensive solo is given over to tenor sax (Shirley Greene). The final chorus sets the sax riff against neat counterpoint from the brass. The latter number is most probably 'Apollo Groove', a piece copyrighted by Kirk's lead alto saxophonist of the period, Reuben Phillips, in July 1945. However, without the emergence of the unissued Decca recording of the piece, made in December 1944, we may never know for sure whether it is that number.

The final episode of the film features Kirk's band backing the dancing of the Varietiettes, a troupe of girls from the Katherine Dunham School of Dancing. The band performs 'Basie Boogie' in a version that replaces Basie's piano with René Hall's electric guitar licks. Hall proves that he is a very fine soloist on this track and his playing points towards the rock 'n' roll music that lay on the horizon for popular music. His playing is certainly more energized and together than the dancing girls and it drives both the track and the film to its conclusion.

It was only a year or so after *Killer Diller* that Kirk decided it was time to disband the Clouds of Joy as a full-time enterprise. His decision

---

20 Manning apparently complained that Andy Kirk played their music 'too damn fast' (JSngry 2017).

resulted from a combination of what he saw as the ill-disciplined attitude of the younger players, an unwillingness to downsize his band, and
the difficulties of finding enough work for them when dance halls were
closing in droves. The band made a final quartet of sides for Vocalion (by
then a subsidiary of Decca) in the spring of 1949.[21] They were all covers of
established hits and three of them featured vocals by Jimmy Anderson. In
a token gesture towards the greater racial integration that had followed
the war, these records were advertised under the 'Sepia Records' category in Vocalion's adverts (Vocalion Records 1949: 19). However, they
were clearly still aimed at a market of black consumers. The reviews of
the tracks in *Billboard* suggested the vocals might sell well on jukeboxes
at the bargain price of 49-cents but the only instrumental amongst them,
'The Huckle-Buck' (74923), was described as a 'Rather mediocre etching
of the smash rhythm piece' ('Ratings [100 Point Maximum]' 1949: 117).
If the writing had been on the wall for Kirk for a year or so, it was also
apparent to critics by 1949.

In sum, this chapter has shown that the vocal recordings of the Clouds
of Joy not only account for the success and longevity of Kirk's band, but
they are also crucial in understanding the sorts of negotiations over musical and racial authenticity that went on between black jazz musicians,
record companies, and audiences in the late 1930s and 1940s. I have
argued that such negotiations are embedded in the style of the music that
is heard on the recordings, and I have suggested that critics like Schuller
often went too far in maligning the vocal recordings of the Clouds of
Joy to the extent that they lost sight of the black-jazz identity that was
always evident in the band's music. Even in the ballads that are most
often represented by critics as the most tawdry, inauthentic, and commercial of the recordings, there was still a black-jazz sensibility, despite
the critics being unable or unwilling to hear it in their bid to dismiss Pha
Terrell's falsetto-filled crooning, and, by extension, his songs as a white-
sounding expression of queer-jazz inauthenticity.

The Trianon Ballroom recordings showed that there may well have
been more balance between hot and sweet styles in the live performances
of the Clouds of Joy. However, the success of 'Until the Real Thing

21 In his discography, Rye lists only the sides ('Drinkin' Wine, Spo-dee-o-dee, Drinkin' Wine'
    and 'Little Girl Don't Cry') that were featured on one (Vocalion 55010) of the two Vocalion
    releases in 1949 (Rye, as cited in Kirk 1989: 142). However, the sides on Vocalion 55009 ('The
    Huckle-Buck' and 'Close Your Eyes') were reviewed in the 25 June 1949 issue of *Billboard*
    ('Ratings [100 Point Maximum]' 1949) and also appear in volume 3 of Michel Ruppli's *Decca*
    discography (Ruppli 1996: 237).

Comes Along' and the numerous subsequent sweet ballads meant that the mediated stylistic character that was heard on their records became very much a part of the identity of Andy Kirk and his Clouds of Joy. Moreover, the style of their hit records represented a familiar stylistic voice of the band for its audiences: it allowed the band to call upon its audiences with an instantly recognizable stylistic identity as much as it permitted them to surprise the racial-stylistic expectations of audiences. In that way, the stylistic mask-play of the Clouds of Joy only got more complex and powerful in its Signifyin(g) with their commercial success as a recording band.

June Richmond may have brought back to the Decca records a decidedly black style of performance in her vocals, but her highly theatrical fronting of the band was no less effective in terms of Signifyin(g) on black musical identity relative to the ongoing racist conditions faced by the band. Her voluminous, bodily rooted, and comedic character as a performer was both arresting and entertaining in its apparent blackness in a way that the ballads were not. In this respect, she proved to be the very embodiment of the rhythm 'n' blues, which would become the next popular-music style to be articulated with black identity on records. Kirk's band was equally voluminous by the early 1940s, but his star players had to make the most of the few solo opportunities that they had to air their jazz chops on records.

The invention of mini 'concertos' gave such luminaries as Floyd Smith, Kenny Kersey and Howard McGhee rare spaces in which to show off their virtuosity. In their own way, these records are the non-vocal equivalents of Richmond's Signifyin(g) theatricality. They do important work for critics like Schuller in asserting the hot-jazz credentials of the band in an output in which such apparent blackness is not always evident. If, as jazz critics would have us believe, the 'real thing' of black-jazz identity of the period was represented by hard-driven hot-swing records, then the AFRS broadcast recordings of the wartime represent a vibrant blackness in which a vein of bebop modernism and wartime African American confidence are apparent in a way that is seldom heard on the Decca records.

The move towards R & B, which came through Richmond's singing, reached it apotheosis in pop vocals that came via doo-wop styled recordings that Kirk's band made with the Jubalaires and the Four Knights in the postwar period. Despite its stature as a 'name band', the Clouds of Joy was effectively relegated to a supporting role in these vocal recordings of the late 1940s. However, given the race-political currency of concepts like 'blending' and 'basing' within the black vocal-harmony tradition, such music nevertheless represented a heterogeneous black-musical community that envisioned a society that appreciated rather than expunged differences, whether they were racial, stylistic, or otherwise. In such performative music, musical style was again manipulated as a Signifyin(g) mask of blackness to envision a different sort of American society. It was one well removed from the racist concerns of record producers, critics and audiences, who either fetishized blackness as some authentic primordial hot expression or else would have it conform to the sweet-white norms of American culture. In this sense, Kirk's black band did important political work in recording such Signifyin(g) music that represented the long wait for the real thing to come along.

CHAPTER 4

A MELLOW BIT OF RHYTHM

RECONCEIVING AUTHENTICITY, 1957

ON 4 AND 12 March 1956, Andy Kirk made his last commercial recordings as a band leader. Three recording sessions were held across those two days at the RCA-Victor studios at Webster Hall in New York City (Guiter 1979). March 1956 marked precisely two decades since the Clouds of Joy had first recorded for Decca.[1] That timing was most likely the motivation for Kirk to lead what was predominantly a studio band in recording new arrangements of 12 numbers that he had originally recorded between 1936 and 1942 with the Clouds of Joy.[2] The resulting tracks were issued in 1957 on an LP album entitled *A Mellow*

---

1 March 1956 was also just a few months short of a decade since Kirk had made his last records for Decca in December 1946.
2 Although 'Froggy Bottom' was recorded by the Clouds of Joy in 1929, the version on the 1957 album clearly draws on Mary Lou Williams's 1936 arrangement rather than the original one.

Bit of Rhythm (RCA-Victor LPM-1302). Exploring that album as a 1950s-styled set of recollections of the recordings of Andy Kirk and His Clouds presents an opportunity to reflect on the whole musical and racial enterprise of their recorded output.

This concluding chapter considers the 1957 album as a Signifyin(g) form of musical retrospection that rounded off the recorded output of Kirk as a bandleader in a way that reilluminated the earlier recordings made by the Clouds of Joy but within a 1950s popular-jazz context. We will see that the retrospective album is as much a form of stylistic mask-play as the original recordings were. It served to establish a particular kind of 'authentic' black-jazz legacy for Andy Kirk and his Clouds of Joy within contemporary stylistic parameters, expectations, and desires about the sound of jazz on records. In that respect, the album represented a 'Greatest Hits' compilation of selections, which Emphasized the hot swing output or the band rather than the more numerous sweet numbers that had won them commercial success and lasting popularity in the 1930s and 1940s.

The 1957 LP served to re-define the jazz credentials of Andy Kirk and his Clouds of Joy through a highly selective set of recollections presented in brasher big-band arrangements. Lest there be any doubt about the selective nature of the music on the LP, in its liner notes, the New York Times jazz critic, John S. Wilson, described the rationale for track selection as follows:

> The tunes in this set have been selected as the cream of the beat-conscious library developed by the Kirk band during its twenty years of existence. (Wilson 1957)

This description points to the emphasis of so-called 'rhythm numbers' on the album and thereby to the upbeat or hot-black half of the 1950s race-music descriptor, 'Rhythm 'n' Blues'. In fact, two slower numbers are included on the album: 'Cloudy' and 'Scratchin' in the Gravel'. However, in the 1956 rearrangements, the former number, which was the band's longstanding closing theme in the later 1940s, loses its vocal in favour of a sultry saxophone solo for Al Cohn, and that instrumental treatment brings it in line with the jazz character of the latter solo feature.[3] 'Scratchin' in the Gravel' was conceived by Mary Lou Williams in

---

3 Its difference from the rest of the music on the LP perhaps explains the fact that the RCA-Victor band failed to record a satisfactory take during the 4 March recording session and had to revisit the tune on 12 March (Rye, as cited in Kirk 1989: 143). The seventh take of 'Cloudy' was the one that ultimately made it onto the 1957 record.

1940 as a solo vehicle for trumpet and it is preserved in that form on the LP.[4] Thus these reinvented slower pieces fit within the LP's agenda of presenting the hot-jazz side of the recordings of the Clouds of Joy. In that way, the 12 tracks on *A Mellow Bit of Rhythm* cohere in the work that they do in establishing a jazz legacy for Kirk and his band by disavowing or else reinventing their sweet-jazz output of ballads and instrumentals for dancing.

All of the 1957 album's tracks are revised in their restyling for a bigger band and, as we will see, the differences that become evident from comparing them with the original recordings are revealing in terms of what they say about the Signifyin(g) form of recollection that is represented by *A Mellow Bit of Rhythm*. If the 1957 album represents the 'cream of the beat-conscious library' of the Clouds of Joy, as the liner notes describe the selections, then, in aural terms, it is reinvented as a much thicker or heavier form of cream, which resulted from the original music being re-presented behind a mask of popular 1950s big-band jazz. The weightier sound on the 1957 LP has much to do with the larger band on the album, which was of a type used on several popular RCA-Victor jazz albums of the mid-1950s. Such a big band was utilized because it exploited the sonic potential of contemporary audio technologies.[5]

In August 1952 RCA-Victor introduced a new sound equalization curve for recording and playback, which they branded as providing 'New Orthophonic' sound (Moyer 1957: 11). This curve aimed to optimize both the cutting of record grooves and sound reproduction relative to the capabilities of contemporary playback equipment (Moyer 1953: 19). It subsequently became the standard of the Record Industry Association of America (RIAA) for sound equalization (Powell 1989: 14; Copeland 2008: 157–158). This standardization of RCA-Victor's sound characteristics meant that by the mid-1950s the company was ideally placed to offer records that exploited the sonic potential of 'high-fidelity' playback equipment of the period and contemporary listeners' expectations.

The ideal of high fidelity—to reproduce sound of such quality that it is as if the performers are actually present—was more than half-a-century

4 Mary Lou Williams's 'Toadie Toddle' also loses its vocal on the 1957 album, but the boogie-woogie-styled 'Froggy Bottom' and 'Little Joe from Chicago' keep their sung elements. This was most likely because they are just elements in what are otherwise lively vehicles for jazz improvisation and impressive riff-based hot-jazz ensembles.
5 These albums included *We Could Make Such Beautiful Music* (LPM-1205), *The Hawk in Hi-Fi* (LPM-1281), *Salute to Satch* (LPM-1324), *The Drum Suite* (LPM-1279), *A Bit of the Blues* (LPM-1369), and *Rhythm Was His Business* (LPM-1301).

old by 1952. As Jonathan Sterne documents, that ideal was greatly influenced by the discourses that both accompanied and motivated the development of new sound reproduction technologies (Sterne 2003: 278–280). Sterne shows that a complex of expectations and desires gradually became bound up with notions of high-quality sound reproduction. As a result, he suggests that perceptibly 'better' reproduced sound was most often not that which appeared to precisely reproduce its aural source, but that which better exploited the tonal potential of the recording *and* reproduction technologies relative to expectations of the rewards of sound reproduction.

By the late 1950s, notions of high-fidelity were associated with exploiting the fuller sound that was made available across a wider tonal spectrum than ever before by contemporary audio technologies and RCA-Victor's New Orthophonic equalization curve.[6] The bigger, bolder, and brasher big band that is heard on the 1957 LP was of a sort that was fashionable with record producers and audiences precisely because it showed off the greater dynamic range of 1950s 'high-fidelity' technologies and rewarded listeners' desires in sonic terms. The 1956 recording band that Kirk directed had four or five more players (depending on the session) than the Clouds of Joy carried in the later 1930s. That greater number only enhanced the ability of the 1957 record to appeal to contemporary recording and listening fashions.[7] The music heard on the LP is thus at least as much of the 1950s period as it is reminiscent of the earlier records of the Clouds of Joy.

Although several discographies and reissues credit the 1957 release to 'Andy Kirk and his Clouds of Joy Orchestra' or 'Andy Kirk and His New Clouds of Joy', the front cover of the LP is actually ascribed to 'Andy Kirk and his orchestra'.[8] This wording, which does not specifically mention the Clouds of Joy, is important because it indicates that, with the notable

6 In his 1953 article, Robert Moyer suggested that by the early 1950s, 'Special acoustic effects, changes in normal balance among instruments and soloists, and in some cases—especially in "pop" recordings—unusual electronic sound effects' meant that 'the criterion [. . .] for judging recording fidelity is the degree that the reproduced sound matches the sound heard in the monitor speaker at the recording session rather than the sound that was heard in the studio itself' (Moyer 1953: 19–20).

7 The 4 March 1956 session featured Kirk conducting eight brass, five reeds, and four rhythm players. In the 12 March session vibes were apparently added to that 17-piece lineup, although I struggle to hear Marty Wilson playing on any of the five tracks that came from that later session.

8 These inaccurate attributions include those in Rye's discography in the back of *Twenty Years on Wheels* (Rye, as cited in Kirk 1989: 120–143) and Tom Lord's *The Jazz Discography Online* (Lord 2015). The original RCA-Victor LP (LPM-1302) is confusing as it bills the band

exception of Ken Kersey, none of the musicians on the record were with Kirk during the heyday of his band, when the music on the album was originally created.[9] Thus, Kirk directed a band of session musicians that, as *Billboard*'s reviewer complained, was made up of 'the same men one hears on nearly every Victor jazz disk of the Jack Lewis era' ('Reviews and Ratings of New Jazz Albums' 1957: 38).[10] What might seem odd about this use of RCA's resident band is that at the time of the 1956 recordings, Kirk was actually still running a band of his own, albeit a rather ad hoc ensemble.

In the early 1950s, Kirk put a function band together with the help of Ray Copeland, an up-and-coming young trumpeter that he had met when he moved to New York City. Kirk noted, 'I still had Harry "Big Jim" Lawson on trumpet. He first joined me in 1926 and was the only original member who stuck the whole way' (Kirk 1989: 117). However, Copeland attracted a group of younger musicians to perform alongside Lawson. Most of these, like Kirk by that point, had day jobs outside of music and many also had young families. Thus, the Kirk-Copeland band was not a full-time professional concern, like the Clouds of Joy, but played only at weekends and public holidays for 'deb[utante] parties and dances and for affairs for the social clubs, sportsmen's clubs, and organizations like that' (Kirk 1989: 117).

The fact that the youngster, Ray Copeland, rather than Lawson, was included in the studio band heard on the 1957 album, underlines that the aim of the LP was not to recreate past recordings in the way of the originals but to reinvent them in a contemporary vein.[11] To this end, the album *A Mellow Bit of Rhythm* offers new arrangements written by Manny Albam and Ernie Wilkins. These men both arranged music for several RCA-Victor albums of the late 1950s. They were steeped in earlier styles of big-band jazz, but by 1956 they had developed a post-bop style of arranging by working with the likes of Dizzy Gillespie and Coleman Hawkins. This meant their rearrangements for Kirk made plenty of room for solos, extended the harmonic vocabulary of the original charts

---

differently, as 'Andy Kirk and his Clouds of Joy', on the reverse of the record cover. This is also the billing used on the French RCA reissue of 1979 (PM 42418).

9 Kersey only features in seven of the 12 tracks on the album, as Moe Wechler took his place in the band for the 12 March recording session.

10 Jack Lewis was the executive at RCA-Victor responsible for the famous *The Jazz Workshop* series of recordings (see http://messageboard.tapeop.com/viewtopic.php?p=623710).

11 Lawson may well not have appeared on the 1957 album because of the dental problems that led to him giving up the trumpet in the later 1950s (Chadbourne 2015).

and, most noticeably, exploited the dynamic energy offered by the larger studio band. To further support the fulsome dynamic character of the band's sound, the tempi of most of the numbers on the LP are adjusted from those of the original recordings (see Table 4.1).

The overriding effect of these new arrangements, played by a bigger band that exploited the greater dynamic range and frequency spectrum of contemporary recording and playback technologies, is of a more sonically full and indulgent music that prizes completely different stylistic qualities from the refined, understated, and smooth swing of the Clouds of Joy in the late 1930s and early 1940s. A different sort of volume-driven and brassy excitement is offered on the 1957 album, and thus, if it is approached as if the RCA-Victor band were the Clouds of Joy, the music it contains can seem wanting or overblown by comparison and indistinct from other 1950s big-band records. The *Billboard* reviewer of the album, for example, felt that the 'somewhat up-dated versions of old Kirk specialties have nothing to create new interest' ('Reviews and Ratings of New Jazz Albums' 1957: 38). It is all too easy to write off the 1957 LP in this way, as merely an inauthentic set of 1950s nostalgic recollections of the jazz records of the past. However, the stylistic differences of the album's selections from the original recordings suggests the need to approach the LP more as a 1950s form of recollection that offered a different sort of listening pleasure in its volume-driven re-presentation of Kirk's musical past.

The 1957 album opens with a new version of the Herman Walder and Mary Lou Williams number, 'A Mellow Bit of Rhythm' (G2 JB-2513). It is taken at a notably slower tempo than on the original 1937 recording. This different pace, together with the liberal use of the much fuller sound of the bigger and louder band, immediately gives the revision a greater aural impact. That is apparent throughout the track: from the powerfully swinging new introduction (0'00"–0'18"), through the distinctively 'moaning' tutti-saxophone riffs in the first AABA chorus (0'18"–1'26"), the solos for Al Cohn's tenor sax and Frank Rehak's trombone in the second one (1'43"–2'57"), to the final brassy half-chorus (2'56"–3'36"). The sheer power of the band in this reworking of the 1937 number is an assault on the ears of the listener that is striking (in Mowitt's sense of engaging listener identification) in its comparative fullness and vividness of sound.

If, as I argued in Chapter 2, the original recording was 'mellow' in terms of its understated, smooth, and refined style of 1930s swing, then this later version is laid back in an altogether louder and more exaggerated 1950s way. The RCA-Victor band is much more present in aural

TABLE 4.1 Table of contents of 1957 LP *A Mellow Bit of Rhythm*, comparing tempi of the tracks with that of their original releases.

Track Title	Matrix	Composer Credits	Session Details[a]	BPM/Original	Original Rec. Date
'A Mellow Bit of Rhythm'	G2-JB-2513-10	Herman Walter & Mary Lou Williams	10 a.m.–1 p.m. 4 March 1956	112/158	26 July 1937
'Little Joe from Chicago'	G2-JB-2856-4	Mary Lou Williams & Henry Wells	10 a.m.–1 p.m. 12 March 1956	152/142	12 September 1938
'McGhee Special'	G2-JB-2858-4	Howard McGhee	10 a.m.–1 p.m. 12 March 1956	166/183	14 July 1942
'Hey Lawdy Mama'	G2-JB-2857-6	Lee Wilson	10 a.m.–1 p.m. 12 March 1956	156/158	14 July 1942
'Cloudy'	G2-JB-2517-7[b]	Andy Kirk & Mary Lou Williams	10 a.m.–1 p.m. 12 March 1956	72/100	3 April 1936
'Froggy Bottom'	G2-JB-2512-4	John Williams & Mary Lou Williams	10 a.m.–1 p.m. 4 March 1956	174/143	4 March 1936
'Wednesday Night Hop'	G2-JB-2511-3	Leslie Johnakins & Andy Kirk	10 a.m.–1 p.m. 4 March 1956	165/170	15 February 1937
'Walkin' and Swingin''	G2-JB-2514-4	Mary Lou Williams	2:30 p.m.–5:30 p.m. 4 March 1956	141/176	2 March 1936
'Scratchin' in the Gravel'	G2-JB-2510-10	Mary Lou Williams	10 a.m.–1 p.m. 4 March 1956	90/95	25 June 1940

Song	Matrix	Personnel		Session	Date
'Toadie Toddle'	G2-JB-2955-6	Mary Lou Williams & Sharon Pease	172/160	10 a.m.–1 p.m. 12 March 1956	12 September 1938
'Take It and Git'	G2-JB-2515-6	Lester Melrose, J. Marshall, & M. Chapman	170/160	2:30 p.m.–5:30 p.m. 4 March 1956	4 March 1942
'Boogie-Woogie Cocktail'	G2-JB-2616-12	Kenneth Kersey	248/240	2:30 p.m.–5:30 p.m.4 March 1956	14 July 1942

Band on March 4: Andy Kirk (dir), Conte Candoli, Ray Copeland, Bernie Glow, Joe Newman (tpt), Jimmy Cleveland, Frank Rehak, Chauncey Welsh (trb.), Tom Mitchell (b.trb), Sam Marowitz, Hal McKusick (a.sax.), Al Cohn, Ed Wasserman (t.sax.), Al Epstein (b.sax.), Kenny Kersey (pno.), Freddy Green (gtr.), Milt Hinton (dbs.), Osie Johnson (drms., vcl.), Manny Albam, Ernie Wilkins (arr.).

Band on March 12: Andy Kirk (dir), Conte Candoli, Ray Copeland, Bernie Glow, Ernie Royal (tpt), Jimmy Cleveland, Fred Ohms, Chauncey Welsh (trb.), Tom Mitchell (b.trb), Sam Marowitz, Hal McKusick (a.sax.), Al Cohn, Ed Wasserman (t.sax.), Al Epstein (b.sax.), Moe Wechler (pno.), Jimmy Raney (gtr.), Buddy Jones (dbs.), Osie Johnson (drms.) Manny Albam, Ernie Wilkins (arr.).

Note: dir.: director; tpt.: trumpet; trb.: trombone; b.trb.: bass trombone; a.sax.: alto sax; t.sax.: tenor sax; b.sax.: bass sax.; pno.: piano; gtr.: guitar; dbs.: double bass; drms.: drums; vcl.: vocal; arr.: arranger.

[a] Details from the LP reissue entitled *Andy Kirk and his Clouds of Joy: Clouds from the Southwest.*

[b] A version of 'Cloudy' was recorded in two takes at the end of the sessions on 4 March but proved to be unsatisfactory. A second version was duly recorded on 12 March but, for some reason, it retained the matrix number of the original recording.

terms, but in rhythmical-metrical ones it is forced to 'sit back', even beyond the usual laid-back manner of the Clouds of Joy, through the contrivance of the slower tempo that facilitates the execution of the fuller ensemble figurations by the bigger band. The result is a sort of loud 1950s caricature of the original mellow vibe, but like all caricatures and theatrical masks (including those of blackface minstrelsy), it exaggerates characteristic details—notably the pitch-bending 'moaning' of the saxophone riffs and the contrasting 'shouts' of the brass—and, as a result, it offers a portrait that is engaging and fun in its own voluminous way. Thus, the opening track of the 1957 album sets the tone for a whole series of such caricatured musical recollections and that constitutes the stylistic masking on the album.

The new version of 'Little Joe from Chicago' (G2 JB-2856) also offers stylistic exaggeration, but in the greater sense of powerful drive that is brought to the original track's boogie-woogie character. It is more driving because it was recorded at some 10 beats per minute faster than the original 1938 recording of the piece and, like 'A Mellow Bit of Rhythm', it is much more richly orchestrated. For example, in the first two blues choruses of the arrangement (0'06"–0'42"), Mary Lou Williams's comparatively sparse 1930s orchestration, featuring jaunty riffs for a pair of clarinets, is replaced by a much fuller texture. On the 1957 record, trombones and trumpets trade motifs beneath those same riffs but they are now rendered by the whole of the reed section. This sort of enlargement of the orchestration obscures the comparatively understated and agile boogie-woogie styling of the original 1938 track with what is, in sonic terms, a more massive and impressive stylistic mask.

Another notable change to 'Little Joe from Chicago' is in the lyrics. In the 1956 version, these suggest that it is Little Joe's handling of women, rather than money, that 'makes you know he ain't no fool'. This implies quite a different sort of reflection on Joe Glaser than is in the original 1938 version. If Kirk was responsible for the change to the lyrics, it suggests that he held no regrets over Glaser's financial exploitation of the Clouds of Joy but was able to rationalize them as being in and of the past. The rewording in the context of the brash boogie-woogie music in the 1950s version recasts this reflection of Glaser as wholly celebratory, with no whiff of bitterness. Glaser's representation is transformed into a womanizing rogue and one only has to think of the representations of women on 1950s album covers, to see that this updating was also drawing on contemporary articulations of jazz with machismo and sex appeal.

In fact, the image on the sleeve of the 1957 LP was a photo shot by Wendy Hilty that featured rhythm-section instruments (guitar, bass, and drums) set in the foreground and a couple dancing in close embrace in the background. The woman in the image is white and wears high heels and a 1950s cocktail dress. She embraces a darker-skinned man in a jacket and shades whose position, facing away from the camera, suggests he is a jazz musician that has just abandoned his instrument to engage in a slow, intimate dance with the woman. The bold and lowercase title of the album, *a mellow bit of rhythm*, runs up the left-hand edge of the image in much larger type than 'Andy Kirk and his orchestra', and it forms a relay with the sense of dancing-intimacy conveyed by the picture. The sleeve imagery is thus symbolic of the rhythmic-bodily sex-appeal of this hot-black music for its intended audience.

The transformation of Glaser's representation would surely have been unthinkable had Mary Lou Williams been in the 1956 RCA-Victor band and, not least, because she was prone to much more critical and bitter reflection. As Jack Lawrence recalled, by the 1960s, 'she had grown paranoid about people, publishers, and record companies. Everyone, she felt, was out to cheat her' (Lawrence 2004: 144). The all-male RCA-Victor band, however, clearly delight in realizing the bold counterpointing of the syncopated riffs in this revised depiction of Glaser's roguish qualities. They offer harmonies in their ensemble vocals, which are lacking in the original, and the final 'shout' chorus (2'18"–2'44") is greatly enlivened by call-and-response 'doo-wah' riffs that are played with a rasping-swelling quality that suggests celebratory abandon of a sort that was absent in the more ominous sounding 1938 recording. In this number, then, the 1950s stylistic mask Signifies a celebration of hot jazz's apparent heterosexual machismo and any effeminacy of their old sweet ballads is eclipsed.

On the 1957 album, Howard McGhee's 1942 'concerto' number, 'McGhee Special' (G2 JB-2858), becomes a vehicle for the trumpeter Ernie Royal. Unlike the first two tracks on the 1957 LP, this one is strikingly similar to the original recording, and Royal, who was regarded as a high note specialist and 'an imaginative improviser, capable of producing fine melodic lines', proves to be a great stand-in for McGhee (Ostransky 1994: 1066). This is especially true of his tone, even if he is not quite so driving, dramatic and fiery towards the end of the piece as McGhee was in 1942.[12] In fact, the soloist-led theatrics, which energized the original version, are all the harder for Royal because of the bigger and brasher

12 This is especially noticeable in the final section of the arrangement, in which the key is twice shifted up a semitone. In the original these shifts give a sense of ever-increasing excitement to the already stratospheric energy level of McGhee's playing—one imagines, 'Surely he cannot go any more?' followed by, 'Oh, yes he can!' and then, 'Oh, and some more still!'

ensemble over whom he must be heard. Furthermore, the slower tempo of the 1956 track facilitates the band more than him. Nevertheless, the overriding effect of this fairly faithful update is to offer a vivid recollection of the original track, albeit behind a mask of 'New Orthophonic' sound.

The fourth track on the 1957 album, 'Hey Lawdy Mama' (G2 JB-2857), is an easy-going instrumental version of what was originally a hit song for June Richmond in 1942. In his autobiography, Kirk recalled that such vocals may actually have enjoyed more sales than 'Until the Real Thing Comes Along' (Kirk 1989: 110), but in 1956 Richmond's vocal nevertheless became a swinging big-band instrumental. After an introduction (0'00"–0'06") and first blues chorus (0'06"–0'25") for the full band, the 1950s recording features a rather stiff and somewhat squeaky clarinet solo by Hal McKusick (0'25"–1'02"). Moe Wechler takes over on the piano (1'02"–1'21") in a style that is perhaps closer to Basie than Kersey, but it serves to recover the soloists' momentum in the piece. An equally swinging trombone solo (1'21"–1'39"), most likely played by Jimmy Cleveland, leads into a quirkily orchestrated ensemble interlude that pairs McKusick's high-pitched clarinet with tightly muted trumpets (1'39"–1'57"). Ernie Royal's open trumpet is heard in a more extensive solo (1'57"–2'34") that follows that and it leads into a powerhouse of a final strain (2'35"–2'56").

The only nod to Richmond's 1942 vocal performance of 'Hey Lawdy Mama' is the exclamation of the title line of the song by an unidentified voice (probably Kirk), which is heard towards the end of the 1956 track (at 2'34"). This voice has a throaty vocal quality that, in an appropriately comedic-vernacular vein, instantly signifies the sort of fun-filled blackness that was a vital component of June Richmond's success with the original version of the song. This vocal interjection has particular impact on the ear because it occurs just before the fulsome final 'shout' chorus. It thus seems to summon up the sheer power of the 1956 band's swing, the locus of enjoyment for Kirk, his players and 1950s listeners alike. So, even when the 1950s stylistic mask slips a little, it is soon re-established through the powerful sound of the band on the 1957 record.

'Hey Lawdy Mama' is an unusual number on the 1957 album for being taken at almost the same tempo as it was in the original recording, but the following track, 'Cloudy' (G2 JB-2517-7), is performed at some 30 bpm slower than it was in 1936. This means that the 1950s version represents

Royal's more reticent articulation somewhat undermines this sort of building up of momentum, despite the ever more present accompaniment of RCA-Victor's house band.

a comparative indulgence in the number's slow-ballad style, but, again, the original vocal is transformed into a different style of brooding jazz instrumental. The soloists on this number, Al Cohn on tenor saxophone (0'13"–1'06") and Joe Newman on muted trumpet (1'06"–1'59"), squeeze every ounce of emotion out of Kirk's melody. To this end, Cohn employs a characteristically slow vibrato, subtle bending of pitches, portamento between notes and, at times, a breathy tone. Despite Cohn's indulgence in such devices, he is somewhat restrained in his embellishment of the melody and Newman is even more so, as he leaves all ornamentation to Copeland's more tightly muted trumpet counterpoint.

The RCA-Victor band is at its most sensitive and sensuously sonorous on the 1957 album in 'Cloudy', when it is heard before, between, and after the solos on the track. The saxophone section follows Newman's solo with an ensemble interlude (1'59"–2'28") that leads to some impressively swelling chords which colour the following repeated strain (2'28"–2'54") for the full band. Cohn then reappears (2'54"–3'34") to wind the track down to its conclusion. Although the players show a commitment to an admittedly saccharine sense of musical line and emotion, it never gets too cloying or sweet because the band does not shy away from the voluminous big-band style it had established with the earlier tracks but uses it to enhance the 1950s aural 'sexiness' of the music. The original ballad is thus reinvented behind a 1950s big-band mask and presented as if it were always a steamy hot-jazz instrumental rather than a sweet-styled pop song.

Perhaps more than any other track on the 1957 album, 'Froggy Bottom' (G2 JB-2512) is completely reconceived in its 1956 rearrangement. Wilson's liner notes tell us that it 'is taken at a faster tempo than usual' (Wilson 1957). This helps transform Williams's bluesy number from one about 'going down to the bottoms' of Kansas City, in both geographic and psychological terms, into one that is more about the ups of 1950s big-band sound. Thus, the introductory piano solo of the 1936 version is replaced with a swinging riff-based trombone feature (0'00"–0'16"). The trumpets and saxes join in for the next chorus (0'16"–0'30") to leave Ken Kersey to lead in to his driving boogie-woogie styled solo (0'30"–1'06"). This points much more towards rock 'n' roll than Williams could possibly have conceived in 1936, and, in that sense, there is a thread of continuity in this masked musical recollection of a blues orientated hot jazz number from 1929.

Kersey's pounding left hand drives his solo, and this, together with the prominence of the ride cymbal—or else the open high-hat—in a shuffle rhythm, gives the piece a decidedly 1950s rhythmical gloss. When the drummer-singer Osie Johnson takes two vocal choruses (1'06"–1'40") on the 1956 track, he accompanies himself with taps on a choked cymbal and snare strokes. This sparser and more percussive texture contrasts the louder and harder-driving qualities heard elsewhere on the track, and it projects the vocal segment back towards something of the style of the earlier recordings of 'Froggy Bottom'. However, this only proves to be a passing return to the sparser atmosphere of the Clouds of Joy because the vocal's close provides a cue for an ensemble celebration of an entirely different and much more raucous character.

The 'shout' chorus after the vocal (1'40"–1'56") presents juxtaposed ensemble riffs, set in enlivening counterpoint, before driving trumpet solos from Newman (1'56"–2'13") and then Copeland (2'13"–2'29") blast away above the rest of the band. A unison ensemble statement (2'29"–2'36") returns Kersey's piano to the fore for a short break (2'36"–2'46") that leads in to a really rocking final 'shout' chorus (2'46"–3'10"). That final chorus is interrupted towards it end by Kersey's piano again (3'01"–3'06"). This interruption tags a few extra bars on to the end of the chorus to preface the rousing closing cadence. Through all of this, one gets a palpable sense that the band is delighting in the sonic power and drive of this 1950s boogie-woogie reinvention of 'Froggy Bottom'. In the final analysis, this is a track that re-presents the original 1929 one through a double racial-musical mask of 1930s riff-based swing (from Williams's 1936 version) and 1950s hot 'rhythm' music.

'Wednesday Night Hop' (G2 JB-2511) consists of four AABA choruses in both the original 1937 version and the 1950s rearrangement. The instrumentation, however, was handled quite differently for the 1957 album. In the 1937 recording, the agile saxophone riff in the opening AABA chorus (0'00"–0'45") is set against muted brass motifs. The muted brass continue into the second chorus (0'45"–1'30") to back Dick Wilson's tenor sax solo, but they give way in the B section (1'08"–1'18") for Mary Lou Williams's piano solo. The A sections of the third chorus (1'30"–2'16") feature a plunger-muted trombone solo (Ted Donnelly) set against what sound like maracas and reiterated tonic pedal tones from the other low brass and saxes. A clarinet solo (John Harrington), without the pedal-note backing, forms the B section (1'54"–2'04"). The trumpets, now unmuted, lead in the A sections of the final chorus (2'04"–3'02") but pause for a characteristically nimble saxophone-ensemble passage in its B section (2'39"–2'51"). A coda tag (3'02"–3'05"), which simply echoes the final two bars of the last A section, brings the piece to a *sotto voce* close and demonstrates the impressive control of tone and timbre by the Clouds of Joy.

The 1956 rearrangement of 'Wednesday Night Hop' is impressive for its timbral subtlety and dynamic control but even more so for its exhilarating and driving ensemble playing. The muting is also replaced by more 'open' use of the brass instruments. So, in the first chorus (0'00"–0'52"), open trombones are set against the original saxophone riff and unmuted trumpet stabs are added to further enliven the timbre. The vibrant-sounding trumpets go on to lead in the longer-breathed melody of the B section (0'28"–0'40") before returning to their stab chords. These gradually transform into lipped trills in the return of the A section (0'40"–0'52"). As in 1937, a tenor saxophone solo is featured in the second chorus (0'52"–1'39"), but Al Cohn's playing is gruffer in its tone and not as fluid in its phrasing as Wilson's 1937 effort, and it also extends across the B section (1'17"–1'28"). It is accompanied in the A sections by plunger-muted brass motifs that open up to swelling crescendo figures during the B section. They give way to a pulsating ensemble of trombones and saxophones that add rhythmic momentum.

In the version heard on the 1957 album, the third chorus (1'40"–2'27") loses the accompanying maracas, pedal notes and the trombone soloist (Frank Rehak) is relegated to completing adrenaline-charged ensemble phrases, which are all the more striking for starting on an accented second beat of the bar. A short piano-solo phrase (2'16"–2'27") for Kersey leads to the final chorus (2'27"–3'15"), which has much more 'shouting' than in the original version for its trilling trumpet figures, drum breaks, the driving trumpet solo for Joe Newman in its B section (2'51"–3'03"). The final phrase leads to an ending that is no longer an echo, but a triumphant cadence for the full ensemble. It is led by a trumpet (most likely, Royal), playing right at the top of its range, and concludes with Osie Johnson, who works around his tom-toms under the final chord. Like the revision of 'Little Joe from Chicago', this track is impressive for the sonic fullness and powerhouse drive of its 1950s stylistic mask rather than the sort of restrained elegance that was the trademark style of the 1930s Clouds of Joy. There is a great deal of aural pleasure to be had in this masked recollection, even if it is not of the same elegant kind as that on the original record.

The 1956 revision of 'Walkin' and Swingin'' (G2 JB-2514) is another track that indulges in a sort of brassier caricature of the Clouds of Joy, but this one exaggerates the band's laid-back swinging style instead of transforming it into hard-driving sonic power. In the original recording, the unison chord of the opening anacrusis is simply elongated to serve as an introduction to the bright four-to-the-bar tempo of the track. The version heard on the 1957 album shifts this elongated unison to the first two beats of what proves to be a seven-bar-long introduction (0'00"–0'14"), which is built from material featured later on in the piece. This introduces a slower swing tempo than in the original track, and the whole introduction is effectively an orchestrated diminuendo, achieved through a series of similar riffs that move from emphatic brass accentuation, through ever more mellow trombones, to the distinctly *sotto voce* timbres of the saxophones. The saxes dovetail with the melody of the first AABA chorus (0'14"–1'12").

In the A sections of this first chorus, the 'doo-wah' styled plunger-muted brass riffs are much more forward in the audio mix than the saxophone melody, and they lead into a powerhouse of a B section (0'40"–0'56"). The fuller-sounding brassy texture is maintained into the final A section (0'56"–1'12") before Al Cohn takes another solo on his tenor sax in the second chorus (1'12"–2'07"). That features much softer trombones and then tightly muted trumpets backing him. His solo shows some of his most suitable qualities as a Kirk-band soloist. It opens with a confidently swinging swagger that gains further momentum in the second of the A sections, by developing a motif that he firstly repeats at a lower octave and then embellishes (see Figure 4.1). Cohn's phrasing in this liquid passage makes him sound like the rightful heir to Dick Wilson, who featured in the original recording. Unlike Wilson, though, Cohn is unable to sustain this sort of fluidity and resorts to ever more discrete, metrically safe and hesitant statements in the remainder of his solo.

The full band blasts in again for the final AABA chorus (2'07"–3'18") and leads towards Kersey's short solo in the B section (2'35"–2'47"). This is in an entirely different style to Mary Lou Williams's stride-piano

FIGURE 4.1 The second A section of Al Cohn's solo in the 1956 recording of 'Walkin' and Swingin'.

playing in the original recording. In the manner of contemporary big-band pianists, Kersey leaves accompaniment to the rest of the rhythm section and thus gives much greater emphasis to his right hand than his left: his left hand is only really employed in a little dialogue with the right hand's melodic riffs. The full band then returns for the last A section, and, in a contrast to the 'big finish' of the original version, its final riff is repeated ever more quietly to close the 1950s track.

This fade out is greatly aided by the engineering of the audio, and such technological intervention gives the 1956 recording of 'Walkin' and Swingin'" an audible contemporaneity that distances it from the 1936 recording while complementing its 'feel'. The more sedate pace, easier-going solos, and technologically facilitated fade out together represent the 1950s Signifyin(g) on 'Walkin' and Swingin'" in a way that places even more emphasis on the 'Walkin'" of the title than the 1936 version did. However, the 1950s version is no less swinging, and in its own caricatured or masked way, it is a highly engaging celebration of the riff-based character of Williams's original composition.

The 1956 rearrangement of Mary Lou Williams's 'Scratchin' in the Gravel' (G2 JB-2510), is quite similar to the 1940 version of this trumpet feature. It lacks the cadenza-like coda section heard on the 1940 recording, but otherwise it has the same introduction and the same order of soloists (trumpet, tenor sax, piano) featured across similar AABA choruses. It also employs a similar, if slightly slower, tempo. It is thus, like the revision of 'McGhee Special', a comparatively faithful 1950s recreation of the original track, but like the other tracks on the album it still sounds different for the fuller timbres of the orchestration, the updated style of the soloing (Newman, Cohn, and Kersey), and the recorded sound which together represent the stylistic mask through which it is mediated.

'Toadie Toddle' (G2 JB-2855) also follows the same basic structure as the 1938 recording of the piece by the Clouds of Joy, but a saxophone solo for Cohn (1'02"–1'29"), which follows the introduction (0'00"–0'11"), two ensemble 12-bar choruses (0'11"–0'44"), and an interlude (0'44"–0'56"), replaces the original's tongue-twisting 'novelty' vocal with instrumental jazz. After Cohn's two phrases, the band introduces its own playful eight-bar riff-filled phrase (1'30"–1'41"), based on meter-defying wide-interval leaps that are more exaggerated than in the original recording. As in that original, these leaps continue beneath the clarinet solo phrase (1'41"–1'52"), played by McKusick, but it sounds to me as though Royal missed coming in with the trumpet solo phrase (1'52"–2'03") that followed the clarinet one in 1938. The band nevertheless continues with its 'leaping' riffs until the saxophone melody of the opening chorus reappears in counterpoint with them to drive the piece to its conclusion in a final chorus (2'03"–2'20") and coda (2'20"–2'31").

Although the original 'Toadie Toddle' featured the 'leaping' ensemble riffs for a few phrases after the vocal, they are ultimately replaced by different counterpoint for the final 'shout' chorus of the number. By contrast, in the 1956 rearrangement, the playfully leaping riffs are maintained right to the end of the piece to bind the number together and maintain its vitality. Their meter-defying character are what make them pleasurable, for the listener and the performer, and one can almost hear the delight of Kirk and his band in the murmurings that are audible in the background of the 1956 track—unless these represents a telling off of Royal for missing his solo!

It is this sort of attention that is given to the more playful details of the original music as well as the greater volume possibilities of the bigger ensemble that constitutes the stylistic masking in the track and which brings 1950s pleasure for Kirk, the RCA-Victor band, and contemporary listeners. The emphasis that is placed on such specifics is the form of caricature that was afforded by the new arrangements of the Clouds of Joy's numbers and the 1956 band's energizing of them in their fulsome rendition under Kirk's leadership. Had Kirk been set on being authentic in recreating the track of 1938, there is no way he would have let that missed trumpet solo pass onto the 1957 album. However, as Kirk suggested in his comment on the album, the emphasis was otherwise placed on the band's 1950s reinvention of the 'feel' of the Clouds of Joy's music and not on fidelity to the letter of the original tracks (Kirk, as cited in Wilson 1957). In other words, Kirk all but acknowledged that 1950s stylistic mask-play is at work in its Signifyin(g) on notions of musical-racial authenticity in the original tracks.

'Take It and Git' (G2 JB-2515) was already a light-hearted, entertainment number when the Clouds of Joy recorded it in March 1942. It was surely the fun of its call-and-response chorus form that, in October of that year, made it the first No. 1 hit in *Billboard*'s 'Harlem Hit Parade' chart. Wilson's liner notes describe the 1956 version as a 'bright, jabbing game of musical chairs', but, if anything, it is more a musical game of throw and catch (Wilson 1957). The piece is built from double choruses founded on the 12-bar blues changes. As in the original record, the first chorus in each pair contrasts the players chanting of the title line, with solo breaks. The chanted calls provoke the second chorus, which follows shouts of acceptance like 'Ok, I got it!' from the soloist, and extends short breaks for individuals into a full-blown solo chorus.

The original 1942 solos are dominated by Kersey's piano because it features in two of these double choruses. Kersey's solos are preceded by Floyd Smith's guitar solo and they surround a trombone solo from Ted Donnelly. Although very close in structure to the original arrangement, the 1956 version heard on the 1957 album has more variety in the solo offerings. After the opening ensemble chorus (0'06"–0'23"), McKusick is heard in an alto saxophone solo (0'23"–0'41") before he passes the baton to Kersey (0'57"–1'14") for a piano solo, which is startlingly similar to his 1942 effort and thereby signals a certain sort of authenticity. As in the earlier recording, the piano gives over to a trombone (1'31"–1'49"), but Rehak's solo has quite a different 1950s character. The ever-dependable Cohn then replaces Kersey for the final solo chorus (2'06"–2'22") before tutti saxophones lead in to the last chorus (2'22" --2'48"). That features ensembles within the band trading motifs and the accompanying brass stabs gradually come to dominate as the rearrangement reaches a climactic closing tag. Unlike the closing double chorus in the original recording (the second allowing the brass to lead the saxes), only the first 12 bars are heard on the 1957 record, but they are surely arresting enough in their greater sonic power.

Despite the different solos, the 1956 rearrangement of 'Take It and Git', like those of 'McGhee Special' and 'Scratchin' in the Gravel', is strikingly similar to the original. In terms of the conceit in its form, the original 1942 number is also similar to the 1936 swing-vocal 'Git', which features the same sort of band-vocal 'calls' to prompt various solo 'responses'. In this sense, the 1956 recollection takes its place in a continuum or chain of stylistic Signifyin(g) on musical-racial authenticity within Kirk's recordings: a 1950s number Signifies on a 1940s number that Signifies on the original 1936 track. So, there are multiple layers to the Signifyin(g) stylistic mask-play that Kirk presents in the 1957 album.

The final number on the *Mellow Bit of Rhythm* LP is 'Boogie Woogie Cocktail' (G2 JB-2516), Ken Kersey's piano feature that was first recorded by the Clouds of Joy in July 1942. It was no doubt because Kersey was the only original member of Kirk's Clouds of Joy (aside from Kirk himself) to participate in the 1956 RCA-Victor band that it forms the finale of the 1957 LP's programme of 'beat conscious' recollections. On the 1957 LP, Kersey's showpiece is telescoped somewhat and it is a bit more slapdash and less varied in Kersey's performance than in the original recording.[13]

---

13 This may have been because Kersey was already suffering from the serious illness that Peter J. Silvester reports led to his retirement in the late 1950s (Silvester 2009: 182).

However, it is no less exciting for that, but in a different sense. Even in his four-bar introduction (0'00"–0'03"), Kersey stumbles over the notes a little, and when the band bursts in, with blazing trumpets almost drowning the saxophones' riff-based melody, it marks something of a relief because it seems to secure the track's momentum. It could thus be argued that the tables are turned in the 1957 album in that it is more the voluminous RCA-Victor band than the soloist that gives the updated 'Boogie Woogie Cocktail' its hot-jazz vitality.

The introductory ensemble statement of the original track is extended from eight bars to cover the whole of the 12-bar-blues structure (0'03"–0'15"). As in the original record, Kersey then solos, but his effort is cut down from four to two blues choruses (0'15"–0'38") before the ensemble re-enters. As in the fourth and fifth choruses of the 1942 record, the ensemble presents the first four bars in both of the following solo choruses on the 1957 album (0'38"–1'01"). In the original record these choruses form a contrast with the rest of the arrangement, in the manner of a 'release' (bridge) section, and in them Kersey offers some of his most dynamic and fluid solo playing because of the absence of the incessant boogie-woogie in his left hand. In 1956, however, Kersey opted to keep the boogie-woogie left hand going. This makes his soloing seem less varied, but it more vividly emphasizes the vital beat of the original boogie-woogie style and plays up to the notion of the seductive qualities of hot rhythm as a key feature of the stylistic Signifyin(g) of the 1957 album.

As in the original recording, Kersey is left on his own after the ensemble/solo passages but his three subsequent solo choruses on the original recording are reduced to just one on the 1957 album (1'01"–1'13"). To make up for this foreshortening, his following chorus of dialogue with the saxophones (1'13"–1'24") is doubled in length and the second of these choruses (1'24"–1'36") is embellished with 'screaming' trumpets and counterpointing trombone riffs, which are not in the original recording. They are also greatly enhanced by audio engineering of the balance on the 1957 record.[14] This leads to the final cadenza (1'36"–2'11"), which is similar in design to the Gershwin-like original but perhaps a little more faltering in its execution. As in the original record, this cadenza leads to an explosion of a final chord for the band that is all the

14 To my mind the only way that the trumpets playing at the top of their range could be balanced with the trombones' counterpointing riffs is through careful mixing of the audio.

more explosive on the RCA-Victor record for the bigger band and 'New Orthophonic' sound.

As Kersey seems less secure than in his earlier recording, there is a sense in which this recollection of 'Boogie Woogie Cocktail' represents a musical white-knuckle ride on a fast and powerful musical rollercoaster, from which one expects Kersey to fall at any moment. In his liner notes, Wilson describes the piece as 'Ken Kersey's flash specialty', but as in most of the tracks on the 1957 LP, it is rather the bigger band and the audio engineering and technologies that makes it sound flashy in the revision, as Kersey barely seems to hang on at times (Wilson 1957). But hang on he does, and, if anything, this only makes for an even more exhilarating recording for hearing him do so, supported by a more fulsome and interactive backing. In several ways, then, the 1950s stylistic mask can bring an extra, if different, appeal to the original music as much as it Signifies upon it.

In conclusion, this survey of the tracks on the 1957 album has illuminated how the RCA-Victor band, under Kirk's leadership and through new arrangements, re-presented a carefully selected set of recordings of the Clouds of Joy in a louder, brasher, and more energy-filled 1950s big-band sound. Ultimately the analysis suggests that the agenda of such re-presentations was to positively establish a hot-jazz legacy for the Clouds of Joy by reinventing their old repertoire in a striking 1950s style. The masked re-presentations involved reappropriating even their sweet-styled music as 'authentic' hot-jazz material of the 1950s. Thus, the decidedly black 'stomping' hot jazz that the Clouds of Joy produced for race records in the 1929–1931 period, the elegant form of swing they recorded from 1936 on, the apparent 'whiting up' represented by their popular sweet ballads, and the turn towards rhythm 'n' blues styles in the 1940s, all become something of an echo of Kirk's past negotiations between his band's music and the racist expectations of the music industry and audiences masked beneath a 1950s veneer.

The restyling in the 1957 album shows how its recollections ultimately Signify on the idea that a 'true' black-jazz artistry lay behind all the different forms or layers of stylistic masking that are implied in the band's earlier recording activity. However, we have seen that the 1950s reinterpretation of the band's music involved a set of stylistic features that were not wholly authentic to those heard in the earlier recordings of the Clouds of Joy: they were in themselves parts of a contemporary form of stylistic masking. It traded in late-1950s notions of aural pleasure related to sonic fullness and stereotyped conceptions of heterosexual masculinity and sex that were then associated with hot-black jazz. There is a sense, therefore, that the 1957 album was as much a 1950s form of stylistic Signifyin(g) on musical-racial authenticity, as any other in Andy Kirk's output.

The fact that the 1957 album sought reinvent the past recordings of the Clouds of Joy as part of the canon of 'authentic' hot-jazz music, thereby cementing the identity and legacy of the Clouds of Joy as a hot-black jazz band, only underlines the enterprise, resilience and achievements of black musicians like Kirk in the face of the racist and commercial pressures that they experienced. While the comparison of figures like Kirk with the later bebop generation of more overtly political black jazz musicians might reflect on the Clouds of Joy as prone to 'Uncle Tomming' in their apparent acquiescence with institutionalized racism, their recordings stand within the context of their period as a manifesto for a subtle form of racial politics that paved the way for later activism. Their stylistic mask-play can be heard to Signify on enduring concepts of racial and musical authenticity and ultimately serves to highlight the fraudulence of any such essentialist notions of the authentic in matters of musical style and race that underpin understanding of jazz.

Kirk and his band's engagement with recording culture, through the artifice of Signifyin(g) stylistic mask-play, constantly found ways around the institutionalized racism that they experienced as they continually renegotiated their musical-racial identity through their music and records. If anything, the 1957 album thus shows the lasting vibrancy of music formed as musicians negotiated jazz's racist culture during a crucial period in the commercialization of jazz and the development of lasting critical discourses that came with it. The musical recollections represented on the album are thus as important as any of the past music of Andy Kirk and his Clouds of Joy precisely because of their apparent inauthenticity. In that respect, the album is a loud and proud 1950s celebration of inauthentic black authenticity, a sort of black pride rooted in the undermining racial politics of Signifyin(g) stylistic mask-play.

This book has shown that throughout their recording career Andy Kirk and his Clouds of Joy Signified on notions of black-jazz authenticity through the music that they made and recorded. As this book's introduction suggested, the musical background of Andy Kirk and the origins of the Clouds of Joy were not in lowdown black jazz but in relatively modern, urban, and sophisticated dance music produced mainly for white-society audiences to enjoy. That sort of music not only provided a living for the musicians but it also chimed with an agenda of racial pride for enterprising and aspirational black musicians like Kirk. Chapter 1, however, showed that recording involved Kirk and his band donning stylistic masks of blackness to meet industry and public expectations of a black band. They effectively blacked up in the prevailing styles of black-sounding jazz, helped by Mary Lou Williams's original compositions, to please record producers' racist preconceptions about black-jazz authenticity that derived from critical tropes surrounding jazz.

In this way, Signifyin(g) mask-play around musical styles and expectations of racial-authenticity about them, which to some extent had always come with their live work, became a staple part of the band's music and recordings. They thereby formed a hybrid sort of musical style, which proved uncomfortable for jazz criticism because it was both sweet (inauthentic) and hot (authentic) black music, and thereby did not fit easily within established critical values that were based on notions of racial-stylistic purity. Through their sweet-and-hot stylistic mask-play, the band's music served to question the whole notion of black-authentic expression that underpinned critical judgements of jazz music and its recording. The band's records have this function because a fundamental critical question is left unresolved by their hybrid and varied stylistic output: Is this an inauthentic sweet (commercial, white-sounding) dance band or an authentic hot (modern, black-sounding) jazz band?

Chapter 2 showed how this hybrid and critical style was cemented during the 1930s through the band's addressing of ongoing feedback from the dancing white audiences that they served in live performance. That was married with their experiences of recording race records and partaking in the fertile black-jazz culture of Kansas City. Participating in after-hours jam sessions together with responding to the beating feet of mainly white and regional social dancers helped hammer out a distinctively subtler and more refined style of swing music than was produced by the harder driving New York bands that played for more energetic Lindy Hop dancing. Mary Lou Williams was shown to be instrumental in defining this style along with characteristic soloists, like Dick Wilson. Under Kirk's leadership they brought the hot-sweet identity of the band's jazz into a swing aesthetic. That updated style continued to prove troublesome in terms of its black-jazz authenticity for critics like Gunther Schuller, especially when the band turned to record numerous sweet-styled ballads with their singer Pha Terrell.

Chapter 3 considered the apparent falseness of Terrell's falsetto in those ballads in terms of the way it also raised questions about notions of musical-racial fidelity that have underpinned jazz criticism. Terrell's many ballad recordings were launched in 1936 with the appropriately titled song, 'Until the Real Thing Comes Along'. For critics like Schuller, Terrell's falsetto 'crooning' represented the worst excesses of sweet-styled commercialism in jazz and a musical-racial inauthenticity that, from a homophobic critical perspective, was morally aligned with a simpering effeminacy and homosexuality. Nevertheless, the Trianon Ballroom recordings of 1937 suggest that the popularity of the ballad recordings were such that in live-performance situations, the band increasingly had to wear their own sweet-jazz style as a mask to meet audience expectations while otherwise maintaining a hot-jazz black identity in their repertoire.

We have seen that a watershed moment was reached by 1942 following the death of Wilson and the departure of Terrell and Williams from the Clouds of Joy. The black-vernacular theatricality of June Richmond's vocals returned the band to a subversive and minstrel-like theatrical representation of a modern-black 'authenticity' of a sort they had first recorded with 'Casey Jones Special' back in 1929. However, Richmond also brought a contrasting seriousness into songs like 'Ride On, Ride On' and, together with the 'concerto' numbers for the band's leading soloists, like 'Boogie Woogie Cocktail' and 'McGhee Special', they represented black-jazz authenticity within a repertoire that still courted apparently inauthentic commerciality. That was demonstrated by Richmond's chart successes for the band and their turn towards recording with vocal groups like the Jubalaires in the later 1940s. Even within that race-market output, though, chapter 3 showed that there was always an underlying politic in the stylistic mask-play of the music about the inauthenticity of articulating racial essentialism with musical style.

In this chapter, we have seen that a decade after Kirk wound up his band for commercial reasons, he returned to the studio to reflect on more than twenty years of recordings that he made with the Clouds of Joy. The 1957 album was no less concerned with representing a politic around jazz-authenticity through the 1950s style of big-band music that it contained. While the album represented a canon-forming agenda of hot-jazz authenticity for Andy Kirk and his Clouds of Joy, in the track selections that were drawn from the band's past music it also presented a form of inauthenticity in its translation of those old jazz tracks into a 1950s big-band idiom: only one of Kirk's former players was in the band, it played new arrangements scored for a bigger and brasher ensemble, and it exploited contemporary audio technologies to court audience desires about the rewards of jazz recordings that would have been unthinkable in the 1930s and 1940s.

Although this study has focused on the recordings of a band that has largely been assigned to the margins of jazz history, it has shown that those recordings deal in the mainstream critical values that underpin their marginalization. These entwined values of racial authenticity, musical styles, and artistry have defined the whole of jazz culture and so they extend way beyond the context of Andy Kirk and his Clouds of Joy to more central figures in jazz such as Duke Ellington, Count Basie, and Fletcher Henderson, to mention but three. However, this book suggests that by attending to such marginal figures who don't wholly fit within the established critical paradigms for evaluating jazz, we can reveal the ideologies that are at work behind those paradigms. Furthermore, when such ideologies turn out to be artistically biased, racist, gendered, and homophobic, as this study has illuminated, such an approach can illuminate them for what they are, deep-seated critical prejudices, and show how they were challenged by those jazz musicians that are most often subjected to them.

One of my own preconceptions, which this study has challenged, was the notion that the repertoire outside of the band's 'classic' Brunswick records and the swing charts of Mary Lou Williams are not very interesting or valuable as jazz. This book has turned that idea on its head. In the end, this study has used the most critically problematic music that was recorded by the band to reconceptualize jazz as a broader aesthetic terrain than critical dogma would have us believe: it embraces apparently inauthentic, sweet, and commercial styles of music, as much as critics wish to disavow them. We should consider them a part of jazz rather than shun them, as to do so is to perpetuate deeply prejudiced ideologies. Furthermore, it has shown that racial activism in jazz was not just something that came with the development of bebop in the 1940s, but it was occurring, albeit in a subtler form, in jazz culture of the 1930s, as black jazz musicians, like Kirk's, came to terms with their increasingly apparent commodification at the hands of the white-run industries that they experienced.

This book has shown that when figures like Andy Kirk, Mary Lou Williams, Dick Wilson, Pha Terrell, June Richmond, and the Jubalaires are considered within the context of negotiations over what and how they performed and recorded, they can be heard to play and sing loudly about the ways that their music was always conditioned by their struggle to overcome the racist structures and values that they faced. That music was therefore instrumental in addressing those conditions.

In the course of making this case for the illuminating power of such figures for understanding the critical underpinning of the jazz canon, this study has contributed to, if not opened up, several new avenues that are worthy of further exploration. These include re-conceptualizing the effects of the close relationship between swing music and dance, the articulation of discourses of gender and sexuality with race in jazz criticism, and the influence of developing technologies within the expressive language of jazz recordings.

The book raises a particular challenge for jazz scholars to explore more of the recorded music of apparently marginal figures like Andy Kirk and his Clouds of Joy for what it might say about the values that underpin the mainstream of jazz culture. It also raises an urgent question for jazz criticism: How can we avoid articulating value in jazz with racist notions of authenticity that have prevailed for the last century? Finally, and most importantly, it challenges even casual listeners not to rely on critical biases in their listening. Instead, it suggests we all open our ears to the possibility that the tracks which are most often deemed to be the most problematic or least valuable may, in fact, prove to be the key to understanding jazz musicians and their recorded music. Moreover, they may be vital in revealing the ideologies that serve to keep them in a place that, most often, someone else with more sociopolitical power has determined for them. This suggests we need new ways of listening that are about hearing the disempowered within powerful critical discourses and that is a major future project in itself.

APPENDIX
DISCOGRAPHY
1929–1949

THIS DISCOGRAPHY IS based on the model of Howard Rye's listing in *Twenty Years on Wheels* (Kirk 1989: 120–143). Since Rye's discography was published, some new sources have come to light that correct and add details, particularly concerning the recordings of radio broadcasts made during the 1940s. These sources include the listings in Petersen and Rehak's 2009 biography of Fats Navarro and the catalogues of the AFRS broadcasts produced by the Glenn Miller Archive at the University of Colorado at Boulder. Those sources were cross-referenced with the AFRS *Jubilee* discography compiled by Lotz and Neuert (1985) and the scripts in the Andy Kirk Papers in the Michigan Historical Collections held in the Bentley Historical Library of the University of Michigan. The rest of the discography has been cross-checked against Tom Lord's jazz discography (2015), Ross Laird's Brunswick discography (2001), John R. Bolig's Victor discography (2013), and Michel Ruppli's Decca discography (1996).

Whenever possible, the approach has been to list the matrix number, the title of the track as it appeared on the record (together with any vocalist information), and the original record number for each track. In the cases of the broadcast recordings, however, the programme number has been used in lieu of the matrix number and any commercial reissue has been noted in the record number column. Track information appears under a personnel list (where available) beneath the band name that appeared on the original release. All of the listed records were issued in the US unless the record number contains one of the following abbreviations:

(E)	Issued in England (United Kingdom)
(F)	Issued in France
(J)	Issued in Japan
(S)	Issued in Sweden

Most of the original records are 78 rpm shellac discs that can be hard to obtain but most of the tracks on them have since been reissued on LP, CD, and/or mp3 files to download or stream from the internet. As detailed in the introduction to this volume, most of the Brunswick, Victor, Vocalion, and Decca tracks have been reissued in *The Chronological Classics* series of CDs and those tracks have themselves been reissued as mp3 files under the title 'Complete Jazz Series' that can be downloaded from online retailers for a relatively small cost.

Abbreviations:

AFRS	Armed Forces Radio Service
as	alto saxophone
bs	baritone / bass saxophone
bb	brass bass (sousaphone)
bj	banjo
CCVPSB	Coca-Cola Victory Parade of Spotlight Bands (Radio Show)
cl	clarinet
d	drums
db	double bass
ET	Electrical Transcription (of radio broadcast onto a 16" disc)
g	guitar
ldr	leader
p	piano
tbn	trombone
tpt	trumpet
ts	tenor saxophone
v	vocal
vn	violin

C.7 NOVEMBER 1929   KMBC RADIO STATION, KANSAS CITY

Andy Kirk And His Twelve Clouds Of Joy
Gene Prince (tpt), Harry 'Big Jim' Lawson (tpt, v), Allen Durham (tbn), John Harrington (cl, as), John Williams (as, bs), Lawrence 'Slim' Freeman (ts), Claude 'Fiddler' Williams (vn, g), Mary Lou Williams (p), William Dirvin (bj), Andy Kirk (bb/bs, ldr), Edward 'Crackshot' McNeil (d).

KC591-A	Mess-a-Stomp	Brunswick 4694

John Harrington (cl), Andy Kirk (bs, ldr), Claude 'Fiddler' Williams (vn, g), William Dirvin (bj), Edward 'Crackshot' McNeil (d), Harry 'Big Jim' Lawson (v).

KC592-A	Blue Clarinet Stomp (HL, v)	Vocalion 3255
KC592-B	Blue Clarinet Stomp (HL, v)	Brunswick 4694

Same personnel as for KC591-A, Billy Massey (v)

KC593-A	Cloudy	Brunswick 4653

C.8 NOVEMBER 1929   KMBC RADIO STATION, KANSAS CITY

Andy Kirk And His Twelve Clouds Of Joy
Same personnel as for KC591-A

KC596-A	Casey Jones Special (HL, v BM, v)	Brunswick 4653

C.9 NOVEMBER 1929   KMBC RADIO STATION, KANSAS CITY

John Williams And His Memphis Stompers
Same personnel as for KC-591-A.

KC600-A	Sumpin' Slow and Low	Vocalion 1453
KC601-A	Lotta Sax Appeal	Vocalion 1453

C.11 NOVEMBER 1929   *KMBC RADIO STATION,* KANSAS CITY

Andy Kirk And His Twelve Clouds Of Joy
Same personnel as for KC591-A.

KC618-A	Corky Stomp	Brunswick 4893
KC619-A	Froggy Bottom	Brunswick 4893

29 APRIL 1930   *BRUNSWICK STUDIO, CHICAGO*

Andy Kirk And His Twelve Clouds Of Joy
Edgar 'Puddin' Head' Battle (tpt), Harry 'Big Jim' Lawson (tpt), Floyd 'Stumpy' Brady (tbn), John Harrington (cl, as), John Williams (as, bs), Lawrence 'Slim' Freeman (ts), Claude 'Fiddler' Williams (vn, g), Mary Lou Williams (p), William Dirvin (bj), Andy Kirk (bb, ldr), Ben Thigpen (d), Billy Massey (v).

C4460-A	I Lost My Gal From Memphis (BM, v)	Brunswick 4803
C4462-A	Loose Ankles (BM, v)	Brunswick 4803

30 APRIL 1930   *BRUNSWICK STUDIO, CHICAGO*

Andy Kirk And His Twelve Clouds Of Joy
Same personnel as for 29 April 1930.

C4470	Snag It	Brunswick 4878
C4471	Sweet And Hot	Brunswick 4878
C4472	Sweet And Hot	unissued
C4473	Mary's Idea	Brunswick 4863

1 MAY 1930   *BRUNSWICK STUDIO, CHICAGO*

Andy Kirk And His Twelve Clouds Of Joy
Same personnel as for 29 April 1930.

C4480	Once Or Twice (BM, v)	Brunswick 4863

15 JULY 1930   *BRUNSWICK STUDIO, CHICAGO*

Andy Kirk And His Seven Little Clouds Of Joy
Harry 'Big Jim' Lawson (tpt), Floyd 'Stumpy' Brady (tbn), John Williams (bs), Mary Lou Williams (p), William Dirvin (bj), Andy Kirk (bb, ldr), Ben Thigpen (d, v).

C6017	Gettin' Off A Mess	Brunswick 7180
C6018	You Rascal, You (BT, v)	unissued

30 SEPTEMBER 1930   *BRUNSWICK STUDIO, CHICAGO*

Andy Kirk And His Twelve Clouds Of Joy
Same personnel as for 29 April 1930.

C6177	Okay, Baby	unissued
C6178	Dallas Blues (BM, v)	unissued

9 OCTOBER 1930   *BRUNSWICK STUDIO, CHICAGO*

Andy Kirk And His Twelve Clouds Of Joy
Same personnel as for 29 April 1930.

C6430-A	Dallas Blues (BM, v)	Brunswick 6129
C6431	Traveling That Rocky Road	Brunswick 4981
C6432	Honey, Just For You (BM, v)	Brunswick 4981

Seven Little Clouds Of Joy

Note: Same personnel as for 29 April 1930 despite the band credit.

| C6435 | You Rascal, You (BM, v) | Brunswick 7180 |

15 DECEMBER 1930   *BRUNSWICK STUDIO, NEW YORK CITY*

Andy Kirk And His Twelve Clouds Of Joy
Same personnel as for 29 April 1930, Dick Robertson (v).

| E35750 | Saturday (DR, v) | Brunswick 6027 |
| E35751 | Sophomore (DR, v) | Brunswick 6027 |

2 MARCH 1931   *VICTOR'S CHURCH STUDIO 2, CAMDEN, NEW JERSEY*

Blanche Calloway And Her Joy Boys
Edgar 'Puddin' Head' Battle (tpt), Harry 'Big Jim' Lawson (tpt), Clarence Smith (tpt, v), Floyd 'Stumpy' Brady (tbn), John Harrington (cl, as), John Williams (as, bs), Lawrence 'Slim' Freeman (ts), Mary Lou Williams (p), William Dirvin (bj), Andy Kirk (bb, ldr), Ben Thigpen (d), Billy Massey (v), Blanche Calloway (v).

64068-1	Casey Jones Special (BM, v; CS, v)	Victor 22640
64069-2	There's Rhythm In The River (BC, v)	Victor 22641
64070-2	I Need Lovin' (BC, v) (erroneously issued as 'All I Need Is Lovin'")	Victor 22641

2 MARCH 1936   *DECCA STUDIO, NEW YORK CITY*

Andy Kirk And His Twelve Clouds Of Joy
Harry 'Big Jim' Lawson (tpt), Paul King (tpt), Earl Thomson (tpt), Ted Donnelly (tbn), Henry Wells (tbn), John Harrington (cl, as), John Williams (cl, as, bs), Dick Wilson (ts), Mary Lou Williams (p), Ted Brinson (g), Booker Collins (db), Ben Thigpen (d, v), Pha Terrell (v), Andy Kirk (ldr).

60852-A	Walkin' And Swingin'	Columbia (E) DB5023
60852-C	Walkin' And Swingin'	Decca 809
60853-A	Moten Swing	Decca 853
60854-A	Lotta Sax Appeal	Decca 1046

3 MARCH 1936   *DECCA STUDIO, NEW YORK CITY*

Andy Kirk And His Twelve Clouds Of Joy
Same personnel as for 2 March 1936.

60861-A	Git (BT, v)	Columbia (E) DB5021
60861-B	Git (BT, v)	Decca 931
60862-A	All The Jive Is Gone (PT, v)	Decca 744

Note: Some pressings of Decca 931 use an alternate take of Git: 60861-C.

4 MARCH 1936   *DECCA STUDIO, NEW YORK CITY*

Andy Kirk And His Twelve Clouds Of Joy
Same personnel as for 2 March 1936.

60865-A	Froggy Bottom (BT, v)	Columbia (E) DB5000
60865-B	Froggy Bottom (BT, v)	Decca 729
60866-A	Bearcat Shuffle	Decca 1046
60867-A	Steppin' Pretty	Decca 931

Note: Some pressings of Decca 729 use an alternate take of Froggy Bottom: 60856-B.

7 MARCH 1936   *DECCA STUDIO, NEW YORK CITY*

Andy Kirk And His Twelve Clouds Of Joy
Same personnel as for 2 March 1936.

| 60874-A | Christopher Columbus | Decca 729 |
| 60876-A | Corky | Decca 772 |

11 MARCH 1936   *DECCA STUDIO, NEW YORK CITY*

Andy Kirk And His Twelve Clouds Of Joy
Same personnel as for 2 March 1936.

| 60886-A | I'se A-Muggin' (BT, v) | Decca 744 |
| 60887-A | Until The Real Thing Comes Along (PT, v) | Columbia (E) DB5004 |

31 MARCH 1936   *DECCA STUDIO, NEW YORK CITY*

Andy Kirk And His Twelve Clouds Of Joy
Same personnel as for 2 March 1936.

| 60961-A | Puddin' Head Serenade | Columbia (E) DB5027 |

2 APRIL 1936   *DECCA STUDIO, NEW YORK CITY*

Andy Kirk And His Twelve Clouds Of Joy
Same personnel as for 2 March 1936.

| 60972-A | Until The Real Thing Comes Along (PT, v) | Decca 809 |

3 APRIL 1936   *DECCA STUDIO, NEW YORK CITY*

Andy Kirk And His Clouds of Joy
Same personnel as for 2 March 1936.

60973-A	Blue Illusion (PT, v)	Decca 772
60974-A	Cloudy (PT, v)	Decca 1208

7 APRIL 1936   *DECCA STUDIO, NEW YORK CITY*

Andy Kirk And His Clouds of Joy
Same personnel as for 2 March 1936.

61003-A	Give Her A Pint (And She'll Tell It All) (PT, v)	Decca 853

10 APRIL 1936   *DECCA STUDIO, NEW YORK CITY*

Andy Kirk And His Clouds of Joy
Same personnel as for 2 March 1936.

60961-C	Puddin' Head Serenade	Decca 1208

9 DECEMBER 1936   *DECCA STUDIO, NEW YORK CITY*

Andy Kirk And His Clouds of Joy
Probably the same personnel as for March 1936; Harry Mills (v).

61463-A	Fifty-Second Street (HM, v)	Decca 1146
61464-A	The Lady Who Swings The Band (HM, v)	Decca 1085
61465-A	What Will I Tell My Heart? (PT, v)	Decca 1085
61466-B	Dedicated To You (PT, v)	Decca 1146

29 JANUARY 1937   *TRIANON BALLROOM,*
CLEVELAND, OHIO

Andy Kirk And His Clouds of Joy
Probably the same personnel as for 2 March 1936.

Unknown	Theme (Until The Real Thing Comes Along)	unissued
Unknown	You Turned The Tables On Me	unissued
Unknown	Never Slept A Wink Last Night	Jazz Society (S) AA503
Unknown	Goodnight My Love	unissued
Unknown	You Do the Darnedest Things	unissued
Unknown	Spring Holiday	unissued
Unknown	When I'm With You	unissued
Unknown	Make Believe Ballroom	Jazz Society (S) AA503
Unknown	Sepia Jazz	Jazz Society (S) AA503
Unknown	(I Went To A) Gypsy (PT, v)	unissued
Unknown	Closing theme (Clouds)	unissued

30 JANUARY 1937   *TRIANON BALLROOM,*
CLEVELAND, OHIO

Andy Kirk And His Clouds of Joy
Probably the same personnel as for 2 March 1936.

Unknown	Theme (Until The Real Thing Comes Along)	unissued
Unknown	You're Slightly Terrific	Jazz Society (S) AA503
Unknown	Yours Truly	Jazz Society (S) AA503

Unknown	Trust In Me (PT, v)	Jazz Society (S) AA503
Unknown	All The Jive Is Gone	Jazz Society (S) AA503
Unknown	Dear Old Southland	Jazz Society (S) AA503
Unknown	In The Chapel In The Moonlight	unissued
Unknown	Closing theme (Clouds)	unissued

5 FEBRUARY 1937   *TRIANON BALLROOM, CLEVELAND, OHIO*

Andy Kirk And His Clouds of Joy
Probably the same personnel as for 2 March 1936.

Unknown	Theme (Until The Real Thing Comes Along)	unissued
Unknown	Honeysuckle Rose	unissued
Unknown	There's Frost On The Moon	unissued
Unknown	Medley (PT, v): Boo Hoo One, Two, Button Your Shoe Trouble Don't Like Music One In A Million	Jazz Society (S) AA503
Unknown	Walkin' And Swingin'	unissued
Unknown	Dedicated To You	unissued
Unknown	Oh Say Can You Swing	unissued
Unknown	King Porter Stomp	unissued
Unknown	Liza	unissued
Unknown	Closing Theme (Clouds)	unissued

6 FEBRUARY 1937   *TRIANON BALLROOM, CLEVELAND, OHIO*

Andy Kirk And His Clouds of Joy
Probably the same personnel as for 2 March 1936.

Unknown	Theme (Until The Real Thing Comes Along)	Jazz Society (S) AA503
Unknown	Swingtime in the Rockies	Jazz Society (S) AA503
Unknown	Froggy Bottom	Jazz Society (S) AA503
Unknown	What Will I Tell My Heart (PT, v)	Jazz Society (S) AA503
Unknown	Moten Swing	Jazz Society (S) AA503
Unknown	There, I Love Your From Coast To Coast	Jazz Society (S) AA503
Unknown	Organ Grinder's Swing	Jazz Society (S) AA503
Unknown	Closing Theme (Clouds)	Jazz Society (S) AA503

15 FEBRUARY 1937   *DECCA STUDIO, NEW YORK CITY*

Andy Kirk And his Clouds Of Joy
Harry 'Big Jim' Lawson (tpt), Paul King (tpt), Earl Thompson (tpt), Ted Donnelly (tbn), Henry Wells (tbn), John Harrington (cl, as, bs), John Williams (cl, as, bs), Earl Miller (as), Dick Wilson (ts), Mary Lou Williams (p), Ted Brinson (g), Booker Collins (db), Ben Thigpen (d, v), Pha Terrell (v), Andy Kirk (ldr).

61598-A	Wednesday Night Hop	Decca 1303
61599-A	Skies Are Blue (PT, v)	Decca 1349
61950-B	Downstream (PT, v)	Decca 1531
61951-A	In the Groove	Decca 1261

17 APRIL 1937   *DECCA STUDIO, NEW YORK CITY*

Andy Kirk And His Clouds of Joy
Same personnel as for 15 February 1937.

62133-A	Worried Over You (PT, v)	Decca 1303
62134-B	Foolin' Myself (PT, v)	Decca 1261
62135-A	I'm Glad for Your Sake (But I'm Sorry For Mine) (PT, v)	Decca 1531
62136-A	I'll Get Along Somehow (PT, v)	Decca 1349

26 JULY 1937   *DECCA STUDIO, NEW YORK CITY*

Andy Kirk And His Clouds of Joy
Same personnel as for 15 February 1937.

62446-A	A Mellow Bit of Rhythm	Decca 1579
62447-A	In My Wildest Dreams (PT, v)	Decca 1579
62448-A	Better Luck Next Time (PT, v)	Decca 1422
62449-A	With Love In My Heart (PT, v)	Decca 1477

27 JULY 1937   *DECCA STUDIO, NEW YORK CITY*

Andy Kirk And His Clouds of Joy
Same personnel as for 15 February 1937.

62453-B	What's Mine Is Yours (PT, v)	Decca 1827
62454-A	Why Can't We Do It Again? (HW, v)	Decca 1477
62455-A	The Key To My Heart (PT, v)	Decca 1710
62456-A	I Went To A Gypsy (PT, v)	Decca 1422

Andy Kirk And His Twelve Clouds Of Joy
Harry 'Big Jim' Lawson (tpt), Clarence Trice (tpt), Earl Thomson (tpt), Ted Donnelly (tbn), Henry Wells (tbn, v), John Harrington (cl, as), John Williams (as, bs), Earl Miller (as), Dick Wilson (ts), Mary Lou Williams (p), Ted Brinson (g), Booker Collins (db), Ben Thigpen (d, v), Pha Terrell (v), Andy Kirk (ldr).

62872-A	Lover, Come Back To Me (PT, v)	Decca 1663
62873-A	Poor Butterfly (PT, v)	Decca 1663
62874-A	The Big Dipper	Decca 1606
62875-A	Bear Down	Decca 1606

Andy Kirk And His Clouds of Joy
Same personnel as for 13 December 1937.

63255-A	I Surrender Dear (PT, v)	Decca 1916
63256-A	Twinklin'	Decca 2483
63257-A	It Must Be True (PT, v)	Decca 1827
63258-A	I'll Get By (HW, v)	Decca 1916
63259-A	Little Joe From Chicago	Decca 1710

Andy Kirk And His Clouds of Joy
Same personnel as for 13 December 1937; Rodney Sturgis (v).

64612-A	The Gal That Wrecked My Life (RS, v)	Decca 7550
64613-A	Bless You, My Dear (PT, v)	Decca 2204
64614-A	How Can We Be Wrong? (PT, v)	Decca 2081
64615-A	Mess-a Stomp	Decca 2204

Note: a smaller band was drawn from the ranks of the Clouds of Joy for the Sturgis vocal.

12 SEPTEMBER 1938   *DECCA STUDIO, NEW YORK CITY*

Andy Kirk And His Clouds of Joy
Same personnel as for 13 December 1937.

64642-A	Toadie Toddle (BT, v)	Decca 2127
64643-A	I Won't Tell A Soul (I Love You) (PT, v)	Decca 2127
64644-A	What Would People Say? (PT, v)	Decca 2277
64645-A	How Much Do You Mean To Me? (PT, v)	Decca 2081

24 OCTOBER 1938   *DECCA STUDIO, NEW YORK CITY*

Andy Kirk And His Clouds of Joy
Same personnel as for 13 December 1937.

64694-A	Jump Jack, Jump	Decca 2226
64695-A	Breeze (Blow My Baby Back To Me) (PT, v)	Decca 2261
64696-A	Ghost of Love (PT, v)	Decca 2226
64697-A	What A Life (Trying To Live Without You) (PT, v)	Decca 2617

25 OCTOBER 1938   *DECCA STUDIO, NEW YORK CITY*

Andy Kirk And His Clouds of Joy
Same personnel as for 13 December 1937.

64698-A	Sittin' Around And Dreamin' (PT, v)	Decca 2261
64699-A	What's Your Story, Morning Glory? (PT, v)	Decca 3306

5 DECEMBER 1938 *DECCA STUDIO, NEW YORK CITY*

Andy Kirk And His Twelve Clouds Of Joy
Same personnel as for 13 December 1937; O'Neill Spencer (v).

64777-A	Honey (PT, v)	Decca 2326
64778-A	September In The Rain (PT, v)	Decca 2617
64779-A	Clouds (PT, v)	Decca 2570
64780-A	Julius Caesar (OS, v)	Decca 2383
64781-A	Dunkin' A Doughnut	Decca 2723

6 DECEMBER 1938 *DECCA STUDIO, NEW YORK CITY*

Andy Kirk And his Clouds Of Joy
Same personnel as for 13 December 1937.

64782-A	Goodbye (PT, v)	Decca 2570
64783-A	Mary's Idea	Decca 2326
64784-A	But It Didn't Mean A Thing (PT, v)	Decca 2277
64785-A	Say It Again (PT, v)	Decca 2774

16 MARCH 1939 *DECCA STUDIO, NEW YORK CITY*

Andy Kirk And His Clouds of Joy
Harry 'Big Jim' Lawson (tpt), Clarence Trice (tpt), Earl Thomson (tpt), Ted Donnelly (tbn), Henry Wells (tbn), John Harrington (cl, as), Earl 'Buddy' Miller (as), Don Byas (ts), Dick Wilson (ts), Mary Lou Williams (p), Floyd 'Wonderful' Smith (g), Booker Collins (db), Ben Thigpen (d, v), June Richmond (v), Pha Terrell (v), Andy Kirk (ldr).

65188-A	You Set Me On Fire (PT, v)	Decca 2383
65189-A	I'll Never Learn (PT, v)	Decca 2510
65190-A	Close to Five	Decca 2407
65191-A	Floyd's Guitar Blues	Decca 2483

23 MARCH 1939 *DECCA STUDIO, NEW YORK CITY*

Andy Kirk And His Clouds of Joy
Same personnel as for 16 March 1939.

65249-A	Then I'll Be Happy (JR, v)	Decca 2723
65250-A	S'posin' (PT, v)	Decca 2510
65251-A	I'll Never Fail You (PT, v)	Decca 2407
65252-A	Why Don't I Get Wise To Myself? (PT, v)	Decca 2774

15 NOVEMBER 1939 *DECCA STUDIO, NEW YORK CITY*

Andy Kirk and His Clouds of Joy
Same personnel as for 16 March 1939.

66877-A	I'm Getting Nowhere With You (PT, v)	Decca 2957
66878-A	I Don't Stand A Ghost Of A Chance With You (PT, v)	Decca 2915
66879-A	Please Don't Talk About Me When I'm Gone (JR, v)	Decca 3033
66880-A	Big Jim Blues	Decca 2915

2 JANUARY 1940 *DECCA STUDIO, NEW YORK CITY*

Andy Kirk And his Clouds Of Joy
Harry 'Big Jim' Lawson (tpt), Clarence Trice (tpt), Earl Thomson (tpt), Ted Donnelly (tbn), Jim Robinson (tbn), John Harrington (cl, as, bs), Earl 'Buddy' Miller (as), Don Byas (ts), Dick Wilson (ts), Mary Lou Williams (p), Floyd 'Wonderful' Smith (g), Booker Collins (db), Ben Thigpen (d), June Richmond (v), Pha Terrell (v).

67010-A	Wham (Wham-re-bop-boom-bam) (JR, v)	Decca 2962
67011-A	Love Is The Thing (PT, v)	Decca 2962
67012-A	Why Go On Pretending? (PT, v)	Decca 3033
67013-A	It Always Will Be You (JR, v)	Decca 2957

Note: Some pressings of Decca 2962 use an alternate take of Wham: 67010-B.

20 MARCH 1940   *COTTON CLUB, NEW YORK CITY*

Andy Kirk And his Clouds Of Joy
Harry 'Big Jim' Lawson (tpt), Harold 'Short' Baker (tpt), Clarence Trice (tpt), Ted Donnelly (tbn), Fred Robinson (tbn), Rudy Powell (cl, as), John Harrington (cl, as), Edward Inge (cl, ts), Dick Wilson (ts), Mary Lou Williams (p), Floyd 'Wonderful' Smith (g), Booker Collins (db), Ben Thigpen (d), June Richmond (v), Pha Terrell (v), Andy Kirk (ldr).

Unknown	The Sheik of Araby	unissued
Unknown	Cherokee	unissued

5 MAY 1940   *COTTON CLUB, NEW YORK CITY*

Andy Kirk And His Clouds of Joy
Same personnel as for 20 March 1940.

Unknown	The Sheik of Araby	Everybody's EV3006
Unknown	Marchetta	Everybody's EV3006

6 MAY 1940   *COTTON CLUB, NEW YORK CITY*

Andy Kirk And His Clouds of Joy
Same personnel as for 20 March 1940.

Unknown	The Riff	Everybody's EV3006

24 MAY 1940   *COTTON CLUB, NEW YORK CITY*

Andy Kirk And His Clouds of Joy
Same personnel as for 20 March 1940.

Unknown	The Riff	unissued

25 JUNE 1940   *DECCA STUDIO, NEW YORK CITY*

Andy Kirk And His Clouds of Joy
Same personnel as for 20 March 1940.

67893-A	Fine And Mellow (JR, v)	Decca 3282
67894-A	Scratchin' In The Gravel	Decca 3293
67895-A	Fifteen Minutes Intermission (JR, v)	Decca 3282
67896-A	Take Those Blues Away (JR, v)	Decca 3293

8 JULY 1940   *DECCA STUDIO, NEW YORK CITY*

Andy Kirk And His Clouds of Joy
Same personnel as for 20 March 1940.

67917-A	Now I Lay Me Down To Dream (PT, v)	Decca 3306
67918-A	(There is) No Greater Love (PT, v)	Decca 3350
67919-A	Midnight Stroll (JR, v)	Decca 3350
67920-A	Little Miss	Decca 3491

7 NOVEMBER 1940   *DECCA STUDIO, NEW YORK CITY*

Andy Kirk And his Clouds Of Joy
Harry 'Big Jim' Lawson (tpt), Harold 'Short' Baker (tpt), Clarence Trice (tpt), Ted Donnelly (tbn), Henry Wells (tbn, v), Rudy Powell (cl, as), John Harrington (cl, as), Edward Inge (cl, ts), Dick Wilson (ts), Mary Lou Williams (p), Floyd 'Wonderful' Smith (g), Booker Collins (db), Ben Thigpen (d), June Richmond (v), Andy Kirk (ldr).

68317-A	The Count	Decca 18123
68318-A	Twelfth Street Rag	Decca 18123
68319-A	When I Saw You (HW, v)	Decca 3491

18 NOVEMBER 1940 · *DECCA STUDIO, NEW YORK CITY*

Andy Kirk And His Clouds of Joy
Same personnel as for 7 November 1940.

68363-A	If I Feel This Way Tomorrow (HW, v)	Decca 3582
68364-A	Or Have I? (HW, v)	Decca 3582

3 JANUARY 1941 · *DECCA STUDIO, NEW YORK CITY*

Andy Kirk And His Clouds of Joy
Same personnel as for 7 November 1940.

68546-A	Cuban Boogie Woogie (JR, v)	Decca 3663
68547-A	A Dream Dropped In (HW, v)	Decca 3619
68548-A	Is It A Sin (Loving You)? (HW, v)	Decca 3619
68549-A	Ring Dem Bells	Decca 3663

17 JULY 1941 · *DECCA STUDIO, NEW YORK CITY*

Andy Kirk And his Clouds Of Joy
Harry 'Big Jim' Lawson (tpt), Harold 'Short' Baker (tpt), Clarence Trice (tpt), Ted Donnelly (tbn), Henry Wells (tbn), John Harrington (cl, as), Earl 'Buddy' Miller (as), Edward Inge (cl, ts), Dick Wilson (ts), Mary Lou Williams (p), Floyd 'Wonderful' Smith (g), Booker Collins (db), Ben Thigpen (d), June Richmond (v), Andy Kirk (ldr).

69519-A	Big Time Crip	Decca 4042
69520-B	47th Street Jive (JR, v)	Decca 4042
69521-A	I'm Misunderstood (HW, v)	Decca 4141
69522-A	No Answer (HW, v)	Decca 4141

14 JULY 1942   *DECCA STUDIO, NEW YORK CITY*

Andy Kirk And his Clouds Of Joy
Johnny Burris (tpt), Harry 'Big Jim' Lawson (tpt), Howard McGhee (tpt), Ted Donnelly (tbn), Milton Robinson (tbn), John Harrington (cl, as), Ben Smith (as), Edward Inge (cl, ts), Al Sears (ts), Kenny Kersey (p), Floyd 'Wonderful' Smith (g, v), Booker Collins (db), Ben Thigpen (d), June Richmond (v), Andy Kirk (ldr).

71050-A	Hey Lawdy Mama (JR, v)	Decca 4405
71051-A	Boogie Woogie Cocktail	Decca 4381
71052-A	Ride On, Ride On (JR, v)	Decca 4436
71053-A	McGhee Special	Decca 4405

29 JULY 1942   *DECCA STUDIO, NEW YORK CITY*

Andy Kirk And His Clouds of Joy
Same personnel as for 14 July 1942.

71239-A	Worried Life Blues (FS, v)	Decca 4381
71240-A	Take It and Git	Decca 4366
71241-A	Hip Hip Hooray (JR, v)	Decca 4366
71242-B	Unlucky Blues (JR, v)	Decca 4436

4 MARCH 1943   *ARMY ADMINISTRATION SCHOOL, ATLANTA UNIVERSITY, ATLANTA, GEORGIA*

Andy Kirk And His Orchestra
Harry 'Big Jim' Lawson (tpt), Theodore 'Fats' Navarro (tpt), Johnny Walker (tpt), Howard McGhee (tpt), Ted Donnelly (tbn), Wayman Richardson (tbn), Bob Murray (tbn), John Harrington (cl, as), Ben Smith (as), Reuben Philips (as), Jimmy Forrest (ts), J. D. King (ts), Johnny Young (p), Booker Collins (db), Ben Thigpen (d), June Richmond (v), Andy Kirk (ldr).

| CCVPSB #142 | New Orleans Jump | unissued beyond original ET |
| CCVPSB #142 | Don't Get Around Much Anymore (JR, v) | unissued beyond original ET |

CCVPSB #142	Blue Skies	unissued beyond original ET
CCVPSB #142	Darktown Strutter's Ball (JR, v)	unissued beyond original ET
CCVPSB #142	Boogie Woogie [Cocktail]	unissued beyond original ET
CCVPSB #142	Ridin' Along	unissued beyond original ET

1 APRIL 1943   *OZARK ORDINANCE WORKS,*
EL DORADO, ARKANSAS

Andy Kirk And His Orchestra
Probably same personnel as for 4 March 1943 without McGhee.

CCVPSB #166	Ridin' Along	unissued beyond original ET

CCVPSB #166	Medley:
	    Taking A Change On Love (JR, v)
	    I Don't Stand A Ghost Of A Chance (JR, v)
		unissued beyond original ET

CCVPSB #166	Boogie Woogie Cocktail (announced as Ozark Boogie Woogie)	unissued beyond original ET
CCVPSB #166	I've Heard That Song Before (JR, v)	unissued beyond original ET
CCVPSB #166	St Louis Blues	unissued beyond original ET
CCVPSB #166	Back Home In Indiana	unissued beyond original ET

29 JUNE 1943   *US NAVAL BASE, ST. JULIEN'S CREEK, PORTSMOUTH, VIRGINIA*

Andy Kirk And His Orchestra
Probably same personnel as for c.4 November 1943.

CCVPSB #242	Ridin' Along	unissued beyond original ET
CCVPSB #242	We Mustn't Say Goodbye (JR, v)	unissued beyond original ET
CCVPSB #242	Liza	unissued beyond original ET
CCVPSB #242	Wednesday Night Hop	unissued beyond original ET
CCVPSB #242	Wake Up	unissued beyond original ET
CCVPSB #242	Back Home In Indiana	unissued beyond original ET

C.4 NOVEMBER 1943   *NBC RADIO CITY, NEW YORK CITY*

Andy Kirk And His Orchestra
Probably Harry 'Big Jim' Lawson (tpt), Art Capeheart (tpt), Theodore 'Fats' Navarro (tpt), Howard McGhee (tpt), Joe Baird (tbn), Wayman Richardson (tbn), Bob Murray (tbn), Ben Smith (as), Reuben Phillips (as), John Harrington (cl, ts), Jimmy Forrest (ts), J. D. King (ts), Eddie Loving (bs), Johnny Young (p), Booker Collins (db), Ben Thigpen (d), June Richmond (v).

AFRS Jubilee! #54	One O'clock Jump (theme, excerpt)	unissued beyond original ET
AFRS Jubilee! #54	Avalon	unissued beyond original ET
AFRS Jubilee! #54	Wednesday Night Hop	Caracol (F) CAR424
AFRS Jubilee! #54	If That's The Way You Want It (JR, v)	unissued beyond original ET

AFRS Jubilee! #54	Hit That Jive Jack (JR, v)	unissued beyond original ET
AFRS Jubilee! #54	Seven Come Eleven	Masters of Jazz (F) MJCD143
AFRS Jubilee! #54	One O'clock Jump (theme, excerpt)	unissued beyond original ET

3 DECEMBER 1943   *DECCA STUDIO, NEW YORK CITY*

Andy Kirk And His Orchestra
Harry 'Big Jim' Lawson (tpt, v), Art Capeheart (tpt), Fats Navarro (tpt), Howard McGhee (tpt), Joe Baird (tbn), Wayman Richardson (tbn), Bob Murray (tbn), John Harrington (cl, as), Ben Smith (as), Reuben Phillips (as), Jimmy Forrest (ts), J.D. King (ts), Eddie Loving (ts, bs), Johnny Young (p), Booker Collins (db), Ben Thigpen (d), June Richmond (v), Andy Kirk (ldr).

71535	Shorty Boo (HL & AK, v)	MCA (J) 3151
71536	Fare Thee Honey, Fare Thee Well (JR, v)	Decca 4449
71537	Baby, Don't You Tell Me No Lie (JR, v)	Decca 4449
71538	Things 'Bout Comin' My Way	unissued

7 JANUARY 1944   *NEWCASTLE ARMY AIRBASE, WILMINGTON, DELAWARE*

Andy Kirk And His Orchestra
Probably similar personnel as for 3 December 1943.

CCVPSB #407	Wednesday Night Hop	unissued beyond original ET
CCVPSB #407	My Heart Tells Me (JR, v)	unissued beyond original ET
CCVPSB #407	Avalon	unissued beyond original ET

CCVPSB #407	When They Ask About You (JR, v)	unissued beyond original ET
CCVPSB #407	Back Home In Indiana	unissued beyond original ET
CCVPSB #407	St Louis Blues (JR, v)	unissued beyond original ET
CCVPSB #407	McGhee Special	unissued beyond original ET
CCVPSB #407	Ridin' Along	unissued beyond original ET

21 FEBRUARY 1944　 *NBC STUDIO C, HOLLYWOOD, CALIFORNIA*

Andy Kirk And His Orchestra
Probably the same personnel as for 3 December 1943.

AFRS Jubilee! #66	One O'clock Jump (theme, excerpt)	unissued beyond original ET
AFRS Jubilee! #66	Ridin' Along (announced as Hallelujah Heaven)	Caracol (F) CAR424
AFRS Jubilee! #66	Get Up Mule (JR, v)	Swing House 39
AFRS Jubilee! #66	Speak Low	Swing House 39
AFRS Jubilee! #66	Paradise Valley	Swing House 39
AFRS Jubilee! #66	One O'clock Jump (theme, excerpt)	unissued beyond original ET

28 FEBRUARY 1944   *NBC STUDIO C, HOLLYWOOD, CALIFORNIA*

Andy Kirk And His Orchestra
Probably the same personnel as for 3 December 1943; *Timmie Rodgers (v).*

AFRS Jubilee! #67	One O'clock Jump (theme, excerpt)	unissued beyond original ET
AFRS Jubilee! #67	Wednesday Night Hop	Caracol (F) CAR424
AFRS Jubilee! #67	McGhee Special	Caracol (F) CAR424
AFRS Jubilee! #67	If You Can Smile and Say "Yes" (TR, v)	unissued beyond original ET
AFRS Jubilee! #67	47th Street Jive (JR, v)	Caracol (F) CAR424
AFRS Jubilee! #67	Peeping Through the Keyhole	Caracol (F) CAR424
AFRS Jubilee! #67	One O'clock Jump (theme, excerpt)	unissued beyond original ET

6 MARCH 1944   *NBC STUDIOS, HOLLYWOOD, CALIFORNIA*

Andy Kirk And His Orchestra
Probably the same personnel as for 3 December 1943.

AFRS Jubilee! #68	One O'clock Jump (theme, excerpt)	Storyville CD 501 1005
AFRS Jubilee! #68	New Orleans Jump	Storyville CD 501 1005
AFRS Jubilee! #68	Basin Street Blues (JR, v)	Storyville CD 501 1005

AFRS Jubilee! #68	Little Joe from Chicago	Storyville CD 501 1005
AFRS Jubilee! #68	Flying Home	Storyville CD 501 1005
AFRS Jubilee! #68	One O'clock Jump (theme, excerpt)	Storyville CD 501 1005

C.2 AUGUST 1944   US NAVAL STATION, HITCHCOCK, TEXAS

Andy Kirk And His Orchestra
Harry 'Big Jim' Lawson (tpt), Art Capeheart (tpt), Fats Navarro (tpt), Claude Dunson? (tpt), Joe Baird (tbn), Wayman Richardson (tbn), Bob Murray (tbn), Ted Donnelly (tbn), John Harrington (cl, as), Ben Smith (as), Reuben Phillips (as), Jimmy Forrest (ts), J.D. King (ts), Eddie Loving (ts, bs), Johnny Young (p), Booker Collins (db), Ben Thigpen (d), June Richmond (v), Andy Kirk (ldr).

CCVPSB #585	Roll 'em	Hindsight HSR227
CCVPSB #585	Together	Hindsight HSR227
CCVPSB #585	Hey Lawdy Mama (JR, v)	Hindsight HSR227
CCVPSB #585	9:20 Special	Hindsight HSR227
CCVPSB #585	St Louis Blues (JR, v)	Hindsight HSR227
CCVPSB #585	Seven Come Eleven	Hindsight HSR227
CCVPSB #585	47th Street Jive (JR, v)	Hindsight HSR227
CCVPSB #585	Boo Wah	Hindsight HSR227
CCVPSB #585	Avalon	Hindsight HSR227

19 DECEMBER 1944   DECCA STUDIO, NEW YORK CITY

Andy Kirk And His Orchestra
Harry 'Big Jim' Lawson (tpt), Art Capeheart (tpt), Fats Navarro (tpt), Claude Dunson? (tpt), Joe Baird (tbn), Wayman Richardson (tbn), Bob

Murray (tbn), John Harrington (cl, as), Ben Smith (as), Jimmy Forrest (ts), J.D. King (ts), Eddie Loving (ts, bs), Johnny Young (p), Lavern Baker (db), Ben Thigpen (d), Andy Kirk (ldr).

72644	Apollo Groove	unissued
72645	So Blue	unissued
72646	Hippy Dippy	MCA (J) 3151
72647	If That's The Way You Want It	unissued

14 MAY 1945   NBC STUDIOS, HOLLYWOOD, CALIFORNIA

Andy Kirk And His Orchestra
Harry 'Big Jim' Lawson (tpt), John Lynch (tpt), Talib Dawood (tpt), Claude Dunson (tpt), Milton Robinson (tbn), Wayman Richardson (tbn), Bob Murray (tbn), Joe Evans (as), Reuben Phillips (as, cl), Jimmy Forrest (ts), Eddie Davis (ts), Johnny Taylor (bs), Hank Jones (p), Floyd 'Wonderful' Smith (g), Lavern Baker (db), Ben Thigpen (d), Lena Horne (v), Andy Kirk (ldr).

AFRS Jubilee! #133	One O'clock Jump (theme, excerpt)	unissued beyond original ET
AFRS Jubilee! #133	Roll 'em	unissued beyond original ET
AFRS Jubilee! #133	Ain't Got Nothin' But The Blues (LH, v)	unissued beyond original ET
AFRS Jubilee! #133	As Long As I Live (LH, v)	unissued beyond original ET
AFRS Jubilee! #133	(I Left My Heart In) Avalon	unissued beyond original ET
AFRS Jubilee! #133	One O'clock Jump (theme, excerpt)	unissued beyond original ET

21 MAY 1945   NBC STUDIOS, HOLLYWOOD, CALIFORNIA

Andy Kirk And His Orchestra
Probably the same personnel as for 14 May 1945; Gwen Tynes (v)...

AFRS Jubilee! #134	One O'clock Jump (theme, excerpt)	unissued beyond original ET
AFRS Jubilee! #134	9:20 Special	Jazum 58
AFRS Jubilee! #134	Don't Take Your Love From Me (GT, v)	Jazum 58
AFRS Jubilee! #134	Seven Come Eleven	Jazum 58
AFRS Jubilee! #134	Together	unissued beyond original ET
AFRS Jubilee! #134	One O'clock Jump (theme, excerpt)	unissued beyond original ET

Note: The session was reissued as AFRS Jubilee! #211.

28 MAY 1945   NBC STUDIOS, HOLLYWOOD, CALIFORNIA

Andy Kirk And His Orchestra
Probably the same personnel as for 14 May 1945; June Richmond (v), Danny Kay (v), Andy Kirk (ldr, v).

AFRS Jubilee! #135	One O'clock Jump (theme, excerpt)	unissued beyond original ET
AFRS Jubilee! #135	Knick Knack	Jazum 58
AFRS Jubilee! #135	47th Street Jive (JR & AK v)	Swing House 39
AFRS Jubilee! #135	Minnie the Moocher (DK, v)	Swing House 39
AFRS Jubilee! #135	Hey Lawdy Mama (JR, v)	Swing House 39
AFRS Jubilee! #135	Together	Swing House 39
AFRS Jubilee! #135	One O'clock Jump (theme, excerpt)	unissued beyond original ET

Note: The session was reissued as AFRS Jubilee! #212.

Andy Kirk And His Orchestra
Harry 'Big Jim' Lawson (tpt), John Lynch (tpt), Talib Dawood (tpt), Claude Dunson (tpt), Milton Robinson (tbn), Henry Wells (tbn), Wayman Richardson (tbn), Bob Murray (tbn), Joe Evans (as), Reuben Phillips (as, cl), Jimmy Forrest (ts), Floyd 'Candy' Johnson (ts), Johnny Taylor (bs), Hank Jones (p), Floyd 'Wonderful' Smith (g), Lavern Baker (db), Ben Thigpen (d), The Jubalaires (v), Andy Kirk (ldr).

73161	Get Together With The Lord (TJ, v)	Decca 18782
73162	I Know (TJ, v)	Decca 18782
73163	Soothe Me	Unissued

Andy Kirk And His Orchestra
Harry 'Big Jim' Lawson (tpt), John Lynch (tpt), Fats Navarro (tpt), Claude Dunson (tpt), Milton Robinson (tbn), Henry Wells (tbn), Wayman Richardson (tbn), Bob Murray (tbn), Joe Evans (as), Reuben Phillips (as, cl), Jimmy Forrest (ts), Floyd 'Candy' Johnson (ts), John Porter (bs), Hank Jones (p), Floyd 'Wonderful' Smith (g), Al Hall (db), Ben Thigpen (d), Beverley White (v), Bea Booze (v), Billy Daniels (v).

73264	He's My Baby (BW, v)	Decca 23870
73265	Alabama Bound (BB, v)	Decca 48073
73266	Soothe Me (BD, v)	Decca 23870
73267	Doggin' Man Blues (BB, v)	Decca 48073

Andy Kirk And His Orchestra
Probably similar personnel to 3 January 1946 but unknown (tpt) replaces Navarro; The Jubalaires (v).

| 73590 | I Don't Know What I'd Do Without You (TJ, v) | Decca 18916 |
| 73591 | I'm So Lonesome I Could Cry (TJ, v) | Decca 18916 |

2 DECEMBER 1946   DECCA STUDIO, NEW YORK CITY

Andy Kirk And His Orchestra
Fip Ricard (tpt), Clarence Trice (tpt), John Lynch (tpt), Unknown (tpt), Milton Robinson (tbn), Henry Wells (tbn), Wayman Richardson (tbn), Bob Murray (tbn), Joe Evans (as), Reuben Phillips (as, cl), Jimmy Forrest (ts), Floyd 'Candy' Johnson (ts), John Porter (bs), Hank Jones (p), Floyd 'Wonderful' Smith (g), Al Hall (db), Four Knights (v), Joe Williams(v).

73751	Now You Tell Me (JW, v)	Decca 23959
73752	Louella (JW, v)	Decca 23959
73753	So Soon (FK, v)	Decca 24139
73754	I'm Falling For You (FK, v)	Decca 24139

13 MAY 1949   DECCA (VOCALION) STUDIO, NEW YORK CITY

Andy Kirk And his Clouds Of Joy
Unknown personnel except Jimmy Anderson (v), Kenny White (v) and Andy Kirk (ldr).

74920	Close Your Eyes (JA, v)	Vocalion 55009
74921	Little Girl Don't Cry (JA, v)	Vocalion 55010
74922	Drinkin' Wine, Spo-dee-o-dee (KW, v)	Vocalion 55010
74923	The Huckle-Buck (KW, v)	Vocalion 55009

REFERENCES

Abbot, Sam. (1944, 25 March). 'Vaudeville Reviews'. *Billboard*, 56(13), p. 26.

Adorno, Theodor W. (1936). 'On Jazz' (Jamie Owen Daniel, Trans.). In Richard Leppert (Ed.). (2002). *Essays on Music: Theodor W. Adorno* (pp. 470–492). Berkeley: University of California.

Auslander, Philip. (2008). *Liveness: Performance in a Mediatized Culture* (2nd ed.). New York: Routledge.

Baggenaes, Roland. (1974, July). 'Mary Lou Williams: Interview with Roland Baggenaes'. *Coda*, 11(10), pp. 2–4.

Bastin, Bruce. (2012). *Melody Man: Joe Davis and the New York Music Scene 1916–1978*. Jackson: University Press of Mississippi.

Berliner, Paul F. (1994). *Thinking in Jazz: The Infinite Art of Improvisation*. Chicago: University of Chicago.

Bolig, John R. (2015). *The Victor Black Label Discography: 22000, 23000, 24000, v-38000, v-38500 and v-40000 Series*. Denver, Colorado: Mainstream Press.

Brooks, Tim. (2005). *Lost Sounds: Blacks and the Birth of the Recording Industry, 1890–1919*. Urbana: University of Illinois Press.

Bryant Weeks, Todd. (2008). *Luck's in My Corner: The Life and Music of Hot Lips Page*. New York: Routledge.

Buehrer, Theodore E. (Ed.). (2013). *Mary Lou Williams: Selected Works for Big Band*. Music of the United States (Vol. 25). Middleton, WI: A-R Editions.

Chadbourne, Eugene. (2015). 'Artist Biography by Eugene Chadbourne'. Retrieved from http://www.allmusic.com/artist/harry-lawson-mn0001554328/biography·

Chilton, John. (1985). *Who's Who of Jazz* (4th ed.). London: Macmillan.

Clark, John L., Jr. (2009). 'Archie Bleyer and the Lost Influence of Stock Arrangements in Jazz'. *American Music*, 27(2), pp. 138–179.

Collier, James Lincoln. (1994). 'Holiday, Billie'. In Barry Kernfeld (Ed.). *The New Grove Dictionary of Jazz* (pp. 533–534). London: Macmillan.

Copeland, Peter. (2008). *Manual of Analogue Sound Restoration Techniques*. London: British Library. Retrieved from http://www.bl.uk/britishlibrary/~/media/subjects%20images/sound/analoguesoundrestoration.pdf

Courlander, Harold. (1963). *Negro Folk Music U.S.A.* New York: Columbia University Press.

Dahl, Linda. ([1999] 2001). *Morning Glory: A Biography of Mary Lou Williams*. Berkeley: University of California Press.

Dance Gossip. (1929a, 13 September). *Kansas City Call*, p. 8.

Dance Gossip. (1929b, 20 September). *Kansas City Call*, p. 2.

Dance, Stanley. (1983). *The World of Earl Hines*. New York: Da Capo.

Dance, Stanley. (1989). 'An afternoon with Mary Lou Williams'. *Jazz Journal International*, 42(10), pp. 8–10.

Decker, Todd. (2015). *Who Should Sing Ol' Man River? The Lives of an American Song*. New York: Oxford University Press.

Deffaa, Chip. (1992). 'Andy Kirk: "A Mellow Bit of Rhythm"'. In *In the Mainstream: 18 Portraits in Jazz* (pp. 76–90). Studies in Jazz No. 11. Metuchen, NJ: Scarecrow Press and the Institute of Jazz Studies, Rutgers University.

Driggs, Frank, & Haddix, Chuck. (2005). *Kansas City Jazz: From Ragtime to Bebop—A History*. New York: Oxford University Press.

Dunning, John. (1998). *On The Air: The Encyclopedia of Old Radio*. New York: Oxford University Press.

Ennis, Philip H. (2006). *The Seventh Stream: The Emergence of Rocknroll in American Popular Music*. Hanover, CT: Wesleyan University Press.

Evans, Joe, & Brooks, Christopher. (2008). *Follow Your Heart: Moving with the Giants of Jazz, Swing, and Rhythm and Blues*. Urbana: University of Illinois.

Evensmo, Jan. (ca. 1977). *The Tenor Saxophones of Budd Johnson, Cecil Scott, Elmer Williams, Dick Wilson, 1927–1942*. Jazz Solography Series (Vol. 7). Oslo: Evensmo (self-published).

Evensmo, Jan. (2017). *The Trumpet of Paul King*. Retrieved from http://www.jazzarcheology.com/artists/paul_king.pdf

Fernett, Gene. ([1971] 1993). *Swing Out: Great Negro Dance Bands*. New York: Da Capo.

Floyd Jr., Samuel A. (1995). *The Power of Black Music: Interpreting Its History from Africa to the United States*. New York: Oxford University Press.

Forbes, Camille F. (2008). *Introducing Bert Williams: Burnt Cork, Broadway and the Story of America's First Black Star*. New York: Basic Civitas Books.

Friedwald, Will. (1990). *Jazz Singing: America's Great Voices from Bessie Smith to Bebop and Beyond*. London: Quartet.

Garrod, Charles. (1991). *John Kirkby and His Orchestra: Andy Kirk and His Orchestra*. Zephyrhills, FL: Joyce Record Club.

Gates, Henry Louis, Jr. (1988). *The Signifying Monkey: A Theory of African-American Literary Criticism*. New York: Oxford University Press.

Giordano, Ralph G. (2007). *Social Dancing in America: A History and Reference. Vol. 2: Lindy Hop to Hip-Hop, 1901–2000*. Westport, CT: Greenwood Press.

Goalby Cressey, Paul. ([1932] 2008). *The Taxi-Dance Hall: A Sociological Study in Commercialized Recreation and City Life*. Chicago: University of Chicago.

Goehr, Lydia. (1992). *The Imaginary Museum of Musical Works: An Essay in the Philosophy of Music*. Oxford: Oxford University Press.

Goffin, Robert. ([1930] 1946). *Jazz: From Congo to Swing* (Ray Sonin, Trans.). London: Musicians Press.

Goldstein, Howard. (2001). 'Crooning'. In Stanley Sadie (Ed.). *The New Grove Dictionary of Music and Musicians* (p. 720) (2nd ed., Vol. 6). New York: Grove.

Goosman, Stuart L. (1997, Spring). 'The Black Authentic: Structure, Style, and Values in Group Harmony'. *Black Music Research Journal*, 17(1), pp. 81–99.

Goosman, Stuart L. (2005). *Group Harmony: The Black Urban Roots of Rhythm & Blues*. Philadelphia: University of Pennsylvania.

Gronow, Pekka, & Saunio, Ilpo. (1999). *An International History of the Recording Industry* (Christopher Morley, Trans.). London: Cassell.

Guiter, Jean-Paul (1979). *Andy Kirk and his Clouds of Joy: 'Clouds from the Southwest'* (Liner notes to RCA PM42418. Black and White Series: Vol. 194). France: RCA.

Hasse, John Edward. (1993). *Beyond Category: The Life and Genius of Duke Ellington*. New York: Da Capo.

Hersch, Charles. (2009). *Subversive Sounds: Race and the Birth of Jazz in New Orleans*. Chicago: University of Chicago.

Hobson, Wilder H. (1939). *American Jazz Music*. London: Dent and Sons.

Hodeir, André. ([1954] 1955). *Jazz: Its Evolution and Essence* (David Nokes, Trans.). New York: Grove Press.

James, Willis Lawrence (1955). 'The Romance of the Negro Folk Cry in America'. *Phylon*, 16(1), pp. 15–30.

Jones, Max. (1988). *Talkin' Jazz*. New York: W. W. Norton.

JSngry. (2017) 'Who's in This 1947 Kirk Band?' [Online forum thread]. Retrieved from http://www.organissimo.org/forum/index.php?/topic/80213-whos-in-this-1947-andy-kirk-band/

Keil, Charles. (1966). 'Motion and Feeling Through Music'. *The Journal of Aesthetics and Art Criticism*, 24(3), pp. 337–349.

Kernodle, Tammy L. (2004). *Soul on Soul: The Life and Music of Mary Lou Williams*. Boston: Northeastern University Press.

Killer Diller. (2018). 'KILLER DILLER—Starring Nat King Cole, Andy Kirk, and His Orchestra, Beverly White, and More (1948)' Retrieved from https://www.youtube.com/watch?v=ijadwFEvCB0&t=1345s%29

Kirk, Andy. (1959, February). 'My Story by Andy Kirk as Told to Frank Driggs'. *The Jazz Review*, 2(2), pp. 12–17. Retrieved from http://www.jazzstudiesonline.org/files/jazzreviewVolTwoNoTwoFeb59.pdf

Kirk, Andy. (1977, April). 'The Candid Andy Kirk' Interview with Kent Hazen. *Mississippi Rag*, pp. 6–8.

Kirk, Andy. (1989). *Twenty Years on Wheels by Andy Kirk as Told to Amy Lee*. Oxford: Bayou Press.

Laird, Ross. (2001). *Brunswick Records: A Discography of Recordings, 1916–1931. Volume 3. Chicago and Regional Sessions*. Westport, CT: Greenwood Press.

Lawrence, Jack. (2004). *They All Sang My Songs*. Fort Lee, NJ: Barricade Books.

Lomax, Alan. ([1950] 2001). *Mister Jelly Roll: the fortunes of Jelly Roll Morton, New Orleans Creole and 'inventor of jazz'*. Berkley and Los Angeles: University of California Press.

Lord, Tom. (2015). *The Jazz Discography*. Retrieved from https://www.lordisco.com

Lotz, Rainer E., & Neuert, Ulrich. (1985). *The AFRS "Jubilee" Transcription Programs: An Exploratory Discography*. Frankfurt: N. Reucker.

McCarthy, Albert. (1971, December). 'Andy Kirk and his Clouds of Joy' *Jazz and Blues*, 1(8), pp. 18–23.

Middleton, Richard. (2006). *Voicing the Popular: On the Subjects of Popular Music*. New York & Abingdon: Routledge.

Monson, Ingrid. (1996). *Saying Something: Jazz Improvisation and Interaction*. Chicago: University of Chicago.

Mordden, Ethan. (2005). *Sing for Your Supper: The Broadway Musical in the 1930s*. Basingstoke, UK: Palgrave Macmillan and Houndmills.

Morrison's Jazz Orchestra. (1920). 'I Don't Know Why'. Recorded by Columbia (A2945). YouTube. Retrieved from https://www.youtube.com/watch?v=DAzkJNozAoo

Mowitt, John. (2002). *Percussion: Drumming, Beating, Striking*. Durham, NC: Duke University Press.

Moyer, Robert C. (1953, July). 'Evolution of a Recording Curve' *Audio Engineering*, 37(3), pp. 19–22. Retrieved from http://www.americanradiohistory.com/Archive-Audio/50s/Audio-1953-Jul.pdf

Moyer, Robert C. (1957, October–November). 'Standard Disc Recording Characteristic' *RCA Engineer*, 3(2), pp. 11–13. Retrieved from http://www.americanradiohistory.com/ARCHIVE-RCA/RCA-Engineer/1957-10-11.pdf

Murray, Albert. (1976). 'The Blues as Dance Music' In Robert Gottlieb (Ed.) (1997), *Reading Jazz: A Gathering of Autobiography, Reportage, and Criticism from 1919 to Now* (pp. 992–996). London: Bloomsbury.

Nations, Opal Louis. (2004). *Jubalaires: The Singing Waiters 1947–1948* (CD liner notes). Bexhill on Sea, UK: Interstate Music (Heritage HT CD 48).

Oliphant, Dave. (2002). *The Early Swing Era, 1930–1941*. Westport, CT: Greenwood Press.

Ostransky, Leroy. (1994). 'Royal, Ernie'. In Barry Kernfeld (Ed.). *The New Grove Dictionary of Jazz* (p. 1066). London: Macmillan.

Panassié, Hugues. ([1934] 1936). *Hot Jazz: The Guide to Swing Music* (Lyle and Eleanor Dowling, Trans.). New York: M. Witmark.

Panassié, Hugues. (1942). *The Real Jazz* (Anne Sorelle Williams, Trans.). New York: Smith and Durrell.

Pearson, Nathan, W. (1988). *Goin' To Kansas City*. Music in American Life. Basingstoke, UK: Macmillan.

Petersen, Leif Bo, & Rehak, Theo. (2009). *The Music and Life of Theodore 'Fats' Navarro: Infatuation*. Studies in Jazz, No. 59. Lanham, MD: Scarecrow Press.

Peterson Jr., Bernard L. (1993). *A Century of Musicals in Black and White: An Encyclopedia of Musical Stageworks by, About, or Involving African Americans*. Westport, CT: Greenwood.

Powell, James R. (1989). 'The Audiophile's Guide to Phonorecord Playback Equalizer Settings" *ARSC Journal*, 20(1), pp.14–23.

Prögler, J. A. (1995). Searching for Swing: Participatory Discrepancies in the Jazz Rhythm Section' *Ethnomusicology*, 39(1), pp. 21–54.

Ramsey, Guthrie P. (2004). *Race Music: Black Cultures from Bebop to Hip-Hop*. Los Angeles: University of California Press.

'Ratings (100 Point Maximum)' (1949, 25 July). *Billboard*, 61(26), p. 117.

Ravens, Simon. (2014). *The Supernatural Voice: A History of High Male Singing*. Woodbridge, UK: The Boydell Press.

Razaf, Andy, & Berry, Leon. (1936). *Christopher Columbus: A Rhythm Cocktail*. New York: Joe Davis.

'Reviews and Ratings of New Jazz Albums' (1957, 9 March). *Billboard*, p. 38.

Ruppli, Michel. (1996). *The Decca Label: A Discography. Volume 3. The Eastern Sessions (1943–1956)*. New York: Greenwood.

Russell, Ross. ([1971] 1983). *Jazz Style in Kansas City and the Southwest*. Berkeley: University of California Press.

Rye, Howard. (2015). 'Richmond, June'. *The New Grove Dictionary of Jazz* (2nd ed.). *Grove Music Online. Oxford Music Online*. Oxford University Press. Retrieved from http://www.oxfordmusiconline.com/subscriber/article/grove/music/J379200

Sampson, Henry T. ([1980] 2013). *Blacks in Blackface: A Source Book on Early Black Musical Shows*. Lanham, MD: Scarecrow Press.

Sargeant, Winthrop. ([1938] 1975). *Jazz, Hot and Hybrid* (3rd ed.). New York: Da Capo Press.

Schirmer, Sherry. (2002). *A City Divided: The Racial Landscape of Kansas City, 1900–1960*. Columbia: University of Missouri Press.

Schuller, Gunther. ([1968] 1986). *Early Jazz: Its Roots and Musical Development*. New York: Oxford University Press.

Schuller, Gunther. ([1968] 1986). *Early Jazz: Its Roots and Musical Development*. New York: Oxford University Press.

Schuller, Gunther. (1989). *The Swing Era: The Development of Jazz, 1939–1945*. New York: Oxford University Press.

Shipton, Alyn. (2010). *Hi-De-Ho: The Life of Cab Calloway*. New York: Oxford University Press.

Silvester, Peter J. (2009). *The Story of Boogie-Woogie: A Left Hand Like God*. Lanham, MD: Scarecrow Press.

Sotiropoulos, Karen. (2006). *Staging Race: Black Performers in Turn of the Century America*. Cambridge, Massachusetts: Harvard University Press.

Spragg, Denis M. (2015). ' "EELIBUJ": The Jubilee Story' Retrieved from https://www.colorado.edu/amrc/sites/default/files/attached-files/Eelibuj%20The%20Jubilee%20Story%20.pdf

Spragg, Denis M, Hällström, Carl A., & Scherman, Bo F. (2014). AFRS Jubilee. University of Boulder, Colorado: Glenn Miller Archives, American Music Research Centre. Retrieved from https://www.colorado.edu/amrc/glenn-miller-archive/gma-catalogs/jubilee

Spring, Howard. (1997). 'Swing and Lindy Hop: Dance, Venue, Media, and Tradition' *American Music*, 15(2), pp. 183–207.

Sterne, Jonathan. (2003). *The Audible Past: Cultural Origins of Sound Reproduction.* Durham, NC: Duke University Press.

Stiles, Steve. (2017). *On the Road With Gasoline Alley: A Cradle to Maturity Family Saga.* Retrieved from http://stevestiles.com/gasalley.htm

Strasmayr, Robert. (2015). *Dance Halls—Encyclopedia of Cleveland History.* Retrieved from http://ech.case.edu/cgi/article.pl?id=DH1

Sultanof, Jeffrey (Ed.). (2010). *Messa Stomp: As Recorded by Andy Kirk, 1929.* Saratoga Springs, NY: Jazz Lines.

Taylor, Yuval, & Jake Austen. (2012). *Darkest America: Black Minstrelsy from Slavery to Hip-Hop.* New York and London: Norton.

Tucker, Mark. (2001). 'Lombardo, Guy' In *Grove Music Online.* Retrieved from http://www.oxfordmusiconline.com/grovemusic/view/10.1093/gmo/9781561592630.001.0001/omo-9781561592630-e-0000048198

'Vocalion Records: All New Recordings—No Re-issues' (1949, 16 July). *Billboard,* 61(29), p. 19.

Waterman, R. A. (1952). 'African Influences on American Negro Music'. In S. Tax (Ed.). *Acculturation in the Americas.* Proceedings of the Nineteenth International Congress of Americanists (pp. 207–218). Chicago: Chicago University Press.

Whitburn, Joel. (2004). *Top R&B/Hip-Hop Singles, 1942–2004.* New York: Record Research Inc.

Whitburn, Joel. (2006). *The Billboard Book of Top 40 R&B and Hip-Hop Hits.* New York: Billboard.

Williams, Mary Lou. ([1954] 1997). 'Mary Lou Williams'. In Robert Gottlieb (Ed.) (1997), *Reading Jazz: A Gathering of Autobiography, Reportage, and Criticism from 1919 to Now* (pp. 87–116). London: Bloomsbury.

Wilson, John S. (1957). *A Mellow Bit of Rhythm* (Liner notes to RCA Victor LPM-1302). New York: Radio Corporation of America (RCA).

Zwicky, Theo. (1971). 'Lloyd Hunter's Serenaders and the Territory Bands' *Storyville,* 35, pp 3–12.

INDEX

Tables and figures are indicated by an italic *t*, and *f* following the page number.

blending (black vocal quartet technique),
    164–65, 166, 180–81
Bleyer, Archie, 33n.6, 58, 69
'Blue Clarinet Stomp', 23, 30–32, 31n.3,
    36–37, 57–58
Blue Network (radio network), 167–68
Boogie-woogie, 79, 200
'Boogie Woogie Cocktail' (1942 re-
    cording), 154, 155, 204
'Boogie Woogie Cocktail' (1956 re-
    cording), 199–201
Booze, Bea, 167
Brady, Floyd 'Stumpy', 61, 66, 68
Brinson, Ted, 86, 100–1
Brooks, Orville, 166
Brooks, Ted, 166
Brooks, Tim, 8, 9
Brown, Walter 'Piney', 79
Brunswick (record label), 27, 38–40,
    56, 65, 66
    imposing songs on contracted
        bands, 65
    'Popular Records' series, 39–40, 56
    race records series, 38–39, 56
Buehrer, Theodore E., 63, 87, 102–3

Cahn, Sammy, 122n.24, 132–33, 134
Calloway, Blanche, 66–67
    as black proto-feminist, 67
    as redefining minstrel stereotypes, 67
Calloway, Cabel 'Cab', 66–67, 160
Calloway, Harriet, 133–34, 134n.2
'Casey Jones Blues', 69–72
'Casey Jones Special', 23, 41–42, 69–72, 204
Castle, Vernon and Irene, 91
Chaplin, Saul, 122n.24, 132–33, 134
'Christopher Columbus', 23, 74, 93–99,
    131, 147
    as a hit in the race records market, 91
    as atypical of the swing music of the
        Clouds of Joy, 93–94
    as blacking up in riff-based swing, 96–97
    as sweet and hot styled swing, 99
    attributions of the arrangement, 93
    authorship of, 94

blackface minstrelsy in sheet music
    cover image, 95–96
    Fletcher Henderson's recording
        of, 97–99
    Fats Waller's recording of, 96–97
    lyrics of, 95
    proposed for recording by Jack Kapp
        and Joe Davis, 94–95, 131
    racial authenticity of, 96–97
    royalties earned by Davis, 95n.12
    sales compared to 'Until the Real Thing
        Comes Along', 138, 138n.3
Chronological Classics (CD series), 20–21
Clark Brothers, 175, 177–78
Cleveland, Jimmy, 192
'Close to Five', 154
'Close Your Eyes', 179n21
'Clouds', 145–47
Clouds of Joy, The
    as a dance band, 37, 40–41
    as a white-sounding band, 41, 74, 85
    camaraderie within, 85
    changes in line up of, 86, 86–87n.4, 171
    classified as a territory band, 84
    collaborative creative process of, 35,
        36n.8, 47–48, 60
    compared with Moten's band, 42–43
    commercialism of, 130, 138, 139
    decline of, 167, 174–75
    distinctive style of, 83
    effect of the Great Depression on, 83–84
    expansion of brass section, 86
    Kirk's ground rules for, 174
    live repertoire and practices of, 40–41,
        129, 144–45, 148
    melodic emphasis of, 83
    playing for black audiences, 41
    racist management of, 85–86
    record as Blanche Calloway and Her Joy
        Boys, 66
    recording practices of, 148
    reputation with jazz critics, 138
    Restricted to making race records, 84
    secure residency at Pla-Mor Ballroom,
        Kansas City, 38

showmanship of band of, 18
style of band of, 16, 17
tour of band of, 18
Morton, Ferdinand 'Jelly Roll', 17, 17n.5, 42, 51n.17, 54
Moten, Bennie, 18, 41–46, 54, 55, 91
  influence of Henderson on, 44n.15
  Kirk's first impression of band of, 18
  roots of band's jazz in ragtime, 82
'Moten Stomp', 44, 91–92
'Moten's Swing' (aka 'Moten Swing), 91–93, 147–48
  as race records material for Decca, 91
  as Southwestern hot jazz, 91
  as transformation of pop-song material into jazz, 92
  as tribute to Bennie Moten, 91
  'authorship of, 91–92, 92n.8
  in comparison with Moten's recording of, 92–93
  Trianon Ballroom 'live' recording of, 147–48
  Dick Wilson's derivativeness in soloing in, 148–49
Mowitt, John, 23–24, 118–20
Murray, Albert, 75
'My Cuban Dreams', 17–18

Navarro, Theodore 'Fats', 2, 172–73, 174
New Orleans, 9–10
  Jazz style of, 42, 43–44
'New Orleans Jump', 170–71, 172–73
New Orthophonic sound, 184, 185, 200–1
New York (City), 84
  Arcadia Ballroom, 174–75
  Cotton Club, The, 66–67
  Savoy Ballroom, 23–24, 175
  style of jazz in, 23–24
  Webster Hall (RCA-Victor studios), 182–83
Newman, Joe, 192–93, 194
Nichols, Alberta, 132–34
Nichols, Ernest Loring 'Red', 39–40, 65
Northeast Amusement Company (aka Southwest Amusement Corporation), 34–35, 34n.7

Oklahoma City
  Blossom Heath ballroom in, 85
'Ol' Man River', 158
Oliver, Joe 'King', 42, 60
'One O'Clock Jump', 168
'Once or Twice', 61–62
one nighters. See touring

Panassié, Hughes, 6, 6–7n.2
Pantages, Alexander, 18n.7
Parker, Charlie, 2
Patterson and Jackson, 177
Peabody, The (dance), 116
'Peanut Vendor, The' (El Manisero), 90
Pearson, Nathan W., 8
Pease, Sharon, 121–22
Pendergast, Tom, 77–78
Petrillo, James, 162
Philadelphia
  Pearl Theatre in, 66
Phillips, Reuben, 173, 178
Pillar, Hayes, 141–42
Pla-Mor ballroom. See Kansas city
Portsmouth, Virginia, 168–69
Prince, Gene, 37–38
prohibition, 77

race records, 3, 31–32, 38–40, 84, 91, 93, 129, 130–31, 160–61
racial segregation, 84–85, 168
radio broadcasts, 85, 129, 144–45, 150, 167–69, 173–74
ragtime
  as a basis for Kansas City jazz, 82
Ramsey Jr., Guthrie P., 8, 10–12
Rath, Franz, 15–16
Razaf, Andy, 95, 147
Record Industry Association of America (RIAA), 184
recording
  as a racist culture, 28
Redman, Don, 63, 84
Rehak, Frank, 195, 199
Reichner, Bickley 'Bix', 165–66, 168n.14
Revellers, The, 143

figured as gay, 139–40
racial inauthenticity in singing of, 140
signifyin(g) double-voiced falsetto
    of, 144
'That Ain't Nobody's Biz'ness What I Do'
    (aka "'T'ain't Nobody's Biz'ness If I
    Do'), 176–77
'There's Rhythm in the River', 69
Theatre Owners Booking Association
    (TOBA), 79–80
theatricality, 65–72
Thigpen, Ben, 56n.20, 59, 66, 86, 121,
    150–51, 173
    talks Kirk out of disbanding Clouds of
    Joy, 85
Thompson, Earl
    talks Kirk out of disbanding Clouds of
    Joy, 85
Three Chocolate Drops, The, 133–34, 137
'Toadie Toddle' (1938 recording),
    86–87n.4, 121–22
'Toadie Toddle' (1956 recording), 198
Tobias, Charlie, 58
touring, 66, 83–84
'Traveling that Rocky Road', 63
Trent, Alphonso, 19
Trianon Ballroom (Cleveland, Ohio), 129,
    144–45, 179–80, 203–4
    makeup of live sets recorded at,
    145–47, 146t
    recordings of 1937 live broadcasts
    from, 145
Trice, Clarence, 123
'Trust in Me', 145–47
Turner, 'Big' Joe, 79
'Twinklin'', 154

'Until the Real Thing Comes Along', 24,
    128, 129, 132–38, 145–47, 149–51
    adopted as band's opening theme, 149
    allusions to sex in, 134
    as a 'special' song for a black band to
    record, 131–32
    authenticity in, 132
    blackness in, 133–34

comparison of forms of, 133
double-voiced Signifyin(g) in,
    134, 143–44
originally entitled, 'A Slave Song', 133–34
published song sheet of, 133
replacement of allusions to sex with ro-
    mance in, 134–37
rerecording of, 132
revision of lyrics in, 134–37, 135t
sales compared with 'Christopher
    Columbus', 138, 138n.3
similarity between recordings and sheet
    music of, 134
stereotyped 'Southern' context of, 133–34
success with Decca recording of, 138
Sweet style of, 133
Terrell's singing of, 132, 134–37, 144
Toning down blackness in, 134

Vallée, Hubert, 'Rudy', 138–39
Varietiettes, The, 175, 178
Vaudeville, 18, 79–80
Victory Parade of Spotlight Bands (radio
    show), 167–68
Vocalion (record label), 38–39, 178–79
vocals, 56, 128–29
Voynow, Dick, 38–39

'Wake Up', 168
'Walkin' and Swingin'' (1936
    recording), 86–91
    as exemplar of distinctive swing style of
    Clouds of Joy, 90–91
    harmonic scheme of, 87
    innovative orchestration in, 88
    primacy of melodic style in,
    87–88, 90–91
    quasi-improvised ensemble in, 88–89
    quote from 'The Peanut Vendor' in, 90
    references walking dance steps in
    title of, 91
    rhythm changes in, 87
    riffs in, 87–88, 90
    solos in, 89–90
    variance of Wilson's soloing in, 89–90